PLACIDO DOMINGO

My Operatic Roles

Plácido Domingo as Canio in *Pagliacci*. *Photo: Fritz Peyer*

PLACIDO DOMINGO

My
Operatic
Roles

Helena Matheopoulos

CD produced and edited by Bill Park

BASKERVILLE
PUBLISHERS

Library of Congress Cataloging-in-Publication Data

Domingo, Plácido, 1941-
  My operatic roles / by Plácido Domingo with Helena Matheopoulos.
    p. cm. — (Great voices ; 6)
Includes discography (p.   ) and index.
  ISBN 1-880909-61-8
  1. Domingo, Plácido, 1941- 2. Singers—Biography. I. Matheopoulos,
Helena. II. Title. III. Series.

ML420.D63A3 2003
782.1'092—dc21

                                                        2002155557

ISBN 1-880909-61-8

Baskerville Publishers
2711 Park Hill Drive
Fort Worth, Texas 76109

CONTENTS

CONTENTS

Plácido Domingo as Cavaradossi, a role first sung in Mexico City
in 1961. He made his European debut in it at the Hamburg State
Opera in 1967, where he sang it again, as seen here, in 1971.

Photo: Fritz Peyer

AUTHOR'S NOTE

When the idea of producing a book for Plácido Domingo's 60th birthday and the 40th anniversary of his debut in a major role (Alfredo in *La Traviata* in 1961) first occurred to me, it was obvious that one should try for something different, more intriguing than the traditional, "linear" biography, or even a straightforward critical appreciation of his art and career.

For an artist as consumed by his roles as Plácido Domingo, the answer seemed obvious: a portrait of the artist in his own words, through his own portrayals of the various operatic heroes he has so grippingly and hauntingly brought to life over the years; and each of whom he contains, mysteriously, within himself.

So I asked him in a series of interviews, which, in typical Domingo fashion, took place all over the world over several years—from Seville to New York to Vienna and home in Acapulco—to trace his journey into each of his 62 major roles; and, for the benefit of present and future singers, to single out the specific vocal aspects in each role that he considers significant.

I have attached a brief introduction to each role in order to place it in context for the reader. Each opera is given its full title in the heading or the first time it is mentioned in each chapter. From then on, it is referred to in its usual conversational abbreviation in order to avoid tedium. For example *I Pagliacci* becomes *Pagliacci*, and *Un Ballo in Maschera* becomes *Ballo*, and so on.

His minor roles, as well as those he sang only in concert, are listed Appendix I.

Helena Matheopoulos
August 2000

ACKNOWLEDGEMENTS

First and foremost, I should like to thank Plácido Domingo for agreeing to cooperate in the creation of this book, and devoting so much of his very busy time to our many conversations. Mrs. Marta Domingo, for her staunch support and invaluable help in making this book a reality, as well as for the unforgettable days I spent in their home in Acapulco last summer, surrounded by their family and being made to feel almost part of it! I will treasure those days forever...

Also to Plácido Domingo's loyal staff:

Mr. Paul Garner, for those very pleasant afternoons spent researching the book at the New York office;

Mr. Peter Hoffstötter, who provided all the dates and statistics used;

Mrs. Petra Weiss;

Mrs. Michelle Krisel, Mr. Domingo's Personal Assistant at Washington Opera;

Mrs. Suzanne Stevens: Press Officer, Washington Opera;

Mr. Peter Clark: General Press Representative, Metropolitan Opera;

Jonathan Tichler: Press Assistant, Metropolitan Opera;

Mr. Thomas Lehmkuhl: Administrative Press Assistant, Metropolitan Opera;

Mr. Christopher Millard: Director of Press, The Royal Opera, Covent Garden;

Mrs. Ann Richards: Press Officer, The Royal Opera, Covent Garden;

Mrs. Rita Grudgeon: Press Assistant, The Royal Opera, Covent Garden;

Mrs. Helen Sapera, country representative for Greece of the International Plácido Domingo Society for her tireless help in steering both people and material my way.

Tony and Sally Gibbons, country representatives of the International Plácido Domingo Society for the U.K., for their unstinting and always prompt responses to countless SOS calls;

Mrs. Lilo Schoppert of the Plácido Domingo Society, Vienna;

Lourdes Morgades, music critic of El Pais (Barcelona office), for supplying invaluable material at breakneck speed;

Dr. Phryni-Aroni Karayanni and Mrs. Angeliki Rosolatou, enthusiastic members of the Plácido Domingo Society, Athens.

I would also like to thank the following artists for sharing their thoughts on Plácido Domingo: Renata Tebaldi, Birgit Nilsson, Grace Bumbry, Agnes Baltsa, Renée Fleming, Veronica Villaroel, Sherrill Milnes, Costas Paskalis and directors Piero Faggioni and Elijah Moshinsky.

My unique (long-suffering!) editor and friend Alan Samson, editorial director at Little, Brown, who believed in this book from its inception and was 100% involved and committed in every step along its way, and his ever obliging assistants, Becky Quintavalle and Joanna Macnamara; and Alison Lindsay at Little, Brown.

My agent and friend Gillon Aitken, who put so much

time into working out the initial concept of this book; my friend Maria Hadzinassios, whose ideas were instrumental in shaping my approach.

to Marta Domingo
with deep affection and admiration

GLOSSARY

arpeggio: from *arpa* (Italian for harp), meaning the singing or playing of notes in a chord in rapid succession.

bel canto: literally "beautiful singing." A term associated with singing in the eighteenth and early nineteenth centuries when a beautiful vocal performance was more important than the dramatic. Bel canto composers most often referred to in this book include Bellini, Donizetti and Rossini.

cabaletta: in nineteenth-century opera, the fast, concluding section of an aria or ensemble. In the early part of that century, a separate aria in lively tempo.

cantabile: literally, "songful"—denotes legato, expressive singing.

da capo: return to the beginning.

a cappella: unaccompanied singing.

cavatina: technically a short aria, but now used to describe widely differing types of song and therefore virtually meaningless.

coloratura: elaborately embellished singing. The term later came to apply to singers specializing in roles needing great vocal agility.

"covering" a note: darkening the vocal quality, usually of a high note, by keeping the larynx low and not letting it float upward.

fioritura: florid vocal embellishment.

legato: from the Italian verb "legare," meaning to bind or tie. Refers to the smooth passage from one note to another, as opposed to staccato.

lirico-spinto: from the Italian verb "spingere," meaning to push. Identifies a lyric voice leaning towards the dramatic.

messa di voce: a crescendo and diminuendo on a phrase or note.

mezza voce: literally, "half voice." Denotes soft singing that is still not as soft as *piano*. A special way of singing as if under the breath, referring not only to the volume but to a different quality from that achieved when singing full voice.

passaggio: the notes E, F and G, which lie between the head and the chest registers.

piano: term applying to volume, meaning soft; also
  pianissimo: very soft
  forte: loud
  fortissimo: very loud

portamento: from the Italian verb "portare," meaning to carry. A practice by which singers slide from one note to another without a break.

recitative: declamatory passages, imitating speech, which precede arias, duets and ensembles. Particularly common in eighteenth-century opera.

register: a term used to denote a certain area or vocal range— "chest," "middle," "head."

rubato: literally, "stolen time." A way of performing without adhering strictly to musical time.

solfège: an elementary method of teaching sight reading and ear training whereby the names of the notes (do, re, mi…) are pronounced while the notes are sung unaccompanied. The intervals have to be learned by ear. A common teaching method in France and Italy, known in English as "tonic sol-fa."

tessitura: literally "texture." A term used to designate the average pitch of an aria or role. A part can be taxing despite the absence of especially high or low notes due to the prevailing tessitura.

verismo: literally, "realism." The opposite to *bel canto*, where drama is as important as beautiful singing. A term applied to the works of Italian composers after Verdi, including Puccini, Mascagni, Leoncavallo, Zandonai and Giordano. Can also be used as an adjective, *veristic*, meaning realistic, and applied to the way in which the works of these composers is sung—i.e., more freely and less precisely than those of composers such as Mozart.

vocalize: exercise the voice. Can be a specifically composed wordless song or exercise.

PREFACE

I have always believed that there are certain performers who need spotlights to let you know when they enter and where they are on stage. And then there is the performer who brings his own spotlight on stage with him. It shines from within. When Plácido Domingo comes on stage, you know that something special is about to happen. Plácido was blessed with a gorgeous voice, an uncanny musicality and an innate histrionic talent that emanates from a larger than life personality. That he is tall and handsome does not hurt a bit and I, for one, was always grateful not to have to "scrunch" down when we sang together...Singing with him is very special for another reason. He doesn't compete with his colleagues on stage. He rejoices when they succeed, assists when they are in trouble, and is constantly working on his craft for the collective success of the performance. He is the Dream Colleague.

He has the charisma of a rock star, the charm of a movie star, the voice of a god...and Superstar is written all over him. Indeed his personal spotlight shines brilliantly from a human being who has always remained the same warm and generous person that he was at the beginning of his career.

This book is valuable not only for today's opera lovers but also for future generations, because in it Plácido explains how he got to where he wanted to go, often step by hard-working step. At the beginning of his career people were alarmed that he seemed unable to say "no" to certain challenges. Upon retrospect, let's be glad that he preferred "yes." Opera has been the richer for it.

Beverly Sills

INTRODUCTION

THE DOMINGO PHENOMENON

THE ART

When one examines the history of opera in the twentieth century, two giants stand out as having shaped and decisively influenced the role and position of the tenor: Enrico Caruso, 'the Great Caruso,' who became a household name and who established himself as a formidable rival to the primadonna in its first quarter, and Plácido Domingo, who has more than earned the accolade 'the Great Domingo' in its last. Similarly, when one analyzes the art of operatic interpretation in the second half of the past century, two names instantly leap to mind as having invested opera with a unique degree of musico-dramatic unity without which it could not have thrived in an age of cinematic and televisual criteria of dramatic credibility: Maria Callas and Plácido Domingo.

Domingo is both a consummate actor whose interpretations could stand as straight theater – 'The bastard acts it every bit as well as I do and on top of that he has to sing it!' remarked the late Lord Olivier after seeing his Otello – and a consummate musician whose gift for phrasing according to Sir Georg Solti 'borders on the miraculous.' The 'Lion of Madrid,' as Domingo is sometimes referred to, extended

1

the Callas revolution – the movement, spearheaded by Callas and inspired by directors like Luchino Visconti and Wieland Wagner, that turned opera into believable theater – to the domain of the tenor. In populist terms, if Pavarotti is, as his recording company labelled him, the King of the High Cs, then Domingo is undoubtedly the King of Opera.

'Domingo's contribution to opera, and particularly to the tenor in opera – who tended to be seen either as half-witted, or totally indifferent to what's going on around him or the wrong shape or the wrong everything – can hardly be overestimated,' says Sir John Tooley, former General Director of the Royal Opera House, Covent Garden. 'For here's a fine-looking man with a beautiful vocal instrument, an extraordinary, and I mean a really extraordinary musicality plus the ability to use his voice to dramatic ends in a way not matched by anybody. And when he's on form, one can hear him shaping the phrases, not always in the same way from performance to performance, and the results are incomparable. He probes the characters very deeply and recreates them in terms of a singer-actor in a most remarkable, imaginative and indeed compelling way.'

Domingo, who became sixty on 21 January 2001, is poised at the pinnacle of a glorious singing career that spans four decades. He also has an increasingly important career as a conductor and now alternates singing with conducting engagements, often on successive evenings! Indeed, it was as a student of the piano, conducting and composition, rather than singing, that he had enrolled at the Conservatoire in Mexico. So it's not surprising that almost all conductors who work with him have noticed his ability to experience and penetrate the music from viewpoints much more profound and three-dimensional than the average singer's. 'Plácido, you have the brain of a conductor,' remarked James Levine, years ago, when he looked into Domingo's dressing

2

room after a performance of *Tosca*. 'It's a good job you don't have the brain of a tenor!' grinned Domingo with his characteristic spontaneous wit.

As if that weren't enough, he is also Artistic Director of both Washington and Los Angeles Opera. His venture into operatic management began with the latter company in 1984, when he became Artistic Advisor to Peter Hemmings, whom he succeeded at the beginning of 2000 after four years' experience as Artistic Director in Washington. So successful has his tenure in the capital been that his contract was extended for a further four years. When people in general and journalists in particular point out that his vertiginous schedule – which would flatten a man half his age – is crazy, he retorts, 'It's not crazy, it's very well thought out! I think that the amount of work you can cope with depends on your shoulders – I have the shoulders for the amount that I do,' he told Opera Now last year. 'I feel when I'm working just like a child feels when you give it candy – everything is exciting and I am really full of happiness and the energy to do it. And that carries me. It's so marvellous, the career I have chosen. The singing, the conducting and now realizing the ambition of being able to do some executive work.'

Still, he admits that when he decided to extend his responsibilities in Washington and Los Angeles, he never dreamt he would still be singing in 2000! Fifteen years ago, he had told me that he felt the bulk of his singing – then over two thousand performances of over eighty roles – had been done and that although he would like to be able to go on singing for another ten years, if that were to prove impossible he would retire 'content' and become a conductor. But fifteen years, and a further nine hundred and twenty performances later, 'as you see I'm still singing!'

As a singer, his repertoire encompasses a number of roles unique in operatic history: no fewer than 114 parts – 81 on stage and the rest in concert or on disc – that include almost the entire Italian and French tenor repertoire plus Wagner (Lohengrin, Parsifal and Siegmund on stage, and Walther, Tannhäuser and parts of the young Siegfried on disc), Tchaikovsky and contemporary works. His versatility eclipses even that of Caruso who shied away from Wagner and died without fulfilling his dream of singing Otello on stage. (Yet Domingo is the first to point out that Caruso died when he was only 48 and that, had he lived, there is no saying what greater heights he might have scaled.) Be that as it may, Domingo – who is inordinately fond of statistics and anniversaries of all kinds, of debuts in specific opera houses, cities, countries, roles, and who keeps constant records of all his activities in little green performance diaries (counting the totals of his performances along the way) – also surpassed him last autumn when he inaugurated the Metropolitan Opera's season for the eighteenth time, to Caruso's seventeen, in *I Pagliacci* on 27 September 1999, a date which New York's Mayor Giuliani proclaimed 'Plácido Domingo Day.'

The honor is richly deserved. For Domingo has dominated the operatic scene for the past 20 years. One of the most important factors in his rise to the position he now occupies in operatic history is the consistently very high quality of almost all his portrayals. Not just of roles such as Otello and Hoffmann, which he has made uniquely his own, but also Cavaradossi, Des Grieux, Dick Johnson, Don José, Samson, Alvaro, Gustavus, and so on. It is the degree of quality, both vocal and dramatic, that he brings to so many roles that has made Domingo such an outstanding and outstandingly important artist in the world of opera.

Before going on to analyze his artistry and list his achievements one should first dwell on the voice: that glorious, golden, super-expressive, instantly recognizable Domingo lirico spinto sound. It has been described, by myself included, as 'dark, sensuous and velvety, with the resonance of a cello' or by turns as 'honeyed,' 'bronze' and 'burnished.' Domingo's preferred description is the one coined by Italian critics. 'In Italy they call my voice brown. I like that. If I were to compare it to a liquid, I would say it resembles no alcoholic beverage but, rather, dark chocolate. I also like to think of my voice as a long-lined lyrical instrument such as the cello – in fact in rehearsals I often catch myself bowing an imaginary cello as I sing.'

Although its essential color is dark, Domingo's voice is richly colored and resembles a palette from which he can draw subtle shades and hues, depending on how much light he chooses to let into it. He considers the ability to color the voice one of the most important attributes of a tenor's, or indeed any singer's, art. 'Coloring reflects emotion and character and you must color your voice as subtly as you can. Being a tenor doesn't mean you have to sing with the same voice all the time. Although you have only one voice, its color can, and should, vary tremendously according to the character and style of the music and especially the orchestration which, in opera, is everything. The geniuses who created the masterpieces we are trying to interpret and who worked so intensely on the story line, the background and feelings of each character, set the mood and atmosphere of each scene mainly through their choice of a particular kind of instrumentation. They do this so effectively that all we singers have to do is carry the mood a stage further, with our voice.'

Domingo's remarkable gift for shading and coloring is as obvious on disc as on stage and even more noticeable in his solo albums where he changes vocal colors and even the texture of his sound so much from aria to aria, character to character and composer to composer that it precludes aural fatigue in his listeners.

Another remarkable quality of Domingo's vocal artistry is his unique way with the words, a gift singled out by colleagues such as baritone Sherrill Milnes, with whom he sang for many years. Milnes, himself a highly musical singer, emphasizes that by a gift for words he doesn't mean just enunciation. 'Most great tenors have very good enunciation. It's what Plácido makes of the words, the way he chews, caresses, bites and spits them out and milks every ounce of meaning out of them. He brings such musical and rhythmic integrity to the words that they assume a totally different power. For if you sing the words without an underlying rhythm – which adds to their excitement – they have no bite. He has made it impossible for subsequent tenors to ignore the power of the word. This gift, too, is part of his extraordinary musicality and may stem from his piano background – for, as you may know, his piano playing is very good. Added to the visceral thrill produced by the timbre of his voice, his way of milking the words makes for a tremendous power to stir and move.'

When one moves from the vocal to the dramatic side of Domingo's art as an interpreter, a trait that strikes most of the directors who have worked with him is his ability to immerse and surrender himself to the characters he portrays, body and soul, to the point of total identification. He literally lives the life of his characters on stage. By then he doesn't think anymore. He just feels. This is what lies behind his ability to improvise and perhaps also explains why performing doesn't tire him. It's interesting that in his analysis of one of his roles he states that the most awful thing about singing with a cold or any other physical indisposition is that this forces him to think technically, instead of abandoning himself to the character, and this both tires and frustrates him. But on evenings when he is himself, one is not aware of seeing Plácido Domingo onstage but Cavaradossi, Otello, Siegmund or whatever character is being portrayed.

'I find his total, no-holds-barred generosity and capacity for giving all of himself to his operatic characters mysterious. I have never come across it in another singer, with the possible exception of Ruggero Raimondi,' says Piero Faggioni, the enormously gifted director with whom Domingo collaborated in historic productions of *Carmen*, *La Fanciulla del West*, *Otello*, *Tosca* and *Francesca da Rimini*. 'He plunges into each role like a bull into a corrida and at each performance seems to go through a sort of trance, a process of self-liberation through singing. I never get the impression that singing tires him or imposes any sort of physical strain on him. Just a liberation, an explosion of energies which, I feel, can be freed only through singing, like a volcano which can free itself only by erupting.' Domingo's immersion and identification with his roles is even greater when the characters in question suffer a great deal. 'This makes it easier for me to let go and reach their innermost core.'

But while Domingo's abandonment to his roles is boundless, unlike some of his predecessors he does not sing unthinkingly, from the gut, but perfectly balances instinct and intellect. Abandonment is tempered by an innate sense of measure and, above all, by good taste. Indeed, Good Taste with a capital 'G' and 'T' – to paraphrase Domingo's own expression when describing Verdi's music as Bel canto with a capital 'B' – has always been his hallmark as an artist. (And also as a human being.) In this, as in all aspects of his interpretations, he is always guided by the music. However vicious the characters or situations he is called to portray, he will never go further than the music. Indeed, as Elijah Moshinsky, who has directed him in productions of *Otello*,

Samson et Dalila and *The Queen of Spades*, noticed, Domingo refuses to plunge into dimensions of cruelty or viciousness that go beyond what is described in the music. This is an area into which he won't go. 'In fact it is the only area into which he won't go, as generally he is totally open, almost too open, to direction.'

Experiencing and 'living' his roles to such a degree means that he is able to react to his stage partners in an organic way that greatly enhances the momentum of the performance. Unlike many singers who are only concerned with the moments when they are actually singing, Domingo's concentration is such that he is 'present', fully focused, from beginning to end, both – as the distinguished, now retired baritone Kostas Paskalis stresses – 'as an emanator, through his own performance, and as a very sensitive and alert receptor to ours. This is something that needs underlining. For being 100 per cent there, listening, reacting and taking part in what your partners are doing at every turn, is extremely helpful. You have no idea what it does to you, as Iago, for instance, when you are standing behind Plácido and telling him about Cassio's dream, to suddenly feel the muscles of his back tensing up. You feel as if the two of you are creating the drama together, on the spot.'

Domingo's artistry, in all its greatness, is even more remarkable when one considers that he is a self-made, and largely self-taught, tenor. He was not born a tenor but a high baritone of the kind encountered in *zarzuelas* (Spanish operettas) – a genre that was his parents' profession and which he grew up surrounded by. In his own words, he had to fight every step to gain the tenor tessitura and to manufacture his voice, so to speak. 'Many tenors, like Pavarotti and Kraus, were born tenors. They open their mouth and the tessitura is there,' he told the Sunday Times. 'I had to fight for it, I had to gain it step by step.'

But he managed to turn even this into an advantage, by gaining a degree of experience other tenors don't possess: 'so, when they run into vocal problems, they sometimes don't know how to deal with them.' Domingo had to deal with such problems right from the beginning in Mexico as he worked his voice up to the tenor range. First, he simply lightened the sound to get the top notes. Then he gradually built up his breath support, by working every day for two and a half years in Tel Aviv where he acquired his phenomenal technique with the help of his wife, Marta, also a soprano, and baritone Franco Iglesias, a future voice teacher with a profound understanding of the voice. By the end of this period his voice was homogeneous, and his top notes as rounded and full of color and brilliance as the rest of his voice which, unlike that of many tenors, is like a column rather than a pyramid, even from bottom to top.

'Plácido has mastered the physical reflex of playing the air on his body like an accordion,' says Eugene Kohn, the conductor and accompanist who often works with Domingo in both capacities and also coaches him in his Wagnerian roles. 'Although not born with a high tenor range extension including high C and high D, he developed the ability to sing wonderful, ringing, high notes in the same range – B flat, B natural and the occasional high C – mastered by Caruso. Certain great singers dominate the physical aspects of their singing to a degree that enables them to sing roles that would otherwise be unsuitable for their voices. Plácido uses his air efficiently and actively and this skill enabled him to take on Otello and Samson at a young age and enhance his vocal gold in the process.' (Kohn suggests that the very term spinto might mean a lyric voice that can sing more dramatic roles when 'pushed' by the breath rather than the throat.)

The fact that Domingo first had to find his tenor tessitura

before developing and mastering his voice makes his subsequent vocal glory and artistic achievement even more astounding and significant as far as future generations are concerned. Indeed, as the famous mezzo Grace Bumbry points out, this might even be one of the most important parts of his legacy. 'Plácido has contributed to the artist's make-up the lust for improvement, for developing and mastering the voice to the point where it becomes a fine-honed instrument under the singer's total control. I feel that this element of "if you want to, you can," you can find an avenue to the desired way of singing, is a very important part of his artistic testimony.'

THE MAN

Plácido Domingo was born in Madrid on 21 January 1941. The date, which has been questioned, is confirmed not just by his birth certificate and official Spanish identity card – both of which, ill-wishers claim, could be faked – but also by his official certificate of baptism in his local church which could not, because Plácido Domingo's name appears among many others in a long list in the church's register (see photo).

His parents, Plácido Domingo sen. and Pepita Embil, were well-known performers of the indigenous Spanish kind of operetta known as *zarzuela*, so Domingo imbibed music with his mother's milk, so to speak. Don Plácido and Doña Pepita were warm, loving parents as well as being gifted performers. It is in large measure to them that Domingo owes the self-confidence and inner serenity that, combined with his own innately sunny nature, accounts both for his universal popularity and the relaxed way in which he handles his fame and position. According to Eugene Kohn who got to know them well, 'they were loving, strict, morally prin-

10

cipled parents. Their love for Plácido seemed unqualified and a feeling of total naturalness surrounded his subsequent fame and achievement, as if they had always taken it for granted it would happen.'

In 1946, when Plácido was five, his parents left for an extended tour of Mexico with Federico Moreno Torroba's company, leaving him and his younger sister Maria José, to whom he is extremely close, in the care of their Aunt Augustina. Encouraged by their tour, they decided to make their home in Mexico where they formed their own *zarzuela* company. As soon as they felt securely established, about two years later, they sent for their children who travelled to Mexico accompanied by their beloved aunt who also made her home there with them. Domingo – who relished the month-long sea voyage – had a very happy and amusing childhood as a 'theater child', spending most of his free time in his parents' company in which he played small parts and later accompanied singers on the piano. Thus without even being conscious of it, he began to think of the stage as his second home and to this day, as Eugene Kohn notes, 'he is comfortable with who he is and nowhere more so than when he is on stage.'

Throughout his childhood he took piano lessons and it was as a pianist and not as a singer that he enrolled at Mexico's National Conservatory of Music, where he also studied solfège, harmony and composition. The Conservatory was going through a peak period in those days, with the famous composer Carlos Chavez and conductor Igor Markevitch – whose classes Domingo attended as an observer – as members of its faculty. But his formal musical education was interrupted at the age of 16 when, romantic and ardent youth that he was, he took advantage of his parents' absence on a European tour and entered into a hasty and secret marriage to his current sweetheart, which

Plácido Domingo's birth certificate, issued when he applied
to become a Spanish national. (He previously held Mexican
nationality.)

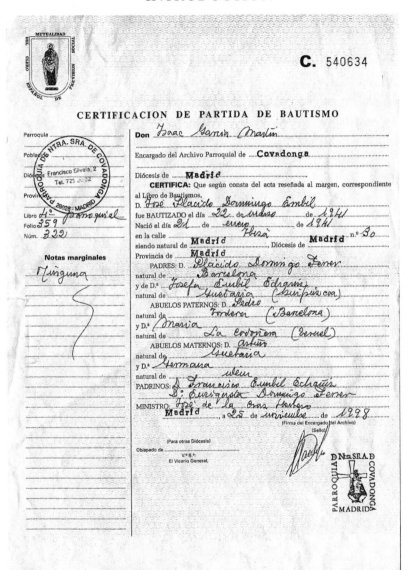

Plácido Domingo's Certificate of Baptism, issued March 22, 1941 by the Madrid parish of Covadonga.

soon resulted in the birth of a son, José, in 1958. To help him support his young family, his parents employed him in their company and he supplemented his income by playing the piano at night clubs and singing baritone parts in musicals such as *My Fair Lady*. (He sang 185 performances of it, in Spanish, every day and twice a day on Sundays!) Barely a year later, the marriage ended in divorce.

Domingo, who had meanwhile begun to be seriously interested in singing and to consider opera, when well done, as the most beautiful thing on earth, felt confident enough to audition for Mexico's National Opera as a baritone. The arias he had prepared were the Prologue from *I Pagliacci* and Gerard's 'Nemico della patria' from *Andrea Chénier*. Although the panel were impressed, they suggested that, in their opinion, he was a tenor and did he know any tenor arias? He did not but ended up sight-reading '*Amor ti vieta*' from *Fedora*. Although he cracked on the A natural, much to his delight he was officially pronounced a tenor and offered a financially decent contract to sing comprimario parts in the house's international season.

He made his debut as Borsa in Rigoletto on 17 May 1959, with Cornell MacNeil in the title role. During the coming seasons – while studying and working on pulling his voice up to the tenor register – he had the opportunity to sing many small roles in operas starring Giuseppe di Stefano and the great Spanish baritone Manuel Ausensi: Remendado in *Carmen*, Spoletta in *Tosca*, Gastone in *La Traviata*, Goro in *Butterfly* and the Emperor Altoum in *Turandot*. His debut in a major role was in Monterrey as Alfredo on 19 October 1961. A few months later he also made his international debut in Dallas as Arturo in *Lucia di Lammermoor* with Joan Sutherland as Lucia, Renato Cioni as Edgardo and the great baritone Ettore Bastianini (who sadly died prematurely in 1967) as Enrico. He also sang

Arturo in New Orleans and finally Edgardo in *Lucia* in Fort Worth with Lily Pons (who had first sung the part with Gigli) in the title role – an experience which he describes with affection in the appropriate chapter.

Having gained some operatic experience and considerable local fame as a presenter of a regular musical show on television, he mustered enough courage to propose to Marta Ornelas, a gifted and musically and socially sophisticated young soprano whom he had been courting assiduously for some time and whose career was then more advanced than his. (She sang Susanna, for instance, in a star-studded production of *Le Nozze di Figaro* with Cesare Siepi as the Count and Teresa Stich Randall as the Countess.) As he points out in several chapters on his early roles, in those days he and Marta often performed together and he looks back on this period as the happiest of his life.

Both were acutely aware, however, that Mexico offered limited opportunities, both for artistic growth and career advancement. So in autumn 1962, a few months after their marriage, they decided to join the Hebrew National Opera in Tel Aviv, then run by the director Edis de Philippe. They were paid $333 a month for the two of them, and had to sing a minimum of ten performances each. They also changed apartments several times during their two-and-a-half-year stay! Still, those were happy, carefree days – despite some cracked notes! As Domingo describes with a hint of nostalgia in the section on *Cavalleria*, he could be found chatting and fooling around in a café next to the theater five minutes before the performance! It was here in Tel Aviv, as will be explained in detail later, that Domingo acquired his now legendary breathing technique, largely responsible both for his astounding vocal longevity – especially when one considers that he has always sung more than most of his colleagues, past or present – and the unblemished condition of his voice on the eve of his sixtieth birthday, both of which have surprised even himself.

After singing 280 performances of eleven roles, the Domingos left Tel Aviv in the summer of 1965, with Marta pregnant with their first son Placi, to settle in New York – or rather, the New Jersey suburb of Teaneck. While still in Tel Aviv, Domingo had auditioned for Julius Rudel, the Music Director of New York City Opera, who had been impressed enough to hire him for *Butterfly*, *Carmen* and the title role in Ginastera's *Don Rodrigo*. 'If he sings as well as he looks, we've got a winner here,' was Rudel's first reaction when Domingo walked into the auditorium for his audition. He describes his impressions in detail in the introduction to the pages on Pinkerton, the role with which Domingo made his New York debut with NYCO in the autumn of 1965. 'A young voice of great natural beauty and a fine acquisition to the company,' wrote the New York Times. Four days after this debut, on the day of his first *Carmen* with the company, Placi was born, the third member of the Domingo dynasty to bear this name!

Marta Domingo had given up her career since they left Tel Aviv to devote her time to her husband and baby. (Three years later, the family was enlarged by the arrival of their second son Alvaro, born on 11 October 1968.) This extraordinary musician has always been a major catalyst in structuring her husband's physical image of each role. The idea is to "create an identity of a real human being that will be painted in tune and body language." Her contribution to Domingo's success can hardly be overestimated. Totally dedicated to him, both as man and artist, she has one of the finest pairs of musical ears in the business (no detail, however seemingly trivial, escapes her), a profound understanding of the voice, vocal technique and stagecraft and an acute critical faculty to match. Her advice, which Domingo takes great heed of, is invariably sound. 'She knows so much about so many things: singing, acting, aesthetics. I trust everything she tells me. And believe me, she is frank about my performances!'

Domingo's first big break came a few months later, on 22 February 1966, when he sang the title role in *Don Rodrigo* in a new production on the night NYCO moved to its new home at Lincoln Center. It was a big international occasion, to which both press and managements from all over the world had been invited. Domingo's triumph led to his European debut. For, present at the premiere of *Don Rodrigo* was Rolf Liebermann, then Intendant of the Hamburg State Opera, who invited Domingo to make his debut there, on 1 January 1967, as Cavaradossi, thus beginning a close and regular association with this house that lasted nearly fifteen years.

This was followed in May 1967 by his debut in Vienna as Don Carlos, Berlin as Riccardo in *Un Ballo in Maschera*, and, in September 1967, by his debut at the Metropolitan Opera as Maurizio in *Adriana Lecouvreur*, opposite Renata Tebaldi. His Italian debut came in summer 1969, at the Verona Arena as Calaf to Birgit Nilsson's Turandot, and in December of the same year he opened the season at La Scala as Ernani. He had already made his London debut, in May 1969, in a performance of the *Verdi Requiem* at the Royal Festival Hall conducted by Carlo Maria Giulini. This was the first time I ever heard Domingo and I shall never forget the *frisson* in the audience the moment he began the '*Hostias*' – the most exquisite hushed singing I have ever heard or probably ever will. His Covent Garden debut came in the 1971–72 season as Cavaradossi.

By then, the early Seventies, Domingo had begun to be recognized as one of the leading tenors of the younger generation. By 1973 he had joined the roster of artists receiving top billing – then $4000 a performance – at the Met. He was already beginning to be accused of singing too much and mortgaging his vocal future through a schedule which – like his diary today – was packed enough to make anyone even looking at it giddy. His career had already begun to be marked by what Bernard Holland of the New York Times called 'an insatiable appetite, almost a gluttony for more roles, more performances, more places to sing.' 'When I discovered opera, I said: "This is a career I want if I can do it big,"' says Domingo. 'So I set myself a limit. I had to make my debuts at both the Met and La Scala before I was 30. Things went well. I was fortunate. I made my debut at the Met when I was 27 and La Scala at 28.'

But some people, including Maria Callas, who admired him at the opening of the 1972–73 season at the Met, wondered if he might be endangering his vocal health. She approached his table when they happened to lunch at the same restaurant to compliment him on his performance: 'You were the only one who was any good, Plácido. But you're singing too much!' she ventured. Birgit Nilsson, a fervent admirer of his even before they sang together in Verona, was quoted in print as saying, 'Plácido, who sings beautifully in six languages, has not yet learnt to say "No" in any of them!' A New York voice teacher went even further: 'Domingo has five years in which to clean up. The managers don't care, the record companies don't care and the opera houses don't care. They'll find another tenor by then. As for Domingo, he'll still be able to get some impresario in Indianapolis to pay him $7500 whether he can sing or not!' Well, as Birgit Nilsson has the good grace to admit, 'he proved us all wrong. Here he is, nearly sixty, and still singing.' Domingo's answer was that the more he sings, the better he sounds, that no one understands his voice better than him – and to no one is it as important. In the event, although he has had to put up with the leitmotiv of doing too much all his singing life, he was proved right with a vengeance! Just as he was proved right when he undertook the role of Otello for the first time, aged only 34, in 1975 in Hamburg, against everybody's so-called expert advice. Otello is a dramatic part and Domingo a lirico spinto tenor. But from the beginning it was clear that this was an ideal role for him – so much so, that he has always found that his voice sounds more lyrical after singing Otello! He thought it's better too soon than too late. If, as in the case of Lohengrin, it proves too soon, you can wait. If it's too late, you will have missed the boat. To sum up, no one should judge Domingo according to their own limitations.

Indeed, Domingo has been able to do all this . . . firstly, because he has been blessed with excellent health and the constitution of an ox. Even his own physician, Dr Andrew Werner of New York, marvels. 'I sometimes wonder if he has superhuman qualities. His cells must produce some chemical that other people don't have.' (Incidentally, Domingo takes no vitamins, supplements or other maintenance drugs.) Once, while playing soccer in 1972, he was knocked semi-conscious and taken to hospital only to discharge himself in time to make it to the theater and sing a double bill of *Cav* and *Pag*!

Secondly, Domingo's legendary capacity to absorb an entire staging in a single rehearsal if need be (which has occasionally offended colleagues who are less gifted in this way and need their rehearsal time with their partner) has also helped him to pack so much singing into his long career. 'One three-hour session with him brings more to the stage director than a rehearsal twice that length with other singers. He listens to a director and is not nearly as vain as some of his colleagues!' said the late August Everding. Thirdly, his ability, thanks to his musicianship and excellent piano playing, 'to learn my roles through my fingers' instead of wasting vocal reserves by learning them with coaches. On top of this he also possesses a prodigious memory which makes it possible for him to learn parts at a vertiginous speed: in his early days he learnt Don José and Riccardo in *Ballo* in three days and to this day he can learn a part – barring German or Russian roles – by himself in a week! (His prodigious memory extends to everything. Domingo never forgets a face, a name or a conversation and can put his finger on them even years later.)

By the 1980s Domingo had risen to the peak of the operatic profession: he had sung in all the great theaters in the world, taken up conducting with considerable success, appeared in hugely popular television specials and was universally honored with awards and decorations. It was towards the second half of this decade, however, that he made the crucial transition to superstardom, culminating in his appearance in the Three Tenors concert in the summer of 1990 at the Terme di Caracalla in Rome. Henceforth he was able to dictate the terms of his engagements, financial or artistic, secure in the knowledge that, in the words of the late Herbert von Karajan, 'they want me everywhere.' He also made three operatic films: *La Traviata*, directed by Franco Zeffirelli with Teresa Stratas in the title role; *Carmen*, directed by Francesco Rosi with Julia Migenes Johnson in the title role and Ruggero Raimondi as Escamillo; and *Otello*, also directed by Zeffirelli, with Katia Ricciarelli as Desdemona and Justino Diaz as Iago.

Yet in the middle of the decade that saw Domingo's rise to superstardom tragedy struck: the Mexican earthquake of 1985 in which an aunt, and an uncle, his wife, a cousin and his little child, died. Domingo, who was released from an important premiere of *Otello* at the Chicago Lyric Opera by the very generous and understanding Ardis Krainik, rushed to Mexico and was seen digging in the rubble with his bare hands. Grief-stricken, he cancelled all his operatic performances for six months – the most eloquent gesture of mourning anyone could offer to the memory of those he loved – and gave only a limited number of concerts for the earthquake victims. (Needless to say, this played havoc with the programming schedules of every major opera house in the world – such is the shortage, nay near total absence, of great tenors in our day.)

Family has always been enormously important to him. 'I am secure because I have the support of those I love' – his parents, sadly now dead, Marta and his beloved boys, his sister, brother-in-law, Marta's family, nephews and nieces. Seeing Domingo with his family, which I have done for more than two decades now, and especially at home in Acapulco, is having a glimpse into one of the two sources from which he draws his near superhuman strength and confidence.

The other source is his seemingly inexhaustible inner center, from which he draws the inspiration, power and spiritual truth he brings to every character he portrays. A deeply religious man and a devout, non-fanatical Catholic (he says a prayer to St Cecilia, patron saint of music, before every performance) and, as anyone who has had dealings with him on any level will testify, he is a profoundly good – both naturally and consciously good – as well as kind, human being. In fact, as I got to know and observe Domingo better, I thought of something that Carlo Maria Giulini had told me nearly 20 years ago for my first book, *Maestro. Encounters with Conductors of Today*. When I asked him which quality he admired most in a human being, he had replied: 'Goodness.' Observing my surprise ('How dull,' I had been stupid and immature enough to think), he explained that "in its supreme expression, goodness contains all other human qualities. Because you cannot be good if you have no courage; you cannot be good without also being intelligent. And it goes without saying that you cannot be good if you are not generous and altruistic.' He then added that, of course, it is impossible for any human being to be truly, 100 per cent good. Well, Domingo comes as close to being truly good as anyone I have ever known. This is what the public senses – beyond the admiration due to him as an artist – and this is why he is so universally liked and loved both by his fans and by those who know and work with him. 'He has always had great contact with the public. His smile and his laughter come from the heart and make instant contact with the heart,' says baritone Kostas Paskalis. According to Caruso this 'something in the heart' is the sine qua non quality of a great singer . . .

THE STUDENT

One might be forgiven for imagining that such an artist, at his age and this stage of his career, who has already achieved so much, might now be content to rest on his laurels and travel the world with a handful of familiar roles, basking in well-earned universal adulation. Not Domingo! He is a man driven and consumed by the need for constant challenge and self-renewal, compelled to move forever onward and discover new musical worlds and new characters to delve into.

Indeed, the Nineties could well be labelled Domingo's Decade of Self-Renewal. He learnt more new roles during this decade than he had since the first decade or so of his career: no less than ten new parts – including Parsifal, Siegmund, Idomeneo, Jean in *Hérodiade* and Jean in *Le Prophète*, Lucero in *Divinas Palabras*, Gabriele Adorno in *Simon Boccanegra*, the title role in *Le Cid*, Don Juan in

Margarita la Tornera and Gherman in *The Queen of Spades*. 'Basically, this is the only way to grow. Taking on a new role such as Gherman, for instance, made me discover an entirely new musical world, Tchaikovsky's world, which is so different, both musically and stylistically, from any of the composers whose works I had sung so far. Of course, it was a great effort because I sang it in Russian, a language I neither speak nor understand. So I had to learn it note by note, word by word and then put the two together.'

Very few superstars of Domingo's stature would, or do, bother to make this degree of effort at this stage in their career. But watching him painstakingly rehearse this role at the Met, day after day, with the humility of a beginner, anxious to get the pronunciation of every syllable and projection of every word right, was a revelation into the source of his greatness. For it is precisely this willingness to test and plunge himself into areas of insecurity for the sake of artistic growth that makes Domingo the gigantic figure he is; an artist towering above any other in today's operatic firmament.

Yelena Kurdina, the Met's leading Russian coach with whom Domingo prepared the role of Gherman intermittently for a year before the production in March 1999, was as surprised as I to see Domingo visibly nervous during rehearsals, worried in case everything didn't come together as it should by the time of the premiere. 'I was amazed to discover,' says Kurdina, with a touch of awe in her voice, 'that, at this stage in his career and stardom, he still cares. He feels the same responsibility to music, to audiences, to whoever, that he did as a young beginner. I found that startling to say the least. Because in my position you see so many artists who are wonderful and talented but accomplish only up to a certain level and then think that this is enough. They can't, or won't, do any more. But here's someone who, you would think, could relax, you know, and rely on what he has already achieved, yet who just goes on to greater things all the time.

'He made me understand, for the first time, that a superstar is not just an accolade, a word, but a super, super, super person who is humble, eager to learn and, amazingly enough, prepared to listen. He learns in a very special way, different from that of other people, who tend to talk quite a lot during coaching sessions, explaining and defending themselves and any mistakes they are making. But Plácido just listens and stores every little thing you say in his memory bank. There is a lot of thinking going on in his mind between sessions, on the plane or wherever he happens to be. At the beginning, I hadn't realized this inner work is going on all the time. But it is and this means that a lot of things to do with characterization don't need to be discussed. Working with him was both an experience and an education.'

Another way in which Domingo has kept himself fresh is through the variety and versatility of his relationships with his leading ladies. He has jokingly pointed out that when he first started performing on stage, he sang with ladies who could have been his mother, then with singers who could have been his elder sisters, then his younger sisters, and finally with girls who could be his daughters. Unlike other colleagues past or present who became closely associated with certain divas (Pavarotti with Joan Sutherland and Carreras with Katia Ricciarelli), Domingo never confined himself to an exclusive artistic partnership with a specific soprano or mezzo but enjoyed fruitful collaborations with most great divas of the past 40 years, barring, to his deep regret, the one with whom he has most in common: Maria Callas. 'I think that one of the most wonderful things that happened in my career is that I have never been associated directly with one particular soprano or mezzo so that people say: "This is the couple." There used to be such standard operatic pairs as Callas and Di Stefano, Tebaldi and Del Monaco, Bjoerling and Albanese. But this has not been the case with me. I worked with all of them – and in perfect harmony. Every soprano has her own qualities.'

Perhaps Domingo's only unfulfilled dream as a singer is never to have performed *Tristan*. He was on the point of doing so three, and then two, years ago but somehow never took the plunge and feels it's too late to attempt it onstage now, though he has plans to record it in 2001. 'It's a very hard and dangerous role, from start to finish. Not just because of the third act, which is really *"massacrante,"* but every act! Act II has some terribly difficult moments in the love duet: phrase after phrase of relentless singing at a very difficult tessitura. And even Act I, where Tristan's part is relatively short, has some terrible moments, just before the ship comes ashore. As a character I like Tristan very much even though, in scenic terms, he is rather static. There isn't much outer movement. Everything happens very much in the mind, it's a very intellectual, esoteric sort of role . . . And it will, perhaps, be the only part that, when the end of my career comes, I will regret not performing on stage.'

Apart from this single, important regret, Domingo faces the future away from the stage with equanimity, profoundly content in the knowledge that, long after he ceases to perform, he will continue to contribute to opera and the art of singing as a conductor and in his position as Artistic Director of the Washington and Los Angeles Operas.

Away from the stage, Domingo's enthusiasms include sport – he is a football and Formula 1 racing fanatic who follows every match and knows the name of every player and racing driver in the business. When flying from New York to Acapulco, for instance, he kept ringing his son regularly to be informed about the progress of a motor race with strict instructions to videotape every minute. He also relishes all the good things of life: food (like a typical Mediterranean man), movies, the sea, sunbathing. In fact, away from the stage Domingo is a very relaxed and normal person. . . . But there is no telling what 'inner work', on which role, might be going on in his mind at the same time. For the true mystery of Domingo, artist and man, begins on stage. This, indeed, is the raison d'être of this book. For I am convinced that the only way of getting to know and portraying the 'real' Domingo is through his operatic characters, to each of whom he brings the essence of his own emotional wealth and spiritual reality.

H.M.

PLACIDO DOMINGO

Major
Operatic
Roles
On Stage

COUNT DANILO

The Merry Widow

Domingo was intimately familiar with Lehár's spar-
kling, much loved operetta since the late Fifties and
early Sixties when he conducted the chorus, sang both
Danilo and Rossillon and made himself generally use-
ful on stage in Mexico. He sang Danilo, its charming
roué of a protagonist, again in February 2000, at the
Metropolitan Opera, in English, in a staging by Tim
Albery that left much to be desired.

Amazingly enough, this was the Met's first ever
staging of the work and in retrospect it is a pity that it
failed to capture a more authentic feel, although it
had some very amusing moments – such as Hannah
Glawari's first entrance, sweeping down a grand stair-
case beneath an imposing Eiffel Tower – and was en-
joyable enough.

Musically speaking, Danilo is hardly a singing role.
It depends much more on appearance, stage presence,
style and lightness of touch, all of which Domingo
brought to the part. He has operetta – both zarzuela,
the Spanish version, and the Viennese genre – in the
blood, as his parents' company performed both, and
it shows. (As also it does in his conducting of Die
Fledermaus.) Yet, characteristically, what he enjoyed
most about this production was the fact that it made
him dance quite a lot, which meant that even now he
learnt something new! This, as everyone who reads

this book will come to realize, is pure oxygen to him. Even though some mean-minded souls professed themselves dissatisfied with his dancing, no one could find fault with his singing or acting!

'Danilo is a prototype of an operetta role and one with which I have been familiar since I was a kid. I sang both Danilo and Camille de Rossillon in Mexico as early as 1960, when I was 19 years old, in Spanish, with my mother and later with Marta in the title role. In fact I think I sang Rossillon about 160 times. I have also prepared the chorus, I have conducted it, and of course I have also sung Danilo. So you can say I know *The Merry Widow* inside out. I remember that when I first conducted *Die Fledermaus* in Vienna, people were surprised that I should have a grasp of the Viennese style. Little did they know that I had imbibed it since my childhood and that it was part of my formation.

'Viennese operetta is a genre created purely for entertainment. The feeling is always gay and lighthearted and all the great composers of operetta – Johann Strauss, Lehár, Kálmán, etc. – wanted to do was to amuse. The genre is very much part and parcel of the Austro-Hungarian Empire. It grew out of the decadence of the time and is steeped in Viennese life: parties, embassy gossip, gypsies and so on and the libretti are full of typically Viennese wit. The only operetta that goes deeper and does not have a happy ending is *The Land of Smiles (Das Land des Lächelns)*. Otherwise, most of them reflect a deep need for escapism into these Ruritanian lands, with those absurd, nonchalant potentates ... *Zarzuelas*, the Spanish kind of operettas, are more down to earth and closer to real life.

'As far as *The Merry Widow* is concerned, dramatically Danilo is a light-hearted part. You can hardly even talk about it vocally. For, unlike Alfred in *Die Fledermaus* which is a difficult role, Danilo isn't. You just have to exude a sense of fun and a languid, sort of bored kind of charm . . . But it was a wonderful contrast and relaxation for me, such a relief, to do this light, fun part in 2000 after all my heavy, dramatic parts. Another role in an operetta I would love to perform before the end of my career is Prince Sou Chong in *The Land of Smiles*, which I hope to do in Washington in a couple of years.'

THE LOVER

Amelia Goes to the Ball

Domingo sang the lover in Gian Carlo Menotti's one-act opera on 28 June 1961, and again in Monterrey with the Chamber Opera Company he had formed with Marta and Franco Iglesias. Amelia Goes to the Ball, *a light-hearted and highly melodic work, composed long before Menotti's sombre, highly successful later works* The Medium *and* The Consul, *was first performed in Philadelphia an 1937 under the baton of Fritz Reiner and at the Metropolitan Opera in 1938. Although the original libretto is in Italian, both productions were in English.*

The story has to do with Amelia, a flippant red-headed socialite determined to attend that night's Ball – against all odds and at any price. But, in the process of getting dressed, she is interrupted by her husband, who has just discovered a love letter signed 'Bubu.' He demands to know the identity of this secret lover in order to kill him! After elaborate denials, Amelia agrees to reveal it – provided her husband promises to take her to the ball without further delay. He does, and leaves to search for her lover (the gentleman from the third floor of their apartment building, who habitually slips down a rope onto their balcony during the night). When the lover, whom Amelia has warned of her husband's impending visit and intentions, climbs down the rope, she offers to hide him so that he can take her to the ball. But the husband, returning, sees the rope dangling on the balcony and discovers the lover in their apartment. After his pistol fails to go off, he and the lover sit down to discuss the situation amicably. Furious and frustrated that she will now have no one to take her to the ball, Amelia hits her husband on the head with a vase and he passes out. Terrified, she screams for help. The neighbours are alerted and call the police. When no less a man than the Chief of Police arrives and demands to know what happened, Amelia says her husband was wounded when he confronted a burglar – her lover! – who is promptly marched off to jail. Amelia then concentrates all her charm and wiles on the one man left to take her to the ball – the Chief of Police, on whose arm she departs!

'This is a charming opera which I greatly enjoyed singing, both in Mexico City and Monterrey. The situation is that Amelia, a frivolous and superficial woman, is hellbent on going to the Ball. Her husband leaves to search for the lover, the latter arrives, expecting to spend a wonderful evening with her. But the only important thing for her that evening is going to the Ball. We don't really know whether, or how much, she cares for the lover. But when he sings of the lovely evening ahead for them, she says no! If her husband won't then he must be the one to take her to the Ball!

'Musically, it's a very enjoyable work, full of beautiful melodies, including an aria for the lover, "*Fu di notte.*" But some of it – the duet and trio – is very difficult music for which you have to be as disciplined as for Rossini, because your singing has to be extremely accurate.

'When I sang it in Mexico City, I had to arrive onstage by climbing down a rope which hung from a platform. But at dress rehearsal I couldn't reach the rope, so I stayed on the platform and instead of making a dashing entrance as the lover, I started to scream "Bring me down, bring me down!" Fortunately everything went smoothly on the opening night!'

ALFREDO

La Traviata

Alfredo was Domingo's first major role. He sang it on 19 October 1961 in Monterrey, about a year after making his professional debut as Borsa in Rigoletto. *During the intervening eighteen months he had sung only minor parts (all of which are listed in the Appendix), including, shortly before Alfredo, Gastone in both Monterrey and Mexico City in April 1961 with Giuseppe di Stefano as Alfredo.*

When asked to single out which among the many productions of La Traviata *stands out most vividly in his memory, spontaneously and unhesitatingly he chose Frank Corsaro's at NYCO in 1966, with the late Patricia Brooks, a moving and accomplished singing actress, as Violetta. On top of the fact that the then doyen of New York critics, Harold Schönberg of the New York Times, called it 'consistently the most intelligent and best acted presentation I have ever seen', this production also demonstrated in the most striking and original way Domingo's impressive technical progress since his days in Tel Aviv: he was able to sing the entire duet 'Parigi, o cara' while carrying Patricia Brooks, luckily as slim a Violetta as one could hope for, in his arms!*

Yet, as Frank Corsaro explains, this spectacular coup de théâtre *happened by chance, through a slip in Domingo's timing in rehearsal, and was incorporated in the production at his insistence: 'Plácido thrives on an offbeat way of doing things,' he told the New York Times. 'During rehearsals he had been asked to carry the dying Violetta to a couch before starting to sing this duet. Domingo was late in picking her up and walking to the couch, so he started singing while walking and holding her in his arms.' While most tenors would recoil in horror at the strain of singing a duet from this awkward position, with a soprano in their arms, Domingo immediately perceived its dramatic possibilities. He told Corsaro that it would be a good idea not only to hold her in his arms at the performance but also to rock her gently, as if this were a lullaby. So he worked on his breathing until it became easier to sing from this position.*

This technical feat did not fail to impress! After the remarks quoted above, Harold Schönberg highlighted it in his review: 'In the last act, he picks Violetta up and carries her to a couch, while singing "Parigi, o cara." This was playing to strength, Plácido Domingo's strength . . . The tenor who had made so much of an impression in last year's Don Rodrigo has a big voice that he skillfully scaled down for this part. He produces good, sturdy tenor sound and all he needs is a little polish.'

By the end of the decade, which saw the onset of his international career in Europe as well as his debut at the Metropolitan Opera, Domingo had acquired the polish and patina that distinguishes greatness. In my opinion, no tenor in our day has combined to the same degree the impassioned, youthful outpouring of feeling needed for Alfredo with the vocal elegance and musical precision Domingo brings to this part. Present and future generations can enjoy this vintage por-

trayal both on record—especially in the Deutsche Grammophon recording conducted by Carlos Kleiber with Ileana Cotrubas in the title role – and in Franco Zeffirelli's 1982 film with Teresa Stratas as Violetta.

'Singing Alfredo in 1961 marked the real beginning of my career, because it was my first important role. Which means that, by 2001, I will have been on the operatic stage for 40 years! I must say it's wonderful to feel that, after all this time, I'm still here and that there are still so many new things I can do!

'As far as Alfredo is concerned, the only thing that changed over the many years I sang the part is that, with the passing of time, I have had to be careful with the characterization. I was getting older and although the stage doesn't show this so much, the fact is that I was getting older . . . Of course, this adjustment in characterization depended very much not just on the production but also on who my Violettas were. Because, as with Otello, I play the part very differently if I have a very young Desdemona, or a very young Violetta, than I do when my partners are more mature. But whatever adjustments you make to your characterization, Alfredo is essentially a very romantic character. The only dramatic moments are in Act II, when he feels ashamed on finding out that Violetta is selling off her possessions to finance their lifestyle and Act III, where because he is feeling betrayed in the worst possible way, he insults Violetta in this brutal fashion.

'Vocally, Alfredo is not one of the most difficult Verdi roles. It's a role for which you need a beautiful lyric voice but with enough reserves of power for the outbursts in Act II and especially Act III. Nevertheless, it needs a very good technique because you are called to do a lot of very tender, piano singing which should express all those romantic feelings as beautifully as possible. But the main problem in this role is intonation. It's very easy to be out of tune at certain very important moments, where you can hardly hear the orchestral accompaniment. In *"Un dì felice,"* for instance, you can barely hear the orchestra because of all those pizzicati and you have to be really careful to ensure that your intonation is perfect. But in this duet I would say that 75 per cent of the time one of the two – either the tenor or the soprano – is either sharp or flat. The same is true of *"Parigi, o cara"* and even *"De' miei bollenti spiriti"* and for the same reason: it's hard to hear the orchestra. But despite the fact that the role is not especially difficult, there are very few good Alfredos around. That's because Alfredo has to have an elegance in his singing line and an elegance in his acting and overall demeanor . . . Yet he has to be very much a man in order to sweep Violetta off her feet to the point where she's willing to give everything up for him. But there are few tenors around who combine this kind of masculinity with elegance and can therefore sing the role the way it's meant to be sung.

'The story, of course, is heartbreaking, with the father breaking up Alfredo and Violetta's happiness. If he hadn't, Violetta would at least have spent her last few months or years happy in love. And who knows, she might even have got better. And it's always so, so sad for you, as Alfredo, when you arrive in the last act full of hope. You sing *"Parigi, o cara"* and she sings it with you and you both believe she's going to get better . . . only to have her collapse and die . . .

'Violetta is one of the greatest operatic heroines, an absolutely beautiful character. Imagine how rare and difficult it is for someone living that kind of life to have a heart such as hers, really fall in love, give that life up and finally make that supreme sacrifice for the sake of her lover's family! And because of what? That egoist father! What really makes her mind up, though, is the thought of Alfredo's sister, the thought that if this young girl cannot get married because of the stigma attached to her family, maybe she, too, might end up living a life like hers, Violetta's . . . Of course one doesn't know if Violetta would have made this sacrifice if she didn't know how ill she is. Probably not . . . But the fact that she is ill makes her aware that, although she's ecstatically happy at this moment, she probably doesn't have very much time ahead.'

CAVARADOSSI

Tosca

Cavaradossi was Domingo's second major role and the one he has sung most often in his career: 225 performances literally all over the world; from Mexico City, where he first sang it on 22 February 1962, and Tel Aviv to the Metropolitan Opera, Covent Garden, the Chicago Lyric, the Vienna, the Bavarian, the Hamburg, the Cologne, the Frankfurt, and the Stuttgart State Opera, as well as Naples, Turin, La Scala, Verona, Madrid, San Francisco, Torre del Lago, Bilbao, Macerata, and many other places, including the Great Lawn in New York's Central Park where, on 1 June 1987, according to Opera News no one was quite prepared for what happened after his rendition of 'E lucevan le stelle.' Some 70,000 people leapt to their feet roaring approval with cheers and tears. Domingo had done what Puccini claimed he wanted his music to do: 'touch that little pocket of sadness around the heart.'

It is a part that fits him like a glove and, as he points out, not one of the most difficult in his vast repertoire. Even when asked at the last minute to substitute for Franco Corelli at the Met on 15 February 1969, shortly after making his debut, at a Saturday matinée, with Birgit Nilsson in the title role, he acquitted himself splendidly: 'He was an incredibly good Cavaradossi,' recalls Nilsson. 'His acting was superb

– he was the part, he lived the part and on top there was his gorgeous singing.' Yet, although he had been singing Cavaradossi since 1961, the single crucial production that opened his eyes to the essence of the role came in 1977, when he sang it in Götz Friedrich's production in Berlin and Munich.

'It was a very powerful production, in which Cavaradossi was shown to have been really tortured, to the point where he could almost not stand up,' remembers Sherrill Milnes who sang the part of Scarpia. 'And his knuckles were broken and bloodied so that he could hardly write his letter to Tosca in the last act. It really showed beyond doubt how totally committed Cavaradossi was to his political ideas and the liberal movement. Plácido would always give me a great deal of resistance in Act II, with his cries of "Vittoria, vittoria," which he really spat out. He challenged me, Scarpia, not the audience. The interplay and tension between us at that moment was almost tangible. Even someone who didn't know the opera would know what was going on in the story at this juncture!'

Future generations can enjoy Domingo's impassioned, noble portrayal of Cavaradossi in two video recordings available commercially. Even more exciting, perhaps, is Andrea Andermann's 1992 film, shot in Rome at the locations and televised live at the times of day specified in the plot – Act I at the Church of San Andrea della Valle on the morning of Day 1, the Palazzo Farnese on the evening of the same day and the Castel Sant'Angelo at dawn of the next day – which meant that Domingo and his co-stars (Catherine Malfitano in the title role and Ruggero Raimondi as Scarpia) were sleepless for nearly two days!

'Cavaradossi is the role I have sung most in my career: a total of 225 times, in every kind of production, with every kind of Tosca and every kind of Scarpia! It was my first Puccini role – and one of my first major roles.

'Like most young, inexperienced singers, I found Puccini the easiest of all composers to sing, because you are less dependent on technique when singing Puccini than when singing Verdi or Mozart. Beginners can sing Puccini's music "spontaneously," without a vocal technique because it's written in a way that makes it apparently easy to sing. But what young singers fail to realize is that there is a catch here. Because although you might be able to sing his music spontaneously, in order to project your voice over Puccini's orchestration and survive, you need as much technique as you do in Verdi. Otherwise you risk doing serious harm to your voice. The greatest danger lurking under this gorgeous, apparently easy, eminently singable music, is that you have to fight a dense orchestration doubling the melody. That's what makes Pinkerton, for instance, so much more taxing than a young tenor might suspect. So what I am saying is that although you can start off singing Puccini without a technique, if you don't acquire one along the way, you're heading for serious trouble.

'Having said that, I always found Cavaradossi a comfortable role. Of course, it has some difficult moments, but overall, it is not especially taxing. The most difficult of all acts is Act I, where he has a big chunk of singing to do: first, "*Recondita armonia*," then his scene with Tosca, followed by the scene with Angelotti and a second duet with Tosca. Yet all of this is so well written that I always enjoyed singing it. I also relished Cavaradossi's cries of "*Vittoria, vittoria*" in Act II. And I cannot imagine any tenor in the world who would not enjoy singing "*E lucevan le stelle*" and "*O dolci mani*" in Act III!

'As a character, I find Cavaradossi very interesting and rewarding to portray. Many tenors make the mistake of portraying him as a sort of "Mr Tosca," just a pretty kind of toy boy, "*com'è bello il mio Mario*," as Tosca sings. But this particular musical phrase can be dramatically misleading as far as the situation between Cavaradossi and Tosca is concerned – especially as Tosca is usually portrayed by mature primadonnas (because young sopranos cannot sing Tosca) behaving in a domineering way, sometimes almost giving the impression that they are about to spank Cavaradossi! Yet nothing could be further from the truth, the real situation between them. Just because Tosca, in desperation, commits the very brave act of murdering Scarpia doesn't mean that Cavaradossi is weak. On the contrary: it is he – an artist, a nobleman, an intellectual with liberal, Voltairian ideals – who is deeply involved in politics and living on the dangerous edge of things. Most of the time he has to humor Tosca – who is really just a girl, a very simple girl with a good voice who developed into a very glamorous woman, a diva, but who was not his intellectual match – and sometimes treat her like a child, with her insane jealousy and the dream world of her art.

'For Cavaradossi knows very well that he's in troubled waters because of his political ideas. He understands his position accurately, but hides this from Tosca almost all the time. And in the last act he knows perfectly well he's going to die. Knowing politics as he does, he realizes there is no way Scarpia would spare his life. You can hear both Cavaradossi's conviction that he's going to die and his acceptance of the fact in his music. But he doesn't have the courage to tell Tosca that this illusion of hers cannot be, that's it's just a joke. So he plays along with her. What else can he do? He knows they cannot escape and this way, at least, they can enjoy five, ten minutes of happiness before the end.

'For me the character of Cavaradossi is so clear and well delineated that I never varied my basic interpretation to suit different partners who, at various stages of my career, have included Renata Tebaldi, Birgit Nilsson, Dorothy Kirsten, Renata Scotto, Gwyneth Jones, Raina Kabaivanska, Grace Bumbry, Hildegard Behrens, Catherine Malfitano, Carol Vaness, Galina Gorchakova, Maria Guleghina . . . What I did, though, was to adjust the way I performed the part depending on what kind of Tosca I was confronted by: if she was very overbearing and bossy, I had to become harder and even bossier! If she was more playful and kittenish, I became gentler, more coaxing, and kind of played with her a little, too, showing her how absurd and unjustified her jealousy was and at the same time enjoying the childish jealousy of this wonderful woman you're so in love with! Because Cavaradossi is truly in love with Tosca (he says so to his jailer in Act III: "*Io lascio al mondo una persona cara*"). He is a very focused man, with no time in his life for anything other than this love, his work and his politics.

'The man who first helped me understand Cavaradossi was Götz Friedrich, with whom I worked on *Tosca* in Berlin. He put me on the right track and also pointed out that in this opera (as we had the opportunity to demonstrate so well in our televised performance filmed in the authentic locations in Rome at the exact hour the action is supposed to take place), everything happens in one day. And Cavaradossi begins this day with an odd, undefined sort of premonition. Without being able to pinpoint the reason, he arrives at the church of San Andrea to begin painting, convinced that this will turn out to be a strange kind of day . . . and you should try to put across this vague sense of malaise. Then, after Angelotti bursts in and asks him to hide him, Cavaradossi realizes why he had this premonition.

Therefore he is almost irritated that Tosca should pick this very dangerous moment to throw a jealous fit and gets almost audibly impatient with her. So there is much more substance to Cavaradossi than his beautiful music. His behavior throughout makes it clear that he is by far the strongest of the two characters – unlike *Turandot*, where both the hero and the heroine are equally strong.'

RODOLFO

La Bohème

Rodolfo, Domingo's second Puccini role, is a proto-
type of the perfect lyric tenor part. This probably ex-
plains why all tenors – both lyric and lirico spinto and
as different as Pavarotti and Domingo – seem to love
it passionately. Despite what even Pavarotti calls 'a
monster of a high C' in 'Che gelida manina' *(which*
Domingo usually transposed down to a B natural), it
is both vocally comfortable and dramatically 'real.'

I remember how surprised I was about 17 years
ago when Domingo told me when I interviewed him
for my book Bravo: Today's Tenors, Baritones and
Basses Discuss Their Art, *that one of the reasons why*
he had not yet committed himself to singing Tristan
on stage was because it would mean losing a good
slice of his lyric repertoire, especially Alfredo in La
Traviata, *the Duke of Mantua in* Rigoletto, *and*
Rodolfo, and 'while I wouldn't mind losing the former
two, I would, ideally, like to be able to sing Rodolfo
for a long time!!'

Indeed, Domingo's last performance of Rodolfo
was at the Metropolitan Opera on 23 February 1991,
which means he performed it for 29 years having sung
it first in Mexico in March 1962. Since then he has
conducted La Bohème *many, many times. He remains*
one of the very few tenors in operatic history who
continued singing Rodolfo after singing Otello – and

doing so with such distinction for a further 16 years.
His amazing technique came up trumps yet again. But,
as he explained at the time – and analyzes in detail in
his discussion of the vocal demands made by Wagner
– this couldn't have happened after singing Tristan:
'If it did, it would have been a miracle!'

Yet as miracles have happened, and continue to
happen, around Domingo with disconcerting fre-
quency, this is a question to which we will never know
the answer.

'Rodolfo is one of the most enjoyable of all tenor roles.
When I first sang it in Mexico in 1962, a few months after
Cavaradossi, I was very young, and if ever there was an
opera about young people it is *La Bohème*! Indeed, the most
enjoyable thing about this opera is the possibility it gives
you to feel young, to experience the complicity of your student years – with all those jokes, pranks and high jinks that
everybody can identify with. The characters are so young
and so real that you can set this opera in any generation,
and any place in the world, and it will still ring true.

'Musically, *La Bohème* is one of the most perfect operas. It's also an ideal way of introducing people to opera
because it has all the right ingredients: sadness and drama
but also joy and happiness, excitement and hilarity. Above
all, when you are introducing people to opera for the first
time, they are usually young, and as this is an opera about
young people, they can identify with those Bohemians.

'Vocally, Rodolfo is a beautiful role and quite a bit more
difficult than Cavaradossi. First of all his first aria, "*Che
gelida manina*," which everyone is waiting for, is very exposed, even though you have had quite a bit of time to warm
up since the beginning of the act . . . The duet "*O soave
fanciulla*" is also difficult and Act III has a lot of singing,

which must be charged with as much feeling and emotion as you're capable of. Yet it's not dramatic singing. The drama is in the action. Vocally speaking, Rodolfo is a purely lyric part. In fact a quintessentially lyric part, but you have to inject feeling and emotion into your singing. And however much more you might like other operas, you couldn't live without *La Bohème*! It's one of the ABCDs of opera – *Aida, Bohème, Carmen, Don Giovanni* – and so on! Puccini's tremendous inspiration at the time of writing is so obvious that it permeates every note and every line. Vocally, it's not one of the most difficult operas, but you certainly have to have everything in place for it.

'I have sung it throughout my career, with very many casts and different Mimis, including Irma Gonzalez in Mexico, Marta in Tel Aviv, Mirella [Freni], Kiri [te Kanawa], Katia [Ricciarelli], and many others. One thing I have tried to do throughout is to preserve a freshness in my sound that enables me to sing so many of those roles even today. There are some I don't sing any longer, but that's because the tessitura starts to get difficult and I certainly don't want to go on singing roles less well than I have sung them in the past. This is what makes me so cagey about doing certain roles when there are so many others I can still do so well.

'You ask me to explain what is so problematic about the tessitura of certain parts. Basically, although I have had a career as a tenor, this tessitura has been difficult for me from day one. Many tenors start singing with their voice completely ready, with its top in place and no problems regarding tessitura. Of course, they have to study and acquire a technique, but their voice is there, by nature. This was not the case with me. I started off as a baritone – a high baritone to be sure, of the kind you encounter in *zarzuelas* – but a baritone. And little by little I worked on bringing the voice up. This is what I meant when I once said that every day I have to fight to gain my tenor tessitura.

'Then, with the passing of time, voices gradually tend to gravitate back to their natural center, their origins. If you look at most tenors who have had long careers, you find that those who had an easy top to begin with don't lose their top as time goes by. They lose the center, the middle voice, which means that they no longer have the same projection. I don't have this kind of problem. I have exactly the same projection as I always had. But, because my voice didn't have an easy top to begin with, the logical, unavoidable process that happens with age will eventually bring it down to its original center. Sometimes, now and then, I put myself through the discipline of singing roles that demand exactly the sort of voice with which I have been singing for over 30 years, precisely in order to prevent the voice from "sinking" down. Some of those roles, such as Gabriele Adorno, are new, some are not.'

FERRANDO

Così Fan Tutte

Ferrando, which Domingo sang in a few – three or four – performances in Mexico in May 1962, and for which, as he confesses, he was technically totally unprepared, is of no importance to his future career. However, his observations about singing Mozart, especially as a young untrained singer, are very important for prospective young singers.

In fact it was Marta Ornelas, before she became his wife, who had first introduced Domingo to Mozart. At the time he was concentrating much more on the Italian and Spanish repertoire, while she, through her Austrian teacher Ernst Romer, was steeped in the German musical world: Mozart, Schubert, Schumann, Brahms, Hugo Wolf and Strauss. In fact in 1962 she was named Mexico's Singer of the Year, after singing Susanna in a production of Le Nozze di Figaro *that included Cesare Siepi as the Count and Teresa Stich Randall as the Countess. But as far as Domingo was concerned he was, as yet, in no way ready for the Mozart challenge at the time.*

In fact Mozart was never destined to become one of the composers associated with Domingo. In the mid-Seventies he turned down an offer to sing Tamino in Salzburg in a production of Die Zauberflöte *by Jean-Pierre Ponnelle. His single 'adult' Mozart role is the tremendously moving and impressive portrayal of*

Idomeneo in 1994 at the Met and, a year later, in Vienna.

'Ferrando was my very first Mozart role. I sang it as long ago as 1961 in Mexico City, with Marta as Despina. Needless to say, I was totally unprepared for such a difficult part. My other major roles to date were Alfredo, Cavaradossi, Rodolfo and Pinkerton, all of which are much easier for my type of voice. For, unless you are a born Mozart tenor, Mozart is the most difficult of all composers to sing. Young singers at the onset of their careers can probably get through Puccini and some other verismo composers without a good technique, at least for a while. But they couldn't get through Mozart (or Verdi) because in Mozart you are totally exposed. You have nothing to hide behind, you are vocally naked! Your ignorance would show up at once ... And it's not true that Mozart cannot harm young voices. On the contrary: if you sing Mozart without a good technique you would soon strangle yourself. The repetitions of certain phrases are written in such a way that they could easily tire your throat. If you sang *"Un aura amorosa"* without a good technique, for instance, you would become unstuck after four bars!

'So how did I cope with this aria back in Mexico? I coped! It was very, very hard for me, because I was always on the point of cracking, but I coped. I very much wanted to impress Marta, who was already much more sophisticated musically, and we had great fun with the staging. It cost me a great deal of effort, but it was the most marvellous time of my life – a time I'll never forget – because it gave Marta and myself a chance to be and work together.

'Of course, *Così* is a fascinating opera, with that cynical Don Alfonso and that bet of his . . . and those two girls who, according to Da Ponte, hail from Ferrara. The Ferrarese women in those days were meant to be very hot, so it all makes for a fabulous comedy. Then we have this poor Ferrando who places such total faith in the fidelity of women that his disappointment at discovering the truth is so great it puts him into a state of shock. The collaboration between Mozart and Da Ponte reaches such a point of identification in this work that you can sense a total complicity between words and music at every turn. I wouldn't attempt a deep character analysis of either Ferrando or the other characters, because this is a comedy. I don't think one should read too much into it or attempt to make it more complex than it is. I never had the chance to sing Ferrando again after my international career took off. I would have loved to, in a "king size" production that would have included Margaret Price as Fiordiligi, Agnes Baltsa as Dorabella and Sherrill Milnes as Guglielmo.'

MAURIZIO

Adriana Lecouvreur

Maurizio was one of Domingo's first major roles, dating back to the beginnings of his career in Mexico, where he sang it on 17 May 1962. He has performed it 25 times over the years, in Newark, Miami, Paris, Munich, nine times at the Metropolitan Opera and lastly in Barcelona in 1989. What renders this relatively insignificant role – dramatically insubstantial and vocally rather banal – important in the context of Domingo's career is the fact that it was as Maurizio that he made his debut at the Metropolitan Opera on 28 September 1968 aged 27, with Renata Tebaldi in the title role.

This was a few days before he was scheduled to make his official debut. At the time he was singing Canio and Luigi at NYCO and standing in at the Met's Turandot rehearsals as he was going to sing Calaf there later on in the season. On the 25th, he had sung Canio at NYCO and on the previous night, the 27th, Luigi. On the afternoon of the 28th he had attended a Turandot *rehearsal at the Met after which he went home to Teaneck, New Jersey for dinner. He intended to return to the Met later on in the evening to watch the last performance of* Adriana *before his own debut. After finishing dinner with Marta, who was then expecting their second child, and his parents who had flown in from Mexico for the birth and Domingo's*

53

Met debut, and while he was shaving before leaving for the theater, the telephone rang. As he describes in his autobiography My First Forty Years, *it was a call from Rudolf Bing, then Managing Director of the Met. 'How do you feel?' he inquired. 'Very well, thank you,' replied Domingo. 'That's wonderful because you are going to make your Metropolitan Opera debut this evening.' Franco Corelli had apparently cancelled 40 minutes before the performance. Domingo was furious. 'I was not planning to arrive for the beginning of the opera,' he murmured. 'I got home late from the extra* Turandot *rehearsal this afternoon.' 'Just come immediately,' replied Bing.*

Leaving his mother with Marta, Domingo drove with his father, ignoring both traffic lights and speed limits and already warming up his voice on West Side Highway. He arrived at the theater on time, but angry because he was convinced that Corelli had cancelled at the last minute – at 7:20 to be precise – on purpose, in order to ruin the Met debut of a very considerable up-and-coming young rival who, he wrongly assumed, would be tired from singing the night before and rehearsing earlier on in the day. But if that was indeed his intention, he reckoned without Domingo's unparalleled, God-given stamina! Although the performance began 20 minutes late and there was an audible gasp of disappointment when Corelli's cancellation was announced, the evening was a triumph for Domingo, with everyone, from Tebaldi to the conductor Fausto Cleva and the Met backstage staff, helping and willing him to do his best in this crucial debut. In one of the intermissions, he rang up his agents, Marianne and Gerald Semon, and announced: 'Guess what! I'm just making my debut at the Met.'

The public and critical response was enthusiastic and Domingo's long and glorious association with a theater he thinks of as a second home had begun. He admits that, if things had been allowed to happen as planned, he would probably have worked himself up into quite a nervous state in the four days before his debut. But, as it turned out, he was hardly aware it was happening until it was over. This way Domingo had the advantage of both an unofficial and an official debut. Most critics were not present at the first, but came to the official debut on 2 October. 'By then,' as Domingo recalls in his book, 'I was feeling calm and relaxed.'

Renata Tebaldi remembers 'waiting an hour for the performance to start. And I must say, I was not disappointed! Plácido, who looked spectacular in his princely costume, gave all of himself to the character, proved a great Maurizio and a wonderful colleague. His personality is reflected in his voice and stage portrayals. He is very hard and demanding on himself but at the same time so simple, humble, ready and happy to learn from colleagues, directors and conductors. He is a great artist and a great friend with whom I later also sang Tosca *and* Manon Lescaut.*'*

'Maurizio is one of my first roles. I sang it in Mexico in 1962. But the most important thing about it, as far as I'm concerned, is that six years later, in 1968, I made my Metropolitan Opera debut in *Adriana Lecouvreur* opposite Renata Tebaldi. I enjoyed it very much because it was wonderful to make my debut at the Met in a role that is not too difficult or taxing.

'Maurizio is a typical romantic character, but not as "good" as people make him out to be because he is literally

55

playing, and very dangerously, too, with two women: Adriana and the Principessa. There is a political game here too, because he is the heir to the Polish throne. For all these reasons, I find him a controversial character. In operatic terms, however, he is a typical verismo hero who finds himself trapped between two ladies. Of course, in the end he is desperately sad that, indirectly, he is the cause of Adriana's death when her jealous rival the Principessa sends her a bouquet of poisoned flowers.

'Vocally, it's not especially demanding. He has two arias, "*La dolcissima effigie*" and "*L'anima ho stanca*" and I would also include "*Non piu nobile*" because that, too, is an aria. In the last act comes the least interesting of all his arias, "*Il russo Mentzikoff*," in which he describes his exploits in a battle he has won. His most beautiful music, though, is in his duets with Adriana and the Principessa, and especially his last-act duet with Adriana. I cannot claim that the rest of the opera is on the same level. Nevertheless, although I haven't sung it all that often, Maurizio is a role that gave me great satisfaction. After those initial performances I sang it once in Caracas with Magda Olivero and at the Met in 1983 with Renata Scotto.'

PINKERTON

Madama Butterfly

Pinkerton was one of Domingo's first big parts. He first sang it in the Mexican town of Torreon on 7 October 1962, and a month later in Tampa. He was already familiar with Puccini by then, having previously sung Cavaradossi and Rodolfo, and with Butterfly *in which he had sung the role of Goro, the marriage broker, the previous year in Mexico City. Later he sang about 15 performances of Pinkerton during his first year with the Edis de Philippe Company in Tel Aviv.*

Although Domingo's debut at New York City Opera is always taken to be the much publicized American premiere of Ginastera's Don Rodrigo *for the inauguration of the company's new home at Lincoln Center, in fact it was as Pinkerton that he made his debut with the company at the old City Center on 17 October 1965, having also sung the part at Binghampton during the previous few days.*

It had already proved a lucky role for him when he auditioned for Julius Rudel, NYCO's Music Director, 'It was clear that this young man had everything it takes to be an important singer: intuition, innate musicianship, good training and, of course, a thrilling voice,' recalls Rudel. 'I hired him on the spot and told him that he would make his debut in Madama Butterfly, *because Pinkerton is a good tenor trial! I say this because every time you hire a young singer, you take a risk. Yes, as at the same time you have no right to jeopardize the audience's pleasure. But Pinkerton is a good trial for the tenor, because here the risk is mini-mized. The tenor doesn't appear at all in Act II and you take care to flank him with a strong Butterfly and a strong Sharpless. But Plácido certainly didn't prove a liability! What he did was both personable and mu-sical. Even then, he was always in control of his voice and constantly working on his technique. He devel-oped very quickly during his seasons at NYCO.'*

Domingo continued to sing Pinkerton at NYCO both in New York City and on tour until the onset of his international career in 1967. His next Pinkertons were in Hamburg in 1969 and on film, directed by Jean-Pierre Ponnelle, conducted by Herbert von Karajan and co-starring Mirella Freni in the title role.

'Pinkerton was my third Puccini role – one of the three I sang in Mexico. Vocally, it's a lot more difficult than people think. If you are not very careful, you can have more trouble with Pinkerton than you could with either Cavaradossi or Rodolfo. It has a number of B flats in Act I which are diffi-cult to tackle. The tessitura of the love duet is quite high and most of the time you have the orchestra doubling the melody. So you have to be careful not to scream, but to sing this music, as beautifully as you can, while ensuring that your voice cuts and projects through the orchestra. There is also a beautiful but very tough B flat in "*Addio, fiorito asil.*" You have to climb to it while accompanied by a very strong orchestra, so you have to try and sail through the orches-tration without ever pushing the voice.

'As a character, Pinkerton is slightly misunderstood. He is usually portrayed as a cad, or given all sorts of "racist-imperialist" connotations that have nothing whatsoever to do with the opera. All this is wide of the mark. Pinkerton is not responsible for the whole tragedy of *Madama Butterfly*. He doesn't either imagine or suspect that things will end the way they do. He is a young officer in the navy, he comes to an exotic place, finds a man who procures girls and settles down to enjoy himself. Okay, he goes through a "marriage" ceremony, but he never dreams or believes that this is the real thing, a lasting thing. He cannot imagine that a girl he "buys" would expect such a thing, either. Sharpless does try to warn him that this girl is different, but he doesn't believe him. He just wants to enjoy this beautiful, exotic girl who arouses terrifically strong passions in him, wonderfully described in his music. Passion is all he goes for. Not love. He expresses his passion very clearly in the text as well as in his music. Both, text and score, show a man who can hardly wait to consummate his passion. He keeps saying, "*Vieni, vieni*" while she keeps expressing herself in poetic terms, romantic feelings and the kind of emotions usually more associated with a woman. Being oriental, she too finds Pinkerton every bit as exotic and fascinating as he finds her.

'The tragedy lies in the huge misunderstanding, the gulf between the needs and motives of the two partners and the fact that she becomes pregnant. And, to my mind the single truly cruel thing Pinkerton does is that when he discovers she has a baby, he comes back to take it away from her. This is the only thing that makes Pinkerton a slightly unpleasant character, not anything that he does in the first act.

'At this point I make up my own story, because Pinkerton and Butterfly have been apart for three years. And I assume that when Pinkerton drinks a toast to his wedding day in Act I, he is thinking of a real marriage, to an American. So he gets married and Kate Pinkerton doesn't produce a child.

So, maybe he confesses that he does have a child, in Japan, and she says, "Okay, let's go get it." What prompts Butterfly's suicide, I think, is the fact that she comes too. I also think that Kate Pinkerton should be portrayed as a very dry, barren woman, incapable of projecting any kind of warmth or feeling. If Pinkerton had come alone, maybe they could have talked things over. But as things are, Butterfly realizes that this child will have a very unhappy life in Japan so she sacrifices herself, she makes this tremendous sacrifice for the sake of her child. It's quite heartbreaking, really . . .'

EDGARDO

Lucia di Lammermoor

Edgardo was the first of Domingo's three major bel canto parts – the others are the title role in Roberto Devereux *and Pollione in* Norma *– and he sang it comparatively little: a total of 25 times. Between the first on 26 November 1962 at Fort Worth, Texas, opposite Lily Pons, and the last two, in Chicago on 8 and 10 December 1986, came one in Guadalajara, two in New Orleans in 1966, two at the Metropolitan Opera (and one on tour with the company in Detroit) in 1970, eight at the Hamburg State Opera in 1971 with Dame Joan Sutherland, one in Piacenza in 1972, two at the Vienna State Opera seven years later, in 1979, and four in Madrid in 1981. Naturally, he treasures the memory of those with Lily Pons and Joan Sutherland.*

Domingo's first Edgardo came after he had already sung Normanno and Arturo in the same opera – the former in Monterrey in 1960 and the latter in Guadalajara and Dallas in 1961 and New Orleans in 1962. This had helped him acquire a good knowledge of the work prior to undertaking its principal tenor role. And although Edgardo never became one of the parts immediately associated with Domingo, singing it was, nevertheless, important in helping him develop his view of how bel canto should be sung or, indeed, of what constitutes bel canto. He came to the conclu-

61

sion that the principles of bel canto – singing long, beautiful legato lines which should never be disturbed by the feelings, or indeed the colors, fed into it – should be applied to all the repertoire, but especially to the Verdi repertoire which he likes to refer to as Bel canto with a capital 'B', even though, because of the power of his music, people have stopped thinking of Verdi as a bel canto composer. 'But if Ernani's aria "Come rugiada al cespite" and Manrico's "A si ben mio" are not Bel canto with a capital "B", what is?' he rightly points out

'Edgardo was my first encounter with a major bel canto part. The first was Normanno, also in this opera, in Mexico and the second was Arturo, this time in Dallas, with Joan Sutherland. So you could say that I know *Lucia* inside out. My first Edgardo, in Forth Worth, was a historical occasion, because my Lucia was Lily Pons, who had sung her first *Lucia* with Gigli and was now singing her last one with me! She was a very, very sweet and extraordinary lady and for me, at 21, it seemed like a dream, a wonder, to be singing my first *Lucia* with such a legend. This was in 1962, one of my last engagements before moving to Tel Aviv for two and a half years. She realized she could be my grandmother, and she was very, very helpful and sweet. The public loved it and for me it was an altogether unforgettable occasion.

'Vocally, Edgardo is the epitome of a bel canto role, and I think I am far from being the ideal bel canto singer!! The unusual thing about me is the fact that I have sung bel canto as well as all the Verdi and veristic repertoire, Wagner, etc. Even in those days my main repertoire centered on heavier parts, such as Rodolfo, Cavaradossi, Pinkerton, Alfredo and Maurizio. But the ideal bel canto singer is someone who can do all kinds of amazing diminuendos, crescendos and *fil di voce*s, who has beauty, purity of sound, purity of line and who has to express so much emotion without ever disturbing this line! I think the most difficult thing in bel canto is to control yourself, control your singing, but still ensure that it has in it some of the excitement of verismo. Just as I feel that verismo should be sung belcantistically, with elegance and light in the sound.

'As a character, he is very intense, and very much a victim of that kind of family feud that existed between noble families in those days, like Romeo and Juliet, but in a Scottish setting. Lucia and Edgardo fall hopelessly in love and her brother is against it and dead set on preventing their marriage at all costs, mainly out of self-interest. Yet the two lovers get secretly engaged and exchange rings. The emotion in the scene when he arrives in the middle of Lucia's wedding, to the man she has been forced to marry against her will, is electric. It's one of the highlights of the entire bel canto repertoire, with that fabulous sextet which, believe it or not, I still sing from time to time with the winners of my voice competition Operalia. If that particular year's winners have the right sort of voices for *Lucia* we still do the sextet together, as we did in Hamburg last year!

'I also like that duet with the baritone which is often cut, probably because the music is a little heavier than the rest of Edgardo's music – requiring almost a full lyric rather than a light lyric voice – because the tessitura here is a lot more dramatic and demands a little more "meat" than the rest of the opera. But Edgardo's most beautiful music, of course, comes at the end with those two fabulous arias "*Fra poco a me ricovero*" and "*Tu che a Dio spiegasti l'ali*" where the music is just about as beautiful as music can get. That exquisite line from the last aria – where you cannot take it any more and commit suicide – amounts to a definition of everything one means by the term "bel canto."

'I was very happy with those Hamburg performances I did with Sutherland, as well as those I did later at the Met. In retrospect, I regret not singing Edgardo more often. For without doubt it is one of the most beautiful roles in the tenor repertoire.'

TITLE ROLE

Faust

Faust, *which Domingo first sang in Tel Aviv on 12 March 1963, was his first French role. It happens to be exceedingly difficult, very high and containing exposed high notes, notably the famous high C at the end of the aria 'Salut demeure' which even seasoned high tenors always find a challenge. The 22-year-old Domingo was totally unprepared for it. I don't wish to detract from the drama of his own graphic description of what happened on the opening night! Suffice it to say that the experience also proved the making of him because more than any other part he had sung to date, Faust convinced him that the acquisition of a good vocal technique was now a matter of utmost urgency. Henceforth, it would be his Number 1 priority.*

Instrumental in convincing him was his wife Marta, who was singing the part of Marguerite and was more nervous on her husband's than her own behalf. On nights when she was not singing, she sat in the auditorium, listening with her incomparable pair of musical ears and assessing his performance. She noticed that his voice was not projecting properly. She commandeered their Mexican friend, baritone Franco Iglesias, to see how they could both help. The three joined forces and got down to some serious work. Every morning, when the theater was not being used, they worked on building up Domingo's breath support.

65

Up to then, the self-taught Domingo was doing the complete opposite of what he should be doing: the sort of 'chest out, stomach in' breathing he had learnt in his gym class. But, as Iglesias explained, before hitting and sustaining a high note the diaphragm should be pushed down and the stomach out, providing room for the lungs to expand and fill up with as much air as possible. This provides enough pressure on the column of air being thrust up between the vocal cords to make them vibrate strongly and produce more sound. As Montserrat Caballé also explains, this is the basis of vocal technique. Yet few singers manage to perfect it and the extraordinary muscular control it requires. Domingo, who first heard about it from Iglesias, proceeded to do just this. 'It felt like being reborn,' he said in an interview to the New York Times.

Domingo's next encounter with Faust *was at the Houston Opera, Orlando, Vienna, the NYCO 1967–68 in New York and on tour, and at the Metropolitan Opera in 1971, by which time he had total technical mastery over the role. During one of the performances, shortly before the Transformation Scene (where, after signing his pact with the Devil, Mefisto, the old Faust's wish to be young again is fulfilled), the catch of his foam-rubber 'old man' mask became loose, causing Domingo to remark, 'I nearly became young before my time!'*

'Faust was not only my first French role, but also the first part I sang in Tel Aviv, with Marta as Marguerite. And, poor Marta, what she had to go through! Pure agony! Because I used to crack all the time! Not just on the high C at the end of "*Salut demeure*" but even on the B natural in the Kermesse "*Je t'aime, je t'aime, je t'aime,*" and bang, I made a big crack. She was nervous enough about her own aria, but before that came my big aria "*Salut demeure*" where I cracked again!

'I was so crestfallen and so, so "down," that at the advanced age of 22 I decided that I had to give up because I didn't think that I could sing after all. And, imagine, that when the reviews were printed two days after the performance, the critic of the main newspaper who was always carping and virtually looking for defects with glee, wrote that I sang the part with a beautiful line, beautiful sound throughout and that I was certainly a promising young tenor and a future star! There was no mention whatsoever of the cracks! It seemed like a miracle to me, a sign from Heaven willing me to continue my career as a singer. It also encouraged me to keep trying to improve. Do I think that, had the reviews been bad, I really would have given up? No! Such things upset you for a day or two but they pass.

'I have to say that I have never, ever had such an embarrassing moment again, in my entire career. To be sure, I did have some more cracked notes in the coming years, up to the late Sixties. In fact all tenors crack now and then. But those cracks were never as obvious or as open or as spontaneous as those ones in *Faust*. After that I was more careful. But on that first night I was not prepared for them so they just went BOOM' [he recalls, laughing]. 'It felt like walking on a tightrope without a safety net underneath you. It was after *Faust* that I began working on my vocal technique in earnest.

'Faust, of course, is an extraordinary role that requires all the lyricism and beauty of phrasing you're capable of. The music for his aria, the Garden Duet, the Kermesse and the quartet is really fabulous. *Faust* was also the opera through which I first came into contact with the French style of singing; putting across a French text and the French language, which was very good for my voice. The fact that before going to Israel I used to attend classes at the Alliance Française in Mexico helped me very much. I also learnt a great deal from Caruso's records. Caruso's French was excellent. In fact some of the arias of Caruso's I like best are from French operas: *La Juive, Le Cid, L'Africaine*, all stunningly beautiful. He had obviously worked very hard on the language and the style and his singing is exquisite.

'Apart from working extra hard on enunciation, French singing demands utmost beauty of voice. As well as singing expressively, powerfully or both, in French operas the voice has to sound very, very beautiful. Otherwise, with all that nasality, those nasal sounds, if you don't make the voice sound very beautiful, it can end up sounding a little . . . precious, a little bit affected. But whether you are singing the French, Italian, German or Russian repertoire, the different "style" emerges spontaneously out of the music and the way it is written. You just know that it has to sound a certain way. In French music, however romantic it might be, it's important to remember not to exaggerate the portamenti and to sing with a very pure line and utmost clarity, especially in romantic roles such as Faust, Nadir, Romeo and Des Grieux.'

DON OTTAVIO

Don Giovanni

Don Ottavio was the first Mozart role Domingo sang in Tel Aviv, on 21 September 1963, then right through the 1963–64 season, and last at NYCO in 1966. However, much later in his career, he was to have two brushes with the role of Don Giovanni: in 1982, when he sang the Champagne Aria in Jean-Pierre Ponnelle's television film Homage to Seville *(available on commercial video); and Don Juan in Chapi's* Margarita la Tornera, *at Madrid's Teatro Real in December 1999. He has interesting things to say about the great seducer in his analysis of both that role and Don Ottavio.*

In the mid-Seventies, Domingo was asked to sing Tamino in Die Zauberflöte *at the Salzburg Festival but declined the invitation. The late Jean-Pierre Ponnelle was directing and he wanted Tamino and Papageno (Bernd Weikl) to be physically similar. But, as he confided to The Times, Domingo was worried about 'the Salzburg Mozart style.' The Don Ottavios he had sung in Tel Aviv were with the sound typical of Domingo whereas Salzburg was more used to the dreamy, more bloodless sound associated with certain German tenors. He was not sure that the same public who accepted him as Don Carlos would also accept him as Tamino. So he declined and it was not until 1994, when he delivered a vintage portrayal of Idomeneo, that one could experience what the combi-*

69

nation of the Domingo sound and spirit could bring to Mozart.

'A year and a half after Ferrando I sang my second Mozart role, this time in Tel Aviv: Don Ottavio, in the autumn of 1963 and 1964. I think I sang a total of about 30 performances, with Marta as Donna Elvira. The production was by the Head of Company, Edis de Philippe, and included a beautiful Greek-Armenian soprano, Athena Lambropoulos, as Donna Anna, the Japanese Michiko Sunahara as Zerlina, the Italian bass Livio Pombeni as Don Giovanni and a black American, William Valentine, as Leporello. The conductor was an Englishman, Arthur Hammond. *Don Giovanni* is an extremely exciting opera and Don Ottavio has some very beautiful music to sing. But I don't like the character. He is neither exciting nor inspirational. In fact, during some moments in the role, I felt almost embarrassed to be singing him – a sensation I have almost never experienced with any of my other characters, however negative.

'The worst of those moments is in Act I, near the beginning where in her recitative "*Era già alquanto avanzata la notte*" Donna Anna is telling Ottavio how Don Giovanni burst into her bedroom. At the point where he realizes that she is still virgo intacta, he whispers that funny aside to himself, "*Ohimè, respiro*," which I don't find very noble on his part. But I suppose this was an attitude typical of a Spanish nobleman of his day, when friendship and a woman's honor were sacrosanct. This is why Ottavio can't believe that another gentleman, Don Giovanni, can possibly be guilty of violating them. Once convinced of his guilt, his reaction is to play it all by the book: wanting to go to the authorities and ask them to take the proper action before he is urged by Donna Anna to swear revenge. So the only thing I could do was to play the part in as strong and dignified a way as possible.

'Vocally I never had any problems with the role, either with his two famous arias – "*Dalla sua pace*" and "*Il mio tesoro*" – or with the trio, the quartet or the ensemble. Of course, by then I had begun working systematically on my singing technique, with Marta and our Mexican friend baritone Franco Iglesias, who was also a permanent member of the company in Tel Aviv. Franco had a deep understanding of the principles underlying good singing: a solid breathing technique that enables you to support the breath from the diaphragm and to sustain this support, through control and manipulation of your air intake.

'Basically it took me all of two and a half years to acquire my technique and be able to sustain the breathing in a way that enabled the voice to cut through the orchestra and project to the back of the theater. By the end of that time my diaphragm felt like a solid wall of cement on which I could lean while singing. But it takes a long time, because those muscles must become so strong that you can depend on them. Once they do, the support comes automatically. While I was in the process of acquiring it, I used to position myself against a piano and try pushing it with my diaphragm.' (Domingo demonstrated this by actually pushing a piano with his expanded diaphragm in a television documentary in which we collaborated in 1984.) 'I also wore an elastic belt – the kind that weightlifters wear to protect their kidneys – so that I could watch and control my diaphragm's increasing capacity to expand.

'Marta, Franco Iglesias and I used to practise this for hours every day, taking turns to listen to one another. In this sense, I am self-taught. This should encourage many of today's young singers who complain that there are no good teachers around any more. This is indeed a problem. Yet once you understand that a good breathing technique is the alpha and omega of good singing, you can set about acquiring one yourself. You need to be very patient, very determined and serious about what you are doing – and you need a good pair of ears, other than your own, to listen and to criticize you. My good fortune was having Franco and Marta. By the time I left Tel Aviv, in 1965, I had the basis of the technique to which I owe my career and vocal longevity.

'This technique enabled me to cope with Don Ottavio as well as the other parts in the repertoire I was then busy acquiring. I sang Don Ottavio again at NYCO in 1966. Once my international career began in earnest, I began to concentrate almost entirely on the Italian and French repertoire. My only other near-brush with Don Giovanni came in the early 1980s when, in the interval interview of a live Met telecast of *Manon Lescaut*, I mentioned that I might quite like to try singing Don Giovanni one day. Next morning came a telephone call from Herbert von Karajan who said let's do it next summer in Salzburg!! I said, dear Maestro, all I said was that I might like to do it one day! Not now! I am in the full bloom of my career, I cannot possibly risk dragging the voice down to the tessitura of a bass-baritone! Later, maybe, who knows? But he didn't like this at all and we didn't work together again until the very last months of his life . . .

'What prompted me to say I would like to try singing Don Giovanni in the first place? Well, he is a riveting character to play, one of the most mesmerizing in the repertoire, and offers you many possibilities. You can play him as a simpatico, fun-loving seducer, or as a dark and satanic soul. But, to be honest, I think that the havoc he wreaks in women's lives is also a little bit the fault of the women themselves. Most of them knew he was Trouble with a capital "T". Yet they still went with him . . . because he made them feel good at that moment. For Don Giovanni lives for the

moment. One thing that you can be sure about, when dealing with him, is that he's not going to stay long with any of
them. Yet although they knew his reputation, women still
fell for him. So I don't think he's entirely to blame except, I
think, in his treatment of Donna Elvira when he makes
Leporello woo her in his stead. That's his worst moment,
really mean. But, like Turiddu in *Cavalleria* who is pursued
by Santuzza – another operatic lady who cannot accept that
when something is finished, it's finished – he reacts like many
men do when they are dealing with a nagging woman: he
becomes cruel . . . So, I feel that portraying Don Giovanni
would have been an exciting and intriguing experience. But
I have now changed my mind about the possibility of my
ever singing it. I'll never do it.'

DON JOSÉ

Carmen

Don José was one of Domingo's first French roles. He sang it as early as 25 June 1963, during his first season in Tel Aviv and during the next season-and-a-half. It was also one of the roles he was engaged to sing at NYCO, in New York and on tour. Not surprisingly, for of all the French parts he had tackled so far, this was the one best suited to his voice, not only then but always! Lyrical in the first two acts and dramatic in the last two, as well as a meaty character to get his teeth into. In short, a part designed to show off Domingo at his best. It is also his third most popular role after Cavaradossi and Otello, with a total of 182 performances worldwide: Hamburg, Vienna, La Scala, Edinburgh, Covent Garden, Paris and the Met. He also performed it in Francesco Rosi's film shot on location in Ronda, Andalusia and featuring Julia Migenes in the title role and Ruggero Raimondi as a most dashing Escamillo.

As is often the case with parts he has sung a great deal and in many different productions, he singles out the one he considers a landmark, the staging that revealed the depths of the character to him, and which helped shape his own view of the role. In the case of Carmen *it is Piero Faggioni's milestone production at the 1977 Edinburgh Festival, which later travelled to Paris, Hamburg and La Scala.*

Alfredo in *La Traviata* with Ileana Cortrubas as Violetta at the Met: Domingo's first major operatic role and one which should 'combine passion with elegance.' © BETH BERGMAN

Cavaradossi in *Tosca*, Mexico City, 1961: One of Domingo's most popular roles, which he has sung more than any other, no less than 225 times. This was Marta's favourite photograph and was used as Domingo's first publicity picture in the United States. COURTESY OF PLACIDO DOMINGO

Count Danilo in *The Merry Widow*, Mexico City 1962: 'A charming, debonair character who should ooze nonchalant charm.' Domingo first sang this in Mexico City with his mother and later with his wife, Marta, (pictured here) in the title role, and last at the Metropolitan Opera in spring 2000. COURTESY OF PLACIDO DOMINGO

Rodolfo in *La Bohème*: 'One of the most enjoyable tenor roles in an opera about young people . . . so real that you can set it in any generation and any place in the world and it would still ring true,' says Domingo, pictured here, with Marta as Mimi in Tel Aviv in 1963 on his 22nd birthday. COURTESY OF PLACIDO DOMINGO

'The most enjoyable thing about *La Bohème* is the possibility it gives you to feel young and experience, once more, the complicacy of your student years.' CLIVE BARDA/ARENA PAL

Domingo as Rodolfo, one of his favourite roles – and which he continued singing even after he took on Otello. With Renata Scotto as Mimi at the Metropolitan Opera in 1977. © BETH BERGMAN

Pinkerton (left) in *Madama Butterfly*: in which Domingo made his New York debut, with NYCO, in 1965. 'A character who is slightly misunderstood and usually portrayed as a cad with 'racist' or 'imperialist' overtones that have nothing whatsoever to do with the opera . . . But he is simply a young naval officer who comes to an exotic place, finds a man who procures girls and settles down to enjoy himself.' © BETH BERGMAN

METROPOLITAN OPERA

SEASON 1968–1969   LINCOLN CENTER PLAZA

Saturday Evening, September 28, 1968, at 8:00

SUBSCRIPTION PERFORMANCE

FRANCESCO CILEA

Adriana Lecouvreur

Opera in four acts   Libretto by A. Colautti
Conductor: Fausto Cleva
Staged by Nathaniel Merrill
Sets designed by C. M. Cristini,
after sketches by Camillo Paravicini

Adriana Lecouvreur	Renata Tebaldi
Maurizio PLACIDO DOMINGO	Franco Corelli *debut*
La Principessa di Bouillon	Irene Dalis
Michonnet	Anselmo Colzani
Il Principe di Bouillon	Morley Meredith
Abbé	Paul Franke
Mlle. Jouvenot	Colette Boky
Mlle. Dangeville	Nedda Casei
Quinault	Paul Plishka
Poisson	Robert Schmorr
La Duclos	Skiles Fairlie
Major-Domo	Edward Ghazal

Maurizio in *Adriana Lecouvreur*: The part in which Domingo made his Metropolitan Opera debut, a few days earlier than scheduled and with only a few hours' notice. He was in such a rush to get to the theatre in time and get into his costume that he 'forgot to be nervous'. (See Met poster with name substitute.)

Domingo as Maurizio in his Metropolitan Opera debut with the great Renata Tebaldi, who said 'he sang marvellously and looked splendid in his princely period costume.'
METROPOLITAN OPERA ARCHIVES

Edgardo in *Lucia Di Lammermoor*: One of Domingo's three *bel canto* roles in which he scored a great success in Fort Worth, where he first sang it with Lily Pons in the title role. COURTESY OF PLACIDO DOMINGO

As Edgardo (right, on stairs) at the Hamburg State Opera with Joan Sutherland as Lucia, Tom Krause as Enrico and Kurt Moll as Raimondo. FRITZ PEYER

Don Ottavio in *Don Giovanni*: Domingo sang this role twice, in Tel Aviv in 1963–64, with his wife Marta as Donna Elvira and at NYCO pictured above. Don Ottavio is a character which, despite the beautiful music and the tremendous excitement of the opera as a whole, Domingo dislikes and finds 'neither exciting nor inspirational. In fact, during some moments, I felt almost embarrassed to be singing him – a sensation I have never experienced with any of my other roles.' © BETH BERGMAN

Title Role in *Faust* at the Metropolitan Opera: A role that gave Domingo a lot of trouble when he first sang it in 1963 at Tel Aviv, but none by the time he sang it here. © BETH BERGMAN

Nadir in *Les pêcheurs de Perles*: Domingo's other Bizet role which he sang just once in Tel Aviv, in Hebrew, with Michiko Sunahara as Leyla, and Franco Iglesias as Zurga.
OPERA MAGAZINE

Turridu in *Cavalleria Rusticana*: One of Domingo's most popular and demanding roles and a character who, contrary to most people's views, isn't a Sicilian gigolo playing with two women, but rather, a man deeply hurt by Lola's betrayal and who only takes up with Santuzza on the rebound. © BETH BERGMAN

Title role in *Hippolyte et Aricie* in 1966 with the opera company of Boston. Domingo's only brush, so far, with baroque opera. 'Although singing baroque music is phenomenally difficult, I have always tried to move from style to style and not be petrified by the exigencies of any particular style or composer'. COURTESY OF PLACIDO DOMINGO

Fiorenza Cossotto as Santuzza at the Met in 1970. CLIVE BARDA/ARENA PAL

Gillian Knight as Lola at Covent Garden. METROPOLITAN OPERA ARCHIVES

Title role in *Andrea Chénier*: 'A dream role for the tenor! Not only is he a dashing, romantic hero but he also has four "showpiece" arias — one in every act.' At Covent Garden in 1985. CLIVE BARDA/ARENA PAL

Title role in *Don Rodrigo* at NYCO in 1966: 'A great experience both vocally and dramatically as well as from a career viewpoint, because it put me on the American and international music map only six months after leaving my first job in Tel Aviv.' © BETH BERGMAN

Title role in *Don Carlos*: Placido Domingo as Don Carlos for his Vienna State Opera debut in 1967. COURTESY OF THE VIENNA STATE OPERA

Below: Domingo in the five-act version of *Don Carlos* with Mirella Freni as Elizabetta. © BETH BERGMAN

Radames in *Aida*: One of Domingo's first major Verdi roles in Hamburg, 1967. Radames is 'the prototype of a lirico spinto role. It needs a lot of brilliance, a lot of stamina and a lot of technique. The character is a great, strong, brave and passionate man of total integrity.' FOTO LIESKE

Luigi in *Il Tabarro* at the Metropolitan Opera in 1989: 'A very short yet very difficult role with a high tessitura.' WINNIE KLOTZ/METROPOLITAN OPERA

Below: Lensky in *Eugene Onegin*: 'An unbelievably sweet, beautiful and tender character, who is madly in love with Olga and insanely jealous.' Domingo sang this role, again in Hebrew, in Tel Aviv only in 1964 (here with Breda Kalef). But he has often performed Ljensky's famous aria in concerts. COURTESY OF PLACIDO DOMINGO

Gustavus III – or Riccardo in *Un Ballo in Maschera* in Hamburg in 1974: One of Domingo's favourite and most exciting roles 'because of the love triangle at its centre and because these triangular situations are what opera is usually about! Vocally it's very difficult, but contains one of the most beautiful love duets in all opera.' GERT VON BASSEWITZ

Des Grieux in *Manon Lescaut* with Magda Olivero: A vintage Domingo portrayal and a great favourite of his: 'one of the longest and most difficult Puccini roles.' ANGELO GUARDINI, LIVERANI

As the Duke of Mantua in *Rigoletto* at the Hamburg State Opera with David Ohanesian as Rigoletto. FRITZ PEYER

As the Duke of Mantua in *Rigoletto* in Hamburg in 1970: The Duke is a character whom Domingo dislikes because 'he is, and remains, a cynic through and through. But he has to sing some of the most beautiful yet difficult music ever written for the tenor every time he steps on stage.' FOTO LIESKO

Left: Calaf in *Turandot*: The role in which Domingo made his debut in Verona in 1969. The white cape in this picture billowing in the night breeze caused Domingo's then tiny son Placi to exclaim 'Look Mami, Papi is flying!' PHOTO BY GIANFRANCO FAINELLO AUTHORIZED BY ARENA DI VERONA FOUNDATION. All rights reserved.

Rodolfo in *Luisa Miller*: A character who reminds Domingo 'of some rebellious juniors of our own day and is vocally a very satisfying, yet far from easy role to sing.' CLIVE BARDA/ARENA PAL

Enzo in *La Gioconda*: The part in which Domingo made his debut in his native Madrid – a highly emotional occasion. The ovation was so tumultuous that it reduced Domingo to tears and made it very difficult for him to continue singing Enzo's 'extraordinary music'. METROPOLITAN OPERA ARCHIVES

Title role in *Roberto Devereux*: One of Domingo's three *bel canto* roles, which he sang in 1970 at NYCO with Beverly Sills as Queen Elizabeth. Domingo's performance drew an ecstatic critical and public response and belied his own contention that he is 'far from being the ideal *bel canto* singer'. © BETH BERGMAN

Arrigo in *I Vespri Siciliani*: 'Without doubt one of the two most difficult yet interesting roles in my repertoire: very rough, very, *very* aggressive, fanatical and, above all, extremely difficult vocally.' In the Paris Opera's 1974 production, where he first sang it, with Peter Glossop as Guy de Montfort. COLETTE MASSON ENGUERAND/BERNAND AGENCY

Title role in *Roméo et Juliette* at the Metropolitan Opera in 1989: 'My first role based on a Shakespearean character and I relished the experience! His music is very beautiful – almost like a non-stop love duet, and very high.' © BETH BERGMAN

Dick Johnson in *La Fanciulla del West* at Covent Garden: A role very dear to Domingo although 'by no means an easy sing!' CLIVE BARDA/ARENA PAL

Otello: Domingo's first Otello seen here in the Hamburg production, where he first sang it in 1975 with Katia Ricciarelli as Desdemona, at the rapturous finale of Act 1. GERT VON BASSEWITZ

Otello (*top left*): Domingo with
Katia Ricciarelli in 1975. GERT VON
BASSEWITZ.

Top right: With Justino Diaz as
Iago in Franco Zeffirelli's film.

Otello: 'The most demanding and
emotionally wearing of all my
roles . . . The combination of the
drama and the singing is so strong
that it drains you completely.'
GERT VON BASSEWITZ

Werther: 'A role I love very much. The beauty is its music, the romanticism, the temperament and the feeling are things I very much associate with myself.' Here with Brigitte Fassbaender as Charlotte, in Munich, 1977. FOTOSTUDIO

Pollione in *Norma* at the Metropolitan Opera: 'One of the most gratifying of *bel canto* roles because it's much meatier than is usual in this repertoire.' © BETH BERGMAN

Loris Ipanov in *Fedora* at the Met: 'Loris is one of the three operatic heroes in my repertoire along with Siegmund and Alvaro, who suffer most. Which is to say that he is a great favourite in mine!' © BETH BERGMAN

Aeneas in *Les Troyens*: 'My only Berlioz part on stage and one of the biggest challenges of my career. A special role for a special occasion – the Centenary of the Metropolitan Opera in 1983.' With the late Tatiana Troyanos as Didon.

Title role in *Goya* at the Washington Opera in 1986: An opera composed especially for Domingo and 'a beautiful melodic piece which I enjoyed singing and believe in so much that I would love to do so again.' Here with Victoria Vergara as the Duchess of Alba at Washington Opera in 1986. WASHINGTON OPERA

Domingo with Walraud Meier as Kundry in La Scala's production of *Parsifal*, December 1991. LELLI & MASOTTI/TEATRO ALLA SCALA

*Faggioni is a director whom Domingo greatly ad-
mires. The two collaborated on several vintage productions, including* Don Carlos *in Verona,* Tosca, *and*
Manon Lescaut *at La Scala,* La Fanciulla del West *in
Turin, at Covent Garden, and Buenos Aires,* Otello *at
the Bregenz Festival and* Francesca da Rimini *at the
Metropolitan Opera.*

*A difficult and eccentric man but undoubtedly a
genius, Faggioni states that he is not sure how much
Domingo liked him at the beginning. 'But gradually I
think Plácido began to feel that special things happened inside him when we worked together. I seemed
able to get things out of him that he didn't know were
there and he came to trust me. We became very close.
I shall never forget one of the rehearsals the first time
we did* Carmen *together in Edinburgh. Of course
Plácido had sung Don José about a hundred times
already, all over the world. Yet when I acted out the
scene of Carmen's death for him, he started to cry. He
was like a child, which I found amazing . . . Perhaps I
shouldn't have, because Plácido has an extraordinary
heart and a generosity that I have never come across
in another artist, a generosity plus a willingness to
give of himself, or rather give all of himself to his roles.
This generosity, which is combined with an outstanding musical intelligence, extends to everyone around
him, although, gradually, with the passing years, he
became a little bit more careful. Even he has had to
learn how to defend himself, to close himself a little
so as not to get hurt. But in the first decade I knew
him, from 1969 to 1979, he was totally open.'*

*Despite the general popularity of Domingo's por-
trayal of Don José on stage, record and film, the dramatic side of his interpretation was sometimes attacked*

and misunderstood by critics who found it a little bit tame by Domingo standards, a bit of a weak character or, to be blunt, a bit of a mamma's boy. But as it turns out this is an essential part of Domingo's concept!

'Don José was one of my first roles in Tel Aviv, all those years ago in 1963, and fortunately I sang it in French right from the beginning. It soon became one of my most popular, because I have sung it close to 180 times. This makes it my third most popular role, after Cavaradossi (225 performances) and Otello (213).

'Although some people disagree with my portrayal, I feel I have a very special understanding of this character, because he hails from Navarra and my own mother was Basque. So I know the character of those people, who are both very proud and very reserved. Therefore, I can sense the sort of explosion of emotions that overtakes Don José the moment he comes face to face with Carmen, a character who is his diametrical opposite: a wholly extrovert, passionate Andaluza, a completely liberated, very modern woman and a gypsy to boot! So initially for him she is almost like an image of the Devil. In fact, the librettist retains Merimée's line where he says: "In my country, if I even looked at a woman like you, I'd cross myself." So, for Don José, Carmen is like a bomb, an explosion; and when she throws him a flower it has the impact of a bullet.

'Central to my portrayal is also the conviction that Micaela, a character who does not exist in Merimée, is not a real, flesh-and-blood rival for Carmen, but a representation by proxy of Don José's mother, and her all-important influence. This is the reason why I always felt that Anglo-Saxons never really understood my portrayal of Don José. Even though less violent in the opera than he is in Merimée

– where he had killed two people in his native Navarra before Carmen – Anglo-Saxon critics often remarked that I played him as too weak a character. But that's because they don't understand a Latin man's tremendously strong bond with his mother. Of course, everybody loves their mother in a unique way, but I think that Mediterranean people in general, and Spaniards and Italians in particular, have an extra special feeling. I made this very clear in Act I when José, through Micaela, is really addressing his mother and is professing himself ready to bow to her wishes. Then boom! Carmen assaults his senses and emotions and breaks through every taboo, through everything he had held sacred up to then. The reason why Bizet replaced the mother with Micaela is because, in theatrical terms, it's more interesting to contrast Carmen with an innocent young girl rather than a saintly old woman. He rightly found the double triangle thus created – Don José/Carmen/Escamillo and Carmen/Don José/Micaela – juicier and more interesting.

'Vocally Don José is one of the more difficult tenor roles, yet far from uncomfortable. Basically it requires two voices: a lyric voice for the first two acts – especially the duet with Micaela and most of the Flower Song – and a dramatic voice for the last two acts, where it has to be able to cut through and ride over the very dense orchestration. Mind you, even the first-act duet, if done without cuts, can also be very exhausting because it goes on and on and at a consistently high tessitura. Nevertheless, it's one of my most vocally satisfying parts. I love going from a lyric to a dramatic voice, from a soft, tender line to more intense, temperamental singing.'

NADIR

Les Pêcheurs de Perles

Like Ferrando and Don Ottavio, Nadir is not a significant role in Domingo's career. He sang it only in Tel Aviv on 21 January 1964 and on tour in other cities in Israel throughout the year. Since then, it has never featured in his repertoire again. Yet, as he himself explains, this second contact with a French role enhanced his love for the French repertoire, which came to occupy a very important slice of his career. Apart from Nadir, his lyrical French parts include Faust, Roméo and Des Grieux in the Massenet Manon. But although he enjoyed singing those, especially Roméo, it is the heavier dramatic French parts such as Hoffmann, Samson, Don José, Vasco da Gama, Jean de Leyden, Le Cid, etc. that Domingo has become identified with. For as Janine Reiss, the distinguished French coach and accompanist, told me some years ago, Italianate voices such as Domingo's or Carreras's are a little bit 'too rich, too luscious and sensuous' for the lighter, lyric French repertoire. 'One feels like pruning them a bit, the way you would a rose bush. The ideal voice for this kind of French part is one whose timbre is sufficiently warm to make it a beautiful voice but which, when compared to an Italianate voice, is a little bit less sunny, and consequently a little bit less warm. If one were to draw a parallel with colors and wines, a French voice would be reseda (mignonette)

78

rather than emerald green and a Bordeaux rather than a Burgundy.'

Domingo's voice is definitely a Burgundy and he thrives in the dramatic French repertoire, although his technique became so fine-honed with the years that, as he explains in his discussion of Gabriele Adorno in Simon Boccanegra, *he can lighten his voice at will.*

'Even though Nadir was my second French role in Tel Aviv, in 1964, I cannot say it taught me all that much about the French style of singing, because I sang it in Hebrew! (The other famous part I also sang in Hebrew was Lensky in *Eugene Onegin*.) This is one of the only two, and lesser known, of Bizet's operas and the music is so gorgeous that I enjoyed singing it very much. It's a very high role and Nadir's aria and famous duet with the baritone Zurga are extraordinary. But I have even less to say about this role than I do about Lensky because I never sang it again.

'Yet this contact with the French repertoire served to enhance my love for French music and sowed the seeds for my future close identification with it. By now, of course, I have sung a huge chunk of it – no fewer than twelve roles on stage and more on record – and feel completely at home in it. One thing I have learnt over the years, though, concerning the French repertoire is that if you sing it absolutely, 100 per cent correctly, with perfect accents, utmost tonal beauty and a sense of measure in everything, it can lose some of its power to move. So you have to compromise a little and while retaining a perfect accent, let go a bit with the voice. It cost me a lot to find the right compromise but I think that finally, I understood. The big difference between the French and the Italian repertoire lies in something Marta pointed out to me: in Italian singing the legato line flows completely seamless whereas in French singing, while you still have to sing legato without cutting the musical line, you nevertheless need to separate the words a little, almost infinitesimally. Otherwise it doesn't sound right, it doesn't sound like French singing.'

LENSKY

Eugene Onegin

Domingo has sung Lensky only once in his career: in September/October 1964 in Tel Aviv with his wife Marta as Tatiana and Franco Iglesias in the title role, and in Hebrew! Since these 30 or so performances, he has occasionally sung Lensky's beautiful, showpiece aria 'Kuda, kuda' in concert. Yet this contact with Tchaikovsky's world made a lasting impression and would culminate years later in his towering portrayal of Gherman in The Queen of Spades.

'It is now so long since I sang Lensky that I hardly remember my experience with him . . . Of course he is such an unbelievably sweet, beautiful, tender character, madly in love with Olga and insanely jealous. What he lacks, totally, is a sense of humor and the ability to see the light side of things. He refuses to believe that it was Onegin's own perverse sense of humor that caused him to flirt with Olga, just to tease him. So we have this tragedy of the duel in which Lensky gets killed.

'Vocally, it's a gorgeous role and I regret not having sung it in Russian. I could do it any time, even now, if anyone were to ask me! Indeed, I would welcome the opportunity to sing this beautiful aria again, in Russian, and those wonderful ensembles, especially the one at the end of the party in Act I, which is really sublime. But I don't expect I'll ever sing such a young character on stage any more. The reason

81

I never sang it earlier is that very soon after those Tel Aviv performances my international career took off and my repertoire became much more Italian-orientated and much "meatier" – *Forza*, *Ballo*, that sort of thing – so that nobody ever thought of asking me to sing Lensky. What I regret even more is never having done a recording. I wouldn't mind doing one right now. In any case, I'm looking at all the Russian tenor repertoire with Valery Gergiev for things to do, and especially at Count Vaudemont in Tchaikovsky's *Iolanta*.'

TURIDDU

Cavalleria Rusticana

Domingo sang his first Turiddu in Tel Aviv on his twenty-fourth birthday on 21 January 1965 and his last in Hamburg on 2 July 1988. In between he clocked up 102 performances in Hamburg, Vienna, Munich, the Metropolitan and the San Francisco Opera, Verona, Barcelona, La Scala, Tokyo, Covent Garden, New Orleans, Hartford and Atlanta, which makes Turiddu one of what Domingo calls his 'Centenary Roles' along with Cavaradossi (225 performances), Otello (213), Don José (182), Rodolfo (121) and Canio (111).

On the dramatic side, Domingo's understanding of this much maligned character's plight – akin, to my mind, to his also very accurate, unusual perception of Pinkerton – invests his scenic portrayal with very subtle undertones and, despite the tremendous passions he is called to express, with a measure of good taste seldom encountered in this role.

This good taste – a hallmark of Domingo's art no matter how searing, heartrending or even savage the passions and emotions in the characters at hand – also extends to the vocal side of his portrayal which, as in all of Domingo's verismo parts, is a model of how to exert every ounce of feeling, passion and abandon out of veristic roles without a hint of vulgar excess. As Turiddu was Domingo's first verismo part, it was cru-

83

cial in helping him shape his approach to this area of the repertoire and his conviction that verismo should be sung 'belcantistically', i.e. with great attention to the line, which must never be broken or interrupted by whatever sighs, gasps or other extraneous sounds characteristic to this repertoire that a singer might have to resort to.

As he has already explained apropos of Edgardo in Lucia, *Domingo applied the opposite approach to bel canto which, like Callas, he tried to imbue with a good dollop of veristic fire and élan. As Callas was a Greek and I also happen to be Greek, I cannot help but perceive both in her and in Domingo's interpretations of verismo and bel canto that idealized Greek sense of economy – the perfect blend of abandon and good taste that the Greeks always strove for in the theater.*

'I always try to look for the positive side of each character I play. In Turiddu's case, I think he is a victim of circumstances. I think he is tremendously in love with Lola. He leaves his village to go to the army and by the time he returns, she is married. He feels very, very bitter inside and goes with Santuzza to console himself – on the rebound, as you say in English. For this reason I don't like portraying Turiddu as a guy who's playing with two women. He's not playing with two women, he's not that kind of man. He really loves Lola very deeply and is suffering very much because she didn't wait for him. Okay, Santuzza is now expecting a baby, which is very unfortunate. But this doesn't mean that Turiddu is playing with two women.

'In some productions I have been asked to portray him as a sort of Sicilian gigolo. And I always refused. I said no, I don't believe this character is this kind of man. In fact there are moments in my duet with Santuzza when I treat her with tenderness, I go to her with tenderness and try . . . I try to make her understand. But she is one of those women who drive you crazy, because every time you go to them, they start crying! They start crying and say, don't do this to me, why do you do this to me, why do you do that to me? And that's exasperating. It explains why Turiddu gets so fed up that he ends up behaving the way he does towards her. It also explains why the opera ends the way it does, with Santuzza's vengeance. She goes and tells Alfio that Turiddu and Lola are lovers knowing he's going to kill him.

'When we first encounter Turiddu, much to his disappointment he has just bumped into Santuzza. He tells her he's looking for his mother and that he can't talk to her now. Of course, he's nervous, because he knows that today he has secretly met with Lola. He is supposed to have gone off to fetch the new wine but he's also seen Lola secretly in the early morning. So he feels guilty. And he is also in despair because he realizes his love for Lola is hopeless. This is an example of what I mean by saying that I always try to find positive things in the characters I portray. And I try to reflect this in my vocal delivery. I try not to make Turiddu sound brutal. But of course, Santuzza keeps insisting and insisting and nagging and nagging, so that his exasperation has to creep into your voice in the end. But you shouldn't sound spiteful. Just exasperated. Turiddu just snaps. If they could have explained things to one another, maybe the tragedy could have been avoided. But this is an opera, so there has to be tragedy!

'Vocally, Turiddu is acutely difficult. The parts I always found hardest are the Siciliana and the "*Addio alla mamma*" ("*Mamma quel vino*"). In the Siciliana the tessitura is very high. You also have to climb very high in the "*Addio alla mamma.*" And the dramatic situation means that it also has to be charged with all the feeling, power and thrust of verismo. It almost destroys you.

'Yet I have sung Turiddu over 100 times! The first time was in Tel Aviv the same evening that Marta was singing Nedda in *Pagliacci*, and I went on to do about 50 performances. But in those days I had a different attitude towards my singing. Five minutes before the performance, I would still be sitting in a café near the theater chatting to members of the public! Of course, I have never done anything like this since! But in those days everything was so natural. You just didn't think about the difficulties in a role. You just sang it! Now it would be unthinkable to be sitting in a café five minutes before the *Siciliana*! But that's what I did then. By that time Marta, whose performance in *Pagliacci* was after *Cavalleria*, was already in her dressing room, getting ready for Nedda. She was always punctilious whereas I was more casual!

'Edis de Philippe, the American soprano and later stage director, founded this company which she headed. She directed this production of *Cavalleria* and was a good stage director with interesting ideas. But I suppose the director with whom I have worked most closely on this opera is Franco Zeffirelli with whom I collaborated in productions at the Metropolitan Opera, Covent Garden, La Scala and Washington. Franco liked the idea of Turiddu as a very macho Sicilian womanizer and this is how he was portrayed by Franco Corelli who first sang the role in his Metropolitan Opera production. But when I took over, we discussed it a lot and I asked him, please, could we do something a little bit more subtle, more human. Because this is one of the most important things about the role . . . But I can never think of Turiddu without thinking also of Canio, because most of my performances of *Cavalleria* have been paired with *Pagliacci*.'

SAMSON

Samson et Dalila

Domingo has been singing Samson throughout his career, ever since 30 July 1965, when he sang it in Chautauqua shortly after leaving Tel Aviv. His last performances to date were in September 1999 in Los Angeles and, even though the part has not reached the status of a 'Centenary Role', it nevertheless totals 86 performances worldwide, which makes it one of the ten parts Domingo has sung most in his career.

Naturally, this means that his portrayal has developed and deepened over the years. When I first caught up with it, at Covent Garden in 1985, with Agnes Baltsa singing her first Dalila, Domingo had already been singing it for 20 years and was in splendid vocal and dramatic form: 'He looked fabulous and sang gloriously,' says Baltsa, 'and exuded such sensuality and eroticism that face to face with him on stage as Dalila, I could actually experience, feel and respond to this chemistry. He remains the best Samson I ever sang with, or ever saw.'

Indeed, the lustrous sheen of Domingo's sound in the great Act II love duet remains forever fixed in one's mind as a yardstick by which all present and future Samsons will be measured. Yet even now, when some of that vocal sheen is not there to the same extent, the depth and inwardness Domingo brings to Act III – down to the way he walks, really like a blind man

(I'm sure he thought himself blind as he crossed the vast setting of the temple at the Teatro Real in Madrid, the last time I saw him as Samson in June 1999), more than makes up for any loss in sheer brilliance of sound.

To prepare for the role, Domingo had studied the Old Testament (Judges: 14–16) in the Bible given to him by Pope Paul VI. As he reveals in greater length in his discussion of Parsifal, he is a devout Catholic and observes his own private rites before every performance. When discussing Samson, 20 years or so ago, he had stressed that in this opera there is the sensual music in the second act and the natural sexual reaction of a man, yet also a great depth of spiritual emotion. 'You must feel God. It is the same feeling like when you sing the Verdi Requiem.'

It is precisely this dimension that Domingo exuded in those last Madrid performances. And in a paradox only made possible when dealing with very great artists, it wiped out all the other times I had seen Domingo's Samson in Act III. It is now joined together with that stupendous Act II in the Covent Garden production. Those two moments, linked across the passage of time, add up to the most complete portrayal of Samson one could ever hope to see and hear.

'Samson – which I first sang shortly after leaving Tel Aviv, in Chautauqua in 1965, Milwaukee and Binghampton – is one of my roles that have now almost reached their centenary. Which is to say I have sung it nearly 100 times. It is a phenomenal role which I always put into a special category, along with Jean in *Hérodiade*, Parsifal and Jean in *Le Prophète*, because all four have something to do with mysticism. As with Jean and Parsifal, the fight is between a woman and God. It's not a fight with the baritone or be-

tween a mezzo and a soprano, but the choice between a
phenomenal woman – in this case Dalila – and Samson's
duty, his mission from God.

'I find it interesting that Samson comes off better in the
opera than he does in the Bible, where he was not all that
saintly and was also having an affair with Dalila's sister.
But in the opera it is he who comes across as the good boy
and Dalila as the bad girl. In reality I think Samson was
both deeper and more controversial. But as it is you have to
portray what is in the libretto and the music. And in the
opera we have the conflict between mysticism – his duty to
lead the people of Israel out of captivity, a mission to which
God has called him – and this woman . . .

'Musically, Samson is so gratifying that I chose to cel-
ebrate my thirtieth anniversary at the Met with this role.
Even the date coincided exactly: 28 September 1998, 30
years to the day since my debut as Maurizio in *Adriana
Lecouvreur*. I chose it because Samson is a role that has
given me great, deep satisfaction. Vocally it's very comfortable. But, you have to be in very, very good physical shape,
because it requires a lot of strength and a lot of stamina to
go through the part which is heavy, both vocally and physically. Not just the exhausting last act with the sawmill, but
all of it. His first entry has to be very powerful and create
an impact right away. You are angry, you encourage and
arouse the Hebrews and you kill Abimelech. So that bit is
difficult. The next thing you must watch for is a line in the
trio, a beautiful line where his real feelings for Dalila start
to come out. Then you have the fabulous love duet in Act II
which is accompanied by a dense orchestration and therefore requires maximum power if you are to project your
voice to thrilling effect. The last act, the Mill Scene, is so
profound, so moving and so painful that it leaves you altogether drained. You can actually hear the pain in the music.

89

And then, you have to summon all your strength, physical and vocal, for the finale where Samson brings down the Temple.'

TITLE ROLE

Les Contes d'Hoffmann

Hoffmann is rightly considered one of Domingo's towering portrayals, on a par with his unforgettable Des Grieux, Cavaradossi, Alvaro, Samson, Aeneas, Siegmund, Gherman and, almost, with his unsurpassed and, in my view, unsurpassable Otello. Even though he first sang it quite early in his career, on 7 September 1965 in Mexico City, Philadelphia, Cincinnati Zoo (with NYCO in 1967 and 1968), the Metropolitan Opera in 1973 and the Chicago Lyric Opera in 1976, it was not until 1980, the Offenbach centenary, that he became wholly identified with the part and it with him. It happened after he sang Hoffmann in three important new productions in quick succession – Jean-Pierre Ponnelle's at the Salzburg Festival, Michael Hampe's in Cologne and John Schlesinger's at Covent Garden.

Of all those productions he prefers Schlesinger's despite the fact that he disagrees with the sequence of the three Acts, which in this staging was Olympia, Giulietta, Antonia rather than his preferred sequence of Olympia, Antonia, Giulietta; and, as Schlesinger himself explained, despite the fact that at the beginning Domingo harbored some initial reservations about the distinguished film director's concept, having first convinced him to put aside the necessary time to stage this, his first opera. Domingo likes to present all his characters in the most positive light, so as to

91

elicit the audience's maximum sympathy for them, however negative those characters might be.

'So he wouldn't commit himself to my view of Hoffmann as an alcoholic, who should be dishevelled and unglamorous at his first entry, because he worried that the audience might take against him. He added that he saw him as more of a poetic character. I replied that you can be poetic but at the same time very self-destructive and that, anyway, there was plenty of time for him to be glamorous in his three personas in the three acts. Then, after seeing him in the Cologne production which didn't correspond to my ideas at all, we didn't meet again until we came to rehearsals at Covent Garden,' remembers Schlesinger.

'Gradually, during rehearsals, I noticed that he began to like the idea of an alcoholic Hoffmann in the Prologue and Epilogue and to develop it very beautifully. The experience of working with him was riveting and also very moving because of his willingness, eagerness almost, to submit himself to difficult or awkward stage movements and positions if he felt that they helped clarify the core of the character. "No, that's too easy. Let me lie down on a plank which is more difficult and therefore bound to be more effective," he would say. I don't know why this surprised me so much. Perhaps because I had this idea in my mind of a divo who would just wish to be center-stage all this time. Well, as you know, but as I didn't know as yet, Plácido is the diametrical opposite of such a creature.'

Domingo's current admirers and posterity can enjoy this vintage portrayal on video, with a star cast that includes Luciana Serra as Olympia, Ileana Cotrubas as Antonia, Agnes Baltsa as Giulietta and Robert Lloyd as Lindorf, Geraint Evans as Coppélius,

Siegmund Nimsgern as Dappertutto and Nicola Ghiuselev as Dr Miracle.

'In the beginning I found Hoffmann an "ungrateful" role to portray. I compared him a little, in my mind, to Beethoven who, despite his towering genius, also had an unpleasant, self-destructive side to his character and was difficult to live with and "not easy to love." Yet people always sought him out, because of his music. The same is true of Hoffmann, who also has a strong self-destructive streak. Yet people are always encouraging him to tell his stories, because he tells them so very well.

'Because of the different editions of the work – the Oeser and the older Choudens – and the fact that Offenbach never established a definite ending, I feel that I have the added advantage of a character not as definitely drawn as most operatic heroes, and this sort of thing sets your imagination free to dream and work him out for yourself. And now, having sung the role in productions of both the existing versions of the work, I still cannot decide which is the right one because, apart from considering it essential to include the Epilogue, I think both have merits and demerits. But in both editions Hoffmann is a role difficult to act and to sing, with a high and uneven tessitura which demands several different kinds of vocal color, ranging from light singing in the Olympia act, a pure lyrical sound for the Antonia act, a rich, passionate voice for Giulietta and dramatic yet kind of destroyed tones for the Prologue and Epilogue. And the tremendous scope provided by this role, not only for vocal but also for emotional and even physical development, is what makes Hoffmann so very challenging and rewarding to portray.

'Unlike many operatic characters, like Cavaradossi, to whom everything happens within a single day, or Otello, where it takes a few weeks, or Werther, where it stretches to a few months, Hoffmann spans almost an entire lifetime. In the Prologue and Epilogue, I see him as a man of 50. Then in the first flashback to his youth – the Olympia act – he is a young and immature man in his early twenties. When we meet him again in the Antonia act which, both for vocal and dramatic reasons – because it's the closest he ever comes to real love – should always be placed before the Giulietta act, he is a man of about 35. And in the Giulietta act he is around 45. And the Giulietta act, by the way, is the most difficult from the vocal point of view because it requires the richest voice towards the end of a long, hard evening's sing, and this leaves you vocally charged for the Epilogue: exhausted, finished, just as the ending requires. So you have to be one man at four very different stages in his life. And each stage requires not only a different vocal color but also a different dramatic approach.

'Yet it is important not to forget that all the characters in the different acts are really one man and that the common denominator is the dissolution of love, with Hoffmann emerging as the loser throughout. For all his love affairs – and I believe that, although he must have had many more, these three represent crucial phases of his emotional development – are unbalanced. He never manages to combine the ideal with the passionate, carnal aspects of love. The Olympia act, with this foolish, illusory love is barely credible. Hoffmann is the only person capable of falling in love with this puppet while everyone around him is laughing and having a ball at his expense. But he believes in it and this shows the rather naive and idealistic side of his character which later develops into this very romantic, almost platonic love for Antonia, the love that never really happens because of her sickness. It is not a complete, fulfilled love, however, only a romantic, platonic version of it, because the only thing those two ever made together is music. Through music they lived this strong, absolutely incredible love story. And Antonia's death is yet another step towards the dissolution of love, a process completed by Giulietta, the courtesan in whom Hoffmann foolishly hopes to find love again. By the end he arrives at the somewhat cynical dimension characteristic of a man who, although completely defeated by love, yet pretends to be a great lover. But he is not, and his failure to find love is largely due to the presence of the devil inside him – not a real devil, of course, but Hoffmann's own self-destructive streak – who possesses him almost completely.

'Do I, also have a devil inside me? Yes! I do. All of us have both God and devil, both good and bad, in us. But you have to negotiate with this devil, find out which way he is trying to lead you and decide on which occasions you may agree to go along with him, to some extent. For in many cases you make a sort of pact with the devil within you, because you see some things in him which you may like or feel you can use creatively, while certain other traits may be too much and lead to chaos. Every human being experiences this sort of conflict because the devil is always right there inside you, telling you "Do this, do that," and some of his exhortations you accept while others you reject. The secret is to find the very delicate dividing line between the creative and destructive side of the devil's influence. In Hoffmann's case, the devil is pushing him in all the wrong directions, but without him ever realizing it, so anxious and desperate he is to find love, real love. But in the end, he is saved by his muse. His love of writing is so strong that when offered another drink he refuses. And nowhere was this made so clear as in John Schlesinger's Covent Garden production which I consider the best staging of this work I have sung in.'

TITLE ROLE

Don Rodrigo

As Domingo describes below, Don Rodrigo was an immensely important role in his career, the role that put him on the international map less than a year after leaving Tel Aviv. It was also the first contemporary part he ever sang. The occasion was momentous: the Gala Opening of the NYCO at its new home in Lincoln Center on 22 Febuary 1966, before a festive audience brimming with celebrities.

The staging of the opera itself – about the last Visigoth King of eighth-century Spain – was lavish. The opera required 19 principals, 84 instrumentalists, a chorus of a hundred, with bells clanging from the balconies and 18 horns sounding forth through the auditorium. There was a five-week rehearsal period of, reportedly, 18 hours of rehearsal a day. 'Everyone worked tremendously hard,' recalls Lil Herbert, a member of the chorus. 'But nobody did so harder than Domingo who attended every rehearsal, always meticulously well prepared.' Journalists from all over the world had been invited and Domingo triumphed in the piece.

He earned well-deserved public and critical acclaim: 'Sung and acted with superb voice, bearing and intensity of feeling,' wrote the New Yorker. The verdict was echoed in publications worldwide. Thus, only four months after his debut with NYCO, Domingo had laid the foundations for his international reputation and he recalls the occasion with special warmth: 'There was a wonderful, wonderful feeling throughout the company. It was very united.'

'Don Rodrigo was my first role in a contemporary opera and it came very early on in my career, in 1966, barely six months after Marta and I left the opera at Tel Aviv, at the age of 25. Unlike the three other contemporary operas I have been involved in and which were written specifically for me, this was not a world premiere. That had taken place two years earlier in Buenos Aires with Carlo Cossutta in the title role. But needless to say, it was a thrilling and vastly challenging experience! It came about after I had auditioned for Julius Rudel, Music Director of New York City Opera. He hired me on the spot for three operas at the old New York City Center – Pinkerton, Don José and Hoffmann – on condition that I would also sing the title role in this opera, which I didn't know. So of course I said yes, little realizing, until I finally got to see the score months later, that it was a completely atonal piece! But musically it proved absolutely gorgeous and the whole production was a great occasion because it marked the opening, on 22 February 1966, of NYCO in its new home at Lincoln Center.

'For me personally, it was a great experience vocally, dramatically and also from the career viewpoint because it put me on the American and international music map barely six months after I left my first job at Tel Aviv. After the first New York performances, the production travelled to Los Angeles and was revived in New York the following season. What I regret, though, is that it was never recorded or televised – of course, those were early days for television – because the opera itself is extraordinary and the production, by Tito Capobianco, so magnificent that I would have treasured a lasting documentation. In fact Julius Rudel and I are still discussing the possibility of reviving it. But we know what a huge effort this would represent for everybody, myself included. Back in 1966, I was in my mid-twenties, I was beginning my career and put everything I had, all my energy, all my enthusiasm into it. I wonder if I could do it the same degree of justice now as I did then, with all that youthful optimism and élan!

'The opera is about the last Visigoth king of Spain and vocally very, very difficult, especially for a beginner like me. Some passages were really phenomenally demanding. Singing atonal music is always very difficult. Of course, there comes a point where it becomes almost second nature. But the whole process of putting the melodies – passages like [demonstrating] his cries of "*Florinda, Florinda*" – into the voice takes much longer to become automatic. No, there is no different technique involved either in the studying or the singing of atonal music. It just takes longer to learn. Another major difficulty lies in how you get the leads, or cues, for your entries from the orchestra, or rather, in the fact that you don't! I asked Ginastera, who was there, present in all the rehearsals and extremely flexible about everything else, about it, but there was nothing he could do. Later, when I came to sing three more contemporary roles, this time composed especially for me, I asked the composers in question to provide such cues.

'But this was my first experience of working with a living composer, and fantastically stimulating. I remember that he was accompanied by an Argentinian pianist named Tauriello, an excellent musician who could play the entire score of *Wozzeck* by heart and knew the score of *Don Rodrigo* even better than the composer himself. He, too, was present at every rehearsal and whenever any of us missed a note, he would rush to the piano and say, "No, no, it doesn't go this way, it goes like that!" But Ginastera himself was amazingly flexible. When I occasionally asked if he could change this or that detail for me as I was still so young and inexperienced, he replied: "Please change anything so that the music becomes comfortable for your voice." A great lesson from a great man! I have found that this flexibility and willingness to adapt the music to the voices at hand is true of all composers I have known and, from what one reads, also of the greats of the past, who also tended to be flexible in this sense as long as it didn't affect the essential truth of their work. Conductors are a different story! But then, they carry the entire responsibility for the realization of a work written by someone else, usually a genius.'

TITLE ROLE

Andrea Chénier

*Domingo first sang the title role in this opera on 3
March 1966 in New Orleans. But this was not his
first contact with the work. He had auditioned at the
National Opera in Mexico in 1959, as a baritone, with
Gérard's famous aria 'Nemico della patria?' (plus the
Prologue from* Pagliacci*). But the panel pronounced
him a tenor and persuaded him to sight-read Loris's
aria 'Amor ti vieta' from* Fedora *instead! The rest is
operatic history.*

*His engagement in New Orleans came about
thanks to the conductor Anton Guadagno, with whom
the Domingos had worked and built a good relationship in Mexico before leaving for Tel Aviv. One
evening, early in 1966, during Domingo's first season
at NYCO, the Guadagnos invited the Domingos to
dinner in their apartment, and Guadagno mentioned
that he was soon off to New Orleans for* Chénier *with
Corelli. Mindful of the latter's penchant for frequent
cancellations, he added laughingly, 'Plácido, be prepared.' Domingo replied that he had never sung
Chénier. 'Well,' replied Guadagno, 'I'm not saying
anything except to be ready.' And, as Domingo recalls in his autobiography, two days later the phone
rang! He learnt the part in two or three days and sped
to New Orleans. The public's anger and disappointment at Corelli's cancellation worked in Domingo's*

favor just as it did, two years later, on the occasion of his debut at the Metropolitan Opera, when he again substituted for Corelli.

Since then Domingo sang Chénier in July of the following year at the Cincinnati Zoo Opera and in August in Santiago, Chile; at the Metropolitan Opera three years later, in October and December 1970, then in Madrid, Mexico City, Barcelona, Torino, Saragossa, San Francisco, again at the Met in 1977, Bilbao, Oviedo, Puerto Rico, Chicago, Vienna, Miami and London. The last time he did so was a special occasion, in Versailles on 15 July 1989, for the 200th anniversary of the French Revolution.

Andrea Chénier is a perfect vehicle for displaying the elegance and taste that are an essential component of Domingo's artistic persona. The real André Chénier had been French Consul in Constantinople and Domingo's demeanor throughout combines the nobility of his birth with the fire of the poet and ardor of the lover.

'Andrea Chénier is a tenor's dream role. Not only is he a romantic, dashing hero, but he also has four showpiece arias, one in every act, and each more beautiful than the other. His duet with Maddalena is also very beautiful. Yet the very beauty of his music and proliferation of tour de force arias also renders Chénier one of the most difficult and demanding roles in the repertoire. You have to be in really good shape to sing it but if you are, then it's a very, very enjoyable sing.

'Of all the arias, the first-act "*Improvviso*" and second-act aria "*Io non l'ho amato ancor*," which nobody realizes is an aria, are the most difficult. The "*Improvviso*" is almost a lesson in good tenor singing. It contains both lyrical

101

and dramatic passages and you should use a completely different vocal color accordingly. The opening of the aria is very poetic. Chénier is hurt by Maddalena's dismissive words and the expression of these feelings should come out in exquisite sound and a beautifully shaped lyrical line. Then, as he gets carried away your sound should become more dramatic and virtually explode at the phrase where he talks about the beauty of life, "*Ecco la bellezza della vita.*" This is where you add power, but without ever detracting from the lyrical beauty of your sound. The aria "*Sì, fui soldato*" in Act III is quite easy. "*Un bel dì di maggio*" in Act IV is more or less easy depending on whether you do it as it's written (in which case it's easy) or in the alternative version, which has a B flat which happens to be a particularly difficult B flat. This comes at the end of the opera, after a long evening's sing, and when you still have the last duet ahead of you.

'Dramatically, Chénier is much more of a romantic hero than a revolutionary. The librettist changed the real story in order to make the drama stronger. In real life Maddalena de Coigny did not die with Chénier. In the opera she does, to enhance the drama. But although Chénier is rewarding to portray, he is not as interesting a character as the baritone, Gérard, who develops much more during the course of the action, while Chénier is always strong from beginning to end.'

HIPPOLYTE

Hippolyte et Aricie

Surprisingly, Domingo's only venture into baroque opera – so far! – took place at the time when he was also performing in the first contemporary opera of his career, Ginastera's Don Rodrigo *at NYCO. The production of Rameau's masterpiece was with Sarah Caldwell's Boston Opera Company, in Boston on 6 and 10 April 1966, with Beverly Sills in the other title role.*

The news of this engagement – which also included performances of La Bohème *with Renata Tebaldi, and Aron in Schoenberg's* Moses und Aron, *which failed to materialize – reached Domingo on a particularly gloomy day: he was deeply upset by an unusually negative review of his recent performances of Hoffmann in Philadelphia in which the critic in question had slain his performance! For the first and almost the last time in his career, Domingo was so affected that he planned to react angrily. But the news that he was about to sing next to two of the world's greatest divas was enough to revive his spirits at a stroke and, as he states in his autobiography, he 'let the critic live in peace'!*

In the event the performances went well and he found working with Sarah Caldwell very interesting. Despite the extreme difficulty of the role of Hippolyte, he relished the musical experience of singing in the baroque style and although he has not done so again since then, he has a surprise in store for all of us at the end of his brief discussion of the role.

'I was thrilled both by the news and later by the experience of singing with Beverly Sills who, needless to say, was absolutely spectacular as Aricie! This made up for the great difficulties that confronted me when I attempted my first brush with baroque opera.

'For, singing baroque music is phenomenally difficult: it requires a lot of discipline, a very clean, clear line, great rhythmic precision and, of course, a great deal of coloratura singing. Basically this was the lightest singing – and by that I refer to vocal weight, not the content of the work – I have ever done. My only preparation had been my earlier brush with Mozart: Ferrando in Mexico and Don Ottavio in Tel Aviv. But Rameau is much, much more difficult and, in addition, I sang it at the same time that I was singing atonal music in *Don Rodrigo*.

'But I have always tried to move from style to style and not to be petrified by the exigencies of any particular style of composer. I consider this an essential part of a singer's musicianship. For moving outside your standard repertoire from time to time gives you new musical insights and this enriches your capacity for performing all, including your standard, roles. As far as the dramatic side of the role is concerned, all I remember is that I was eaten by a dragon – echoes of my later stage-son, the young Siegfried!

'But the beauty and depth of baroque music is such that, although I left it alone throughout the rest of my career, I am thinking of the possibility of Handel's *Tamerlano*, Gluck's *Iphigenie en Tauride* and even, maybe, Monteverdi's *L'Incoronazione di Poppea*, for the future.'

CANIO

I Pagliacci

Canio is another of Domingo's 'Centenary Roles.' It numbers a total of 111 performances, dating from 9 August 1966, when he first sang it at the Lewisohn Stadium with the Metropolitan Opera Company, to 23 October 1999 when he sang it with the same company at Lincoln Center. On many occasions he performed Canio on the same night as Turiddu in Cavalleria *and, more seldom, Luigi in* Il Tabarro.

Canio is one of his most popular portrayals worldwide and always elicits maximum sympathy from the audience. Yet, despite depicting Canio as a good man, Domingo on stage also arouses maximum terror in the sopranos who sing Nedda with him! Veronica Villaroel, who did so in Washington and the Metropolitan Opera, recalls that on both occasions she felt real fear on stage:

'When I play Nedda to Plácido's Canio I am scared to death, I'm scared he'll really kill me, Mamma mia, I feel real terror!' Her experience is similar to that of Renée Fleming who sang Desdemona to Domingo's Otello at the Metropolitan Opera in October 1995. As she was second cast, she had not taken part in the initial rehearsals but did have to rehearse the very dramatic duet in Act III, where Otello hurls Desdemona to the floor. Domingo walked up to Fleming, slapped her face and whispered, 'Hello, I'm Plácido Domingo,

nice to meet you.' 'And,' remembers Fleming, 'after the rehearsal I could hardly walk! I literally had to hold on to the rails in order to climb up a pair of steps because my legs were shaking. Plácido was so terrifying in that scene, so real, that he produced an equally real reaction in me. I had never experienced anything like that on stage before and it was incredibly exciting.'

As both Fleming and Villaroel found out, such stimulating exchanges happen when there is a real collaborative exchange between great artists. It has to do not just with experience but with the aura and intensity of feeling such artists exude on stage. For, again, according to Veronica Villaroel, *'when I go to see Plácido perform, I see in his portrayals authority, love, care, tenderness, passion, a wonderful colleague to his partners, and a great musician and actor. When I'm actually singing with him, he gives me all this plus this energy of his which is so strong that it reaches right inside me and draws incredibly powerful responses out of me to the point where I can react in the same way that he does to anything unforeseen or spontaneous that might occur onstage. On the last of a run of performances in Washington in November 1997 Plácido (who had been suffering from severe toothache throughout the evening), suddenly grabbed me by the waist and swept me into an impromptu waltz. It was completely unrehearsed but I responded at once and it worked.'*

'I have sung Canio many, many times, over 100 times, I think, and greatly enjoyed doing so. As a character, you can portray him in several different ways. You can be a little bit of a brute, a drunkard; or the chief, the padrone, or paterfamilias, of the whole troupe of travelling performers; or a man suspicious of his wife because he feels older; or as a straightforward man, a good man who gets so deeply disappointed, so shocked by the discovery that his wife loves another man that he cracks. And this, the latter view, is the best solution, I think. It has a whiff of *Otello* about it . . .

'The way I imagine the story is that Canio probably took Nedda in as a child. Then, when the child grew, he married her. Nedda feels for him the way she would for a father. So, when she meets a young man she likes and who likes her, she doesn't enter into a relationship because she wants to betray Canio, but because it's a natural thing, she's going for something she's never had. This is the interpretation I prefer because it gives you more leeway, although some of the others were also interesting: coming onstage and being very suspicious and a little bit crude from the beginning, you know sort of watching Nedda all the time, and being a bit cruel the moment she as much as looks at another man. But, the one which works best for me is the interpretation that makes Canio really a good man. He is inclined to be jealous, like most people from Sicily and Calabria are, yet a good person. But he gets this terrible shock when he discovers the truth and realizes what's going on. And of course, his reaction is something he can't control. Something in his heart snaps, and the way she challenges him, by saying I'm not going to tell you his name even if you kill me, goads him to the point where he sees red and stabs her. It's not that he was planning a premeditated crime. It's a bit like Don José in *Carmen*. She goads him and he snaps.

'The first time I sang it was at the New York City Opera, in a very satisfying production by Frank Corsaro whose ideas produced a most interesting and inventive characterization. Apart from Franco Zeffirelli's several productions, I also sang Canio in very good productions by the late Jean-

Pierre Ponnelle in San Francisco and Giancarlo Del Monaco in Munich, where I sang both Turiddu and Canio on the same night. This is what I have tended to do most of the time. Needless to say, singing those two on the same night is a marathon! And as if that weren't enough, once in Barcelona, in the 1970s when the baritone got sick, I did the Prologue as well as Turiddu and Canio. Which of the two characters haunts me most? I think Canio's pain is deeper . . . And I remember that when I sang Canio first and Turiddu second at some rehearsals, I found that Turiddu became easier to sing.

'I'm intrigued you noticed something utterly spontaneous, unrehearsed, that I did on the last of a run of performances in Zeffirelli's Washington production in 1997. I grasped Veronica Villaroel by the waist and swept her into a waltz! It was a spontaneous impulse in response to the craziness of the moment: Canio arrives in the middle of the show and, at least for a little while, tries to pull himself together a little bit and continue with the show as if nothing were wrong, until the situation overwhelms him. Sometimes these things come to you spontaneously, and you have to go with the moment . . . There is no doubt that a lot of what you do in a performance – the way you walk, even the degree of concentration – is affected by who your partners are. One of the most important things for me, in every role I do, is listening to the others, to my partners. You have to be the character but at the same time you have to be so concentrated, so "in character" that you can react even to the way they look at you. Timing can also vary a great deal depending on who you're singing with. Last year I did another interesting production by Liliana Cavani in Ravenna, with Muti conducting. She had very much a film director's approach: she didn't want us to do very much – in fact she wanted very little movement – but she wanted intensity of expression, facial expression. So perhaps this is the opera I have performed with the greatest number of directors.

'As far as the voice is concerned, Canio is one of those roles which have to be sung with the vocal beauty and conviction of a bel canto role but for which you also have to have the temperament of verismo: plenty of passion and abandon. But the music is so beautiful that all the lines of *"Un bel gioco"* and *"Vesti la giubba"* and *"Pagliaccio non son"* have to be sung with utmost beauty of tone. You cannot scream this music. You have to sing it. Nevertheless you have to inject temperament and intensity into your singing. All Canio's pain and despair should be there and yet you have to be careful with what you do vocally. The only easy thing about Canio is that it's short! Otherwise, it can be a killer role. Singing it coupled with *Il Tabarro* – which I did in Vienna in June 1992 – was enjoyable but made no difference to the vocal exhaustion at the end of the evening.'

COUNT ALMAVIVA

Il Barbiere di Siviglia

Domingo sang his only Rossini part, Count Almaviva, very early in his career, in 1966, in Guadalajara, Mexico. In the discussion that follows, he describes the circumstances of this engagement, and his encounter with this role.

An unknown but very important by-product of these performances was also his first contact with an artist with whom he was destined to form a fruitful and lasting partnership that would span two decades: Sherrill Milnes, one of the great Verdi baritones of our day, with whom he has sung hundreds of performances of over 20 roles over the years. 'Our careers converged from the beginning and developed along parallel lines,' says Milnes, 'although the way we got there was different: he from an international launching pad whereas I was still very much a home-grown product.'

In Guadalajara, Milnes sang Figaro to Domingo's Almaviva and Enrico to his Edgardo in Lucia. *'He was very, very good in both parts. Of course, the voice in those days was much lighter and I'm afraid that I didn't know the role of Almaviva sufficiently to notice the cuts he says he made in the part. What was immediately apparent, apart from the beauty of his voice, was a rare and outstanding musicianship, maybe linked to his piano-playing, which is very good. I also*

110

noted that he had a wonderful way with words: he would curve and arch and enjoy and toss them to the audience in a very effective way.

'And he was an instinctive stage animal. You could play ping-pong with him, i.e. bounce emotions at him and know that he would always react and deliver back. I can't tell you what a difference this gift can make to the joy you get out of a performance! Combined with his high quality musicianship, it made him a very adaptable, flexible partner on stage. He could make changes and adjustments if you asked him to. Unlike many dumb singers whose attitude is "This is the way I do this and that's that," you could really discuss roles with Plácido and say: "Let's take a breath here, or let's hold this a fraction longer," and he would do it and enjoy doing it. Normally when I'm singing with tenors I listen to how they phrase and then imitate them because usually they can't change. But Plácido can change even from evening to evening . . . Little did I know then how closely intertwined our careers were destined to become! But I knew that this was someone special.' The only whiff we have of Domingo in this role is a performance of the Duetto del Metallo in the video Homage to Seville, *which is a masterpiece of vocal artistry and dramatic wit. Equally outstanding, although not relevant here, is Domingo's masterly rendition of Florestan's monologue.*

'Count Almaviva is not one of the roles associated with my kind of voice. Yet I sang it once, in 1966 in the beautiful Mexican city of Guadalajara, for a special occasion: the centenary of the city's Teatro Degollado. The management rang to ask whether I could sing two parts: Edgardo in *Lucia*, which I knew well and had sung on several occasions, and

111

Count Almaviva in *Barbiere*. I said I wasn't sure about the latter, I would look at the score and let them know. Well, I decided to sing it and I am glad I did. It was a lot of fun! But, as often happens, I have to confess that this was a very trimmed version of the opera, minus a great many coloratura passages. Yet even so, coping with the first duet was very difficult . . .

'Almaviva is my only Rossini role on stage. Also one of the few opportunities I've had in my career to perform a role in a nice comedy. Yet in 1982 I had another chance to make a fleeting contact with this character, when Jean-Pierre Ponnelle and I had the idea of putting together a television special based on operatic characters who hail from Seville, in which I sang both Almaviva and Figaro as well as Don Alvaro, Don José, Don Giovanni, Florestan, and Rafael Ruiz in *El Gato Montes*. The music was conducted by James Levine and we had already recorded it in the studio before arriving in Seville to start filming. The company sent us a track for me to dub the sound while filming. But when the track arrived, we discovered to our dismay that there was no sound on it! So we had to fly to Madrid, find a studio, put my voice on the track in one single session, and fly back to Seville to film!

'Which of the two roles was the most difficult? Undoubtedly Almaviva, because it's so high, requires great agility and lightness of touch, for which you have to summon all your technique. The Almaviva–Figaro duet on this video, "*Su, vediamo di quel metallo,*" is one of the things I'm happiest and proudest of in my career! The programme ended up winning two Emmy Awards – the television equivalent of the Oscars – and it was a wonderful project to film in Seville. The idea that I should sing both Almaviva and Figaro was Ponnelle's. In fact there is another spot in this programme in which I appear in a scene with myself: during the Champagne Aria where I also play the part of Leporello. I don't sing, and perhaps this is why nobody seems to have noticed. But if you look carefully at Leporello, you will see that it's me!

'You ask how I managed to sing a part as light as Almaviva after so many years of heavy singing. One of the most important things about a tenor voice, any tenor voice, is to keep it fresh, keep it young. If your voice doesn't sound young, you cannot be a tenor, because almost all the characters you have to sing are young. There is nothing technical, no exercises that I do in order to achieve this. I just think young, think the voice light. Because even in heavy, dramatic roles such as Siegmund, there are moments, such as the "*Winterstürme*" where you have to lighten the voice, or literally let light creep into your sound. And as I believe that the best exercise for a singer is just singing, I force myself to undertake some light, youthful parts such as Gabriele Adorno in *Simon Boccanegra* from time to time in order to bring the voice up again.'

LUIGI

Il Tabarro

Domingo first sang Luigi on 8 March 1967 during his second season at NYCO. It is not one of his best-known parts, for he has sung only 17 performances – in New Orleans in November 1968, Philadelphia in February 1972, Hartford in March 1973, Madrid in May 1979, the Metropolitan Opera in October 1989 and September 1994, and the Vienna Volksoper in June 1993 – but he is, nevertheless, very fond of this unhappy hero whose hard lot in life moves him deeply.

Sherrill Milnes, who has sung Michele to Domingo's Luigi, feels that Domingo brings just the right qualities to this working-class hero – so far removed from the usual noblemen and kings in his repertoire, and who 'if he were speaking rather than singing, would be using slang' – to elicit the audience's sympathy and compassion, not only at Luigi's plight as a lover, but at the injustice suffered by men of his position. The New York Times's distinguished critic Bernard Holland noticed this facet of Domingo's portrayal in the 1989 performances.

'Mr Domingo has not sung this role in eight years and never in this production, but he occupies it with great confidence. His big physical frame makes him a credible stevedore and his gait and gesture have a working-man's naturalness. The writing rarely hits Mr Domingo in the sweetest part of his range but the hard

114

muscularity in his tenor on Saturday night was appropriate.'

Domingo's last performance of this role was at the Met on 26 September 1994 as part of the Trittico, *while on other occasions he sang Luigi on the same night as Canio in* Pagliacci. *On what was probably the most amusing of such occasions – the Vienna production in June 1993 – as part of an officially conceived gimmick, after singing Luigi at the Volksoper he took the tram and went on to perform as Canio at the State Opera.*

'This is one of the few Puccini operas not put on very often. When it is, it's usually part of the "*Trittico*" [triptych] which also includes *Suor Angelica* and *Gianni Schicchi*. Less often, it is coupled with Leoncavallo's *I Pagliacci* or Mascagni's *Cavalleria Rusticana*.

'Vocally Luigi is a very short role. Yet being short doesn't stop it from being very difficult. The tessitura is high throughout and, in his duet with Giorgetta, a killer. There is a phrase in this duet which sits on G sharp – bang in the middle of the passaggio – and is repeated again and again before climbing up to B natural. This adds up to a lot of singing at such an uncomfortable tessitura. Yet I adore the part. I love the character of Luigi, who is a very, very bitter character, a man living a very difficult life. He is a stevedore, part of the lowest social strata and acutely aware of social injustice. Indeed, in his aria "*Hai ben ragione*" he sings about that, about how hard he and his coworkers work for a meager living and how badly they are treated. Then there is his passionate love for Giorgetta, who happens to be married, and very unhappily married, to his boss Michele. But even though Giorgetta reciprocates his love, their relationship has a tragic ending. Michele, her jealous husband discovers their affair, stabs Luigi and wraps his corpse with his cloak – *il tabarro* – for Giorgetta to discover, which makes for a highly dramatic ending.'

RADAMES

Aida

*Radames was one of Domingo's earliest Verdi roles.
He sang it first in Hamburg on 11 May 1967 and continued singing it until the end of the Eighties. In the
discussion that follows, he describes Radames as the
perfect lirico spinto role and so it is. It is also a perfect
vehicle for displaying Domingo's outstanding technique and good taste, both vocal and dramatic.*

*Vocally, his unique way of phrasing the passaggio
notes and building up the high notes – in this case no
fewer than 23 B flats – is achieved through a succession of vocal bridges, or arcs, so that the high notes
don't sound weak or insecure in this context but emerge
rounded both above and below, 'rich in vibrato and
harmonics,' in Marta Domingo's words, 'like a column instead of a pyramid (heavy below and tapered
on top), as with many other tenors.'*

*Dramatically, the role is fulfilled through the pro-
found nobility of his portrayal. While there are several kinds of Radameses around, ranging from gruff
soldiers to weaklings whose infatuation makes them
seem like putty in Aida and Amonasro's hands,
Domingo's is a noble Radames through and through,
permeated by an innate dignity that goes far beyond
the pride of a warrior. Never has the pathos of
Radames's veil of self-imposed, self-contained isola-
tion in his Trial Scene, where he tries to reconcile him-*

*self to himself, come across more movingly. And it
was not just a matter of the way Domingo stood, or
even of his facial expressions, but of something he
exuded, or emanated through his whole persona.
Equally convincing was the almost tangible way in
which Radames's initial infatuation with Aida's beauty
was seen to grow into a love so deep as to make his
renunciation of Amneris's offer – to save his life if he
promised never to see Aida again – seem absolutely
logical.*

*Yet Grace Bumbry, who sang Amneris with
Domingo in Vienna in the early Seventies, remembers
that in those days, although already totally secure
vocally, Domingo was not yet the great singing actor
he later became. 'Although he sang the role beautifully, without any vocal problems, I remember him as
rather unsure histrionically: very willing, very friendly
and co-operative on stage as a colleague but by no
means the outstanding actor he was later to become,
and who was to astound me, when five years later we
came together for L'Africaine at Covent Garden. This,
of course, has to do with growth. No, it has to do
with more than that. It has to do with wanting to
grow. Plácido always wanted to stretch himself and
get better all the time. This sort of zeal for self-im-
provement, which Plácido possesses to the nth degree,
is very rare . . . Yet it's the basic difference that distinguishes a fine singer: the realization that the study never
stops.'*

'Radames is the prototype of a lirico spinto tenor role. It
needs a lot of brilliance, a lot of stamina and a lot of technique. It's certainly one of the most difficult in the tenor
repertoire. The moment Radames steps on stage, he has to

sing that very important aria "*Celeste Aida*," which every-body loves, is eagerly waiting for and which, therefore, must be exciting. Yet the fact that this aria, which culminates in a very exposed B flat ("*Un trono vicino al sol*"), comes right at the beginning of the opera is both a disadvantage and an advantage. The disadvantage is obvious: you have to sing this tricky aria "cold," without a chance to warm up the voice. But the advantage is that, having got rid of this hurdle, you then have the rest of the entire opera to make some-thing of! And, if "*Celeste Aida*" has gone more or less well, you can relax and just be the character.

'Of course, after "*Celeste Aida*" you still have plenty more B flats to sing – 22 of them to be precise, including two optional ones and an interpolated one in the ensemble. But you also have some sensational moments ahead, both vocally and dramatically: first, right after this aria, the duet with Amneris, a trio and an ensemble; then, in Act I Scene 2 comes the Temple Scene, followed two scenes later by the Triumph Scene; Act III, the Nile Scene, which is the best of all to my mind, with a wonderful duet with Aida and the trio with her and Amonasro, which gets very difficult around the middle, though. Then comes the Judgement Scene (Act IV Scene 1) and finally the Tomb Scene, which, along with "*Celeste Aida*" is the most difficult music in the role, the part for which you need to summon all your technique: Because after so much dramatic singing in the previous acts, you suddenly have to lighten the voice and sing "*O terra addio*" softly and lyrically.

'As a character, people sometimes think of Radames as somebody who just stands up there and sings. But he is not. He is a great, passionate man, beset with problems. In fact I think he is one of the strongest and most remarkable char-acters in opera: a very honest, very determined person, much more interesting than people think. Also a most unconventional hero, especially in the historical context of the opera, a man of total integrity and single-mindedness, with everything, every advantage anyone could wish for, going for him: he is given the job he wants, he goes to war, returns a hero and is given the hand of Pharaoh's daughter in marriage – which means he will be the next Pharaoh. Yet he falls in love with a slave and is prepared to lose everything for the sake of this love. For, until Aida reveals her true identity in the Nile Scene, Radames thinks she is a slave. But he doesn't care. He loves her and that's it. Of course, as the story also implies, for him to be willing to give up Amneris and all she represents for a mere slave, Aida's beauty should be quite breathtaking. Unfortunately, in practice this doesn't often work out this way! Usually it is the mezzos singing Amneris who tend to be very good-looking! But of course, the theater is the way it is and we have to accept its reality. But the score and the libretto suggest what kind of beauty Aida should be for Radames, the proud warrior, to drop everything he has going for him in order to be with her.

'This integrity and single-mindedness of his is probably what makes both these women, these two princesses, fall so madly in love with him. Yet at the same time, he is clearly ambitious. Right from the beginning, he states that his big dream as a warrior is to be chosen to lead the attacking Egyptian army into Ethiopia. So we have his dream as a warrior and his dream of Aida, his dream as a lover. And he is naïve enough to believe that if he is victorious, he can place Aida, a supposed slave, on the Ethiopian throne! I can't figure out how he imagines he could make that work out in reality . . .

'But be that as it may, Radames is as near-perfect a role as you can hope to get. Because *Aida* is an opera about two ladies fighting for the same man. Their rivalry is ferocious. And what more could any man ask for than two women, two powerful women, in love with him? Because even though it is not convenient for Aida to reveal who she is at first, we find out later that she, too, is a king's daughter. So you have two princesses, each determined to get you, and I cannot think of many operas in which two royal ladies are fighting over one man. And even after Radames has lost everything and is facing death, he is still given a chance to repent and have Amneris free him. But no. He risks everything and fights everyone, knowing he is going to die a horrible death. This is one of the strongest acts of love by any operatic character. His only weak moment comes when he momentarily forgets himself and his duty and reveals a military secret to Aida – the path to be taken by the invading Egyptian armies into Ethiopia. Even though he didn't know that Aida was an Ethiopian princess and that her father Amonasro is hiding and listening to their conversation, he willingly admits that this was unacceptable and is prepared to atone for it with his life. Again, this single act of weakness was committed out of love.

'Since my first *Aida*s at the Hamburg State Opera back in 1967, I sang Radames more or less everywhere. But three productions stand out in my mind: Sonia Frizell's at the Met (with Aprile Millo as Aida and Dolora Zajick as Amneris), Pizzi's in Houston with Mirella [Freni] as Aida, and the production at Luxor in Egypt, which was quite an awesome experience. Those authentic surroundings enabled me to feel the role more than I had ever done before. Imagine, for instance, what it felt like to sing the Judgement Scene in that ancient temple, amidst those vast columns, hearing your name called three times, "Radames, Radames, Radames," by the priest who asks you to defend yourself, and almost hearing the echo of his voice in that setting. Then the damning word *"traditor"* echoing even more loudly. It was quite, quite overwhelming and so was the

Nile Scene . . .

'I was asked to sing it again in October 1999, but declined. I no longer have the vocal ease this role requires. So now I conduct it instead! In fact *Aida* is the single opera I have conducted most often. From a conductor's point of view it is a delight. Because the kind of Verdi opera where you only have to conduct an accompaniment – operas such as *Rigoletto*, *Nabucco*, *Luisa Miller*, *La Traviata* and even *I Vespri Siciliani* – are very difficult to conduct because rhythmic accuracy is everything. But from *Don Carlos* on, we have a completely new kind of Verdi opera, with a symphonic world existing parallel to the vocal element. This means that conducting *Aida* and *Don Carlos* is very different from conducting an early or middle Verdi opera. The turning point is *Un Ballo in Maschera*, a work in which Verdi has already changed his style and inserted a much more robust symphonic dimension. The style of the orchestral contribution is different, bigger than before. Although there are arias which are still very sharply rhythmic, they are different, freer, not just a rhythmic repetition.

'*Aida* is even more advanced and the reason why I find it a delight to conduct is that it is a quasi-symphonic work with all kinds of orchestral color, phenomenal instrumentation and great inventiveness of counterpoint in the way he treats the strings and brass in the Judgement Scene, and in the solos he gives the flute in the Nile Scene. All of this signals a completely new kind of opera. Verdi had, by then, developed into such a great orchestrator that I wonder why he never wrote a symphony. He was a great admirer of Brahms and kept the scores of his four symphonies on his bedside table. So it's really surprising that he never wrote a symphony . . . Hamburg was also the place where I conducted my first *Aida*. Later I did so also in many other places including Vienna, Verona and the Met. And the more I con-

122

duct it the more amazed I am that I was able to sing Radames so many times! Because, as a conductor, I see the vocal difficulties in the role even more clearly!'

TITLE ROLE

Don Carlos

Domingo made his Austrian debut in this role on 19 May 1967 at the Vienna State Opera and later, on 11 August 1975, at the Salzburg Festival. Up to the Eighties he sang it fairly regularly, mostly in the four-act Italian version, Don Carlo, *at the Met in 1971, Hamburg in 1974, Vienna several times again, and La Scala in 1980.*

On many of those performances his partner as Rodrigo, Marquis of Posa, was Sherrill Milnes who found that singing duets with Domingo is a supremely satisfying musical experience, seldom to be savored to the same degree with other tenors.

'One of Plácido's many gifts is his musical precision, which is of the highest level. This is particularly important when you are singing what I call a "parallel" duet (with both of you singing the same line, together) as you do in the famous Don Carlos–Posa duet and, of course, in Otello. *With most tenors, you tend to be more or less together. But with Plácido you can be absolutely together and this hugely enhances both the musical and dramatic impact of the duet.'*

'Another very important aspect in parallel duets is how you release the joint top notes. It should be without any loss in your sustaining power so that they have the impact of a knife slicing through the air. But more often than not, one of the voices hangs on and

124

the duet misses some of that extra sharpness. For it takes energy to release a note. You should push your support through the release and not merely stop singing, just like that! Plácido just knows this and his energy was always the same as mine. Our performances of Ballo, Forza, Don Carlos *and* Otello *– and that's just some of our joint Verdi operas – remain the most enjoyable and artistically satisfying of my career.'*

'Don Carlos was my third Verdi role, after Alfredo and Radames. I sang it quite early in my career, in 1967 for my Austrian debut at the Vienna State Opera and since then more or less everywhere, in all the different versions. But I have to say that my favorite is the four-act Italian version. And not just because it's easier – though it's certainly that – but because I also find it tighter and more immediate, with more tension packed into a shorter space of time. But in all versions, *Don Carlos* is a masterpiece, with a magnificent orchestration. It is the first Verdi opera in which we come across such an important symphonic dimension, probably because Verdi was already deeply influenced by Wagner. I have also conducted *Don Carlos* and have to confess that, as a conductor, I prefer the five-act version, because it gives me more wonderful music to conduct.

'But for me as a tenor, it's a different story. From the vocal point of view, Don Carlos is a very difficult role in all versions. But it becomes even more so in the five-act version, with the Fontainebleau Scene. His aria *"Io l'ho perduta"* is higher than in the shorter version – with a B natural as opposed to a B flat – and the whole shape of it is different because the circumstances in which Don Carlos finds himself when he sings it are diametrically opposite. In the five-act version he sings it in joyful anticipation while in the four-act version he is in despair. In the former, the whole act is overloaded with some very difficult music for the tenor to have to sing so near the beginning, without much real satisfaction, either, because people are used to the aria as it appears in the shorter version. Carlos's ensuing duet with Posa is also difficult. In the next scene his duet with Elisabetta is very difficult and the Garden Scene – where we have the trio with Eboli and Posa – even more so. But the toughest is the ensemble which has a very high overall tessitura plus high notes.

'As a character Verdi's Don Carlos is Verdi's Don Carlos – not Schiller's or even the real historical Don Carlos, who was a very sick, not very good-looking man and an epileptic. And in my own portrayal – which I am proud of because I feel I really followed Verdi's idea very closely – I retained just one flicker from the historical character: in his first scene with Elisabetta, I tried to feign something a little bit like an epileptic fit. I think it conveyed the sadness of this impossible character and situation even more . . .

'A very interesting feature in Don Carlos is that here for the first time we come across the hero's nemesis in the shape of Eboli, the heroine's rival, whose love for the hero is hopeless and who triggers off the disastrous sequence of events that bring about his downfall. This nemesis is usually a mezzo – for like the baritone the mezzo is usually the loser in love – and achieves her apotheosis in Amneris. In the case of Don Carlos, I don't think he is even aware of Eboli's passion until the Garden Scene. I think he is so preoccupied with his own hopeless love for Elisabetta, his involvement with Posa's politics, the fate of Flanders and his non-relationship with his father, that he doesn't realize Eboli is keen on him or that he's making her jealous. Even when he receives her anonymous note "*Nel giardino della Regina*" he assumes it's from Elisabetta and it's her he's waiting for with such ecstatic anticipation. When, instead of her, he is con-

126

fronted by Eboli, he is flabbergasted. Of course, I don't think there is real love on Eboli's side. I think she is simply keen on feathering her own nest. She is the king's mistress, but she's certainly not in love with him, and I don't think she's in love with Don Carlos, either. I think she's just preparing for her future. Musically, the duet with Eboli in this scene and the trio that follows after Posa's entry contain some quite wonderful music.

'One thing I don't understand about this opera, though, is why in an opera titled *Don Carlos* Verdi has his principal hero disappear for an entire act, the most important act in the opera, where, after a highly dramatic and important duet with the Grand Inquisitor he gives the most important aria, "*Ella giammai m'amo*," to King Philip. This is followed by another very dramatic confrontation, this time between the king and Elisabetta, the sublime quartet after they are joined by Eboli and Posa and finally Eboli's showpiece aria "*O don fatale*." Then you have Posa's two arias, while Don Carlos is left completely out of it and appears only at the end of the opera. Maybe Verdi was trying to bring home the essential weakness of this character. But in the last act Don Carlos reappears with a vengeance and has this glorious duet with Elisabetta, "*Ma lassù ci vedremo*."

'And, apropos of this aria, the single performance of *Don Carlos* that is fixed in my mind as the most memorable of my career is the one I sang in 1969 at the Arena in Verona. My actual debut role there was Calaf about a fortnight earlier, but at that performance of *Don Carlos* the atmosphere was unforgettable. The conductor was Eliahu Inbal and the rest of the cast included Montserrat Caballé as Elisabetta, Fiorenza Cossotto as Eboli, Piero Cappuccilli as Posa and Dimiter Petkov as King Philip. You cannot imagine the sensation of singing that final duet "*Ma lassù ci vedremo*" under the stars at 1:30 in the morning (because performances

127

there start at 9 p.m.) with Montserrat floating those magical pianissimi into the air, before she and I walked away from each other. In a space like the Arena where the size of the stage is huge – a distance of maybe 20 to 30 meters – nothing could have conveyed the sense of separation more powerfully and effectively.'

GUSTAVUS (RICCARDO)

Un Ballo in Maschera

Gustavus III, or Riccardo as in this case when the opera was presented in its Boston setting, was the role in which Domingo made his debut in Berlin on 31 May 1967, ten days after his debut at the Vienna State Opera as Don Carlos. Originally, he was meant to make his Berlin debut as Radames, which he had just sung for the first time a few weeks before in Hamburg. But while still in Vienna, he received a call from the Deutsche Opera informing him that as the mezzo scheduled to sing Amneris had fallen ill and as no suitable replacement could be found, the management had decided to replace Aida *with* Ballo.

Domingo hadn't sung and didn't even know the part of Riccardo. But he told the Berlin Opera that he was happy to switch to Ballo! *Trusting his prodigious memory and conspicuous ease for learning scores, he felt confident he could do it. And with Marta's help, plus Gigli's recording of the role, he learnt Riccardo in three days just as he had learnt Don José in Tel Aviv and Andrea Chénier for New Orleans. The performance went well and Domingo was justly proud of having sung three major new Verdi roles and made his Vienna and Berlin debuts within three weeks.*

Riccardo soon became one of his favorite and most popular roles and he has sung it 77 times all over the world – Chicago, Miami, Fort Worth, New Orleans,

129

New York, Milan, Barcelona, Hamburg, London, Caracas, Cologne, Vienna, Salzburg, Seville, Tokyo, Yokohama – up to September 1993, when he said goodbye to the role in Los Angeles.

Domingo prefers the opera in its Swedish setting and singles out John Schlesinger's Salzburg production as among the most memorable of his career. It was prepared and was to have been conducted by Herbert von Karajan, with whom Domingo hadn't worked for many years. But, having first recorded and then rehearsed the work right up to the pre-dress rehearsal, Karajan died a few days before the premiere, on 16 July 1989, and was replaced by Sir Georg Solti.

Domingo treasures the memory of those recording sessions and rehearsals, both as a singer and a conductor. He was especially struck by the humility and diligence with which a conductor of Karajan's age and repute approached this work which he had not conducted since his young days as Kapellmeister in Aachen and especially by the way he conducted the beginning of the scene with Ulrica, 'where the strength, the unbelievable power of his upbeats had to be seen to be believed. They made everybody gasp. No one had ever heard anything like them before.' Domingo learnt a lot from Karajan musically, especially by the emphasis he placed not so much on precision but on expressing every ounce of the feeling in the music.

Watching the video of the Salzburg performance in which Domingo is in resplendent form both vocally and dramatically it is interesting to observe the subtle differences of this portrayal in which he is Gustavus III, King of Sweden, from other performances of Ballo *in which he was merely Riccardo, Governor of New England. Here, as king, he oozes*

130

authority in every stance and gesture. But in either setting, Domingo's portrayal of this character remains one of my personal favorites among Domingo vintage portrayals.

'This is one of my most favorite Verdi roles. From the dramatic point of view, the most exciting thing in this opera is the love triangle at its center, because triangular situations are what opera is usually about! It's true to say that baritones are almost always the losers, which is unfair to them but wonderful for us tenors, who are almost always the winners! Except, perhaps, in the case of *Ballo* where Gustavus is killed without "getting" Amelia in the obvious sense of the word. To me, there is always this puzzle, in this particular Verdi opera, this question mark in my mind about the nature of the relationship between them. For how can music as overwhelmingly, mind-bogglingly passionate as the Gustavus–Amelia duet in Act II apply to a love that is merely platonic? It seems incredible.

'Yet if we believe the plot, and believe it we must, Gustavus assures Anckarström in his dying moments that it was platonic. But why? It seems a pity that with such music, their love was not consummated. Because for me, there isn't a single moment in any opera by any composer in the world that can compare with the climax of this duet, the phrase *"irradiami d'amor"* where Verdi has the orchestra explode in a huge, apotheotic crescendo. It's total beauty, total ecstasy, with the full orchestra coming together with the voice at the word *"irradiami"* . . . of course, one doesn't know what would have happened after the love duet if the traitors hadn't followed Gustavus and if Anckarström hadn't arrived in time to save him. But from the moment he is saved by Anckarström the King decides that, no matter what, he cannot have an affair with the wife of a man who has risked his life to save him. Friendship has to prevail, even if leaving Amelia to her husband is agony for Gustavus.

'Vocally speaking, *Ballo* is one of Verdi's most "rounded" melodic works. Like *Il Trovatore* and Verdi's early operas, it is still founded in the bel canto school, but "Bel canto" with a capital "B". Yet because Verdi's orchestral writing is so strong and virile we have stopped thinking of him as a "bel canto" composer. One of the reasons may be that nowadays orchestras are so much bigger than in Verdi's day. So much so, that they can easily "kill" the singer when doubling the melody. Today's orchestras also tune higher than in Verdi's day, and this can be a problem that renders his roles even more difficult.

'Gustavus is one of the hardest of all Verdi roles, especially in the first two acts which are among the most demanding you will find in any Verdi opera. The tenor simply never stops. He has to sing a string of arias, one after the other. Certain moments such as *"Di' tu se fedele"* in Act I, for example, demand the agility of a light lyric tenor, but pitched against the heavier Verdi orchestration I mentioned a minute ago. One of Gustavus's most important and challenging moments is the romanza *"E scherzo od è follia"* in Madame Arvidson's tent (Ulrica in the opera's Boston setting). At the beginning it is reminiscent of the Duke of Mantua's music in *Rigoletto*. But halfway through, Verdi makes it very clear that the tenor should change his vocal color. By the time we get to the second verse the music, which starts off a little nervous, gets deeper and more brooding as a reflection of the dramatic situation: at first Gustavus tries to laugh off Madame Arvidson's prophecy foretelling his imminent death by the hand of a friend, but little by little he begins to sense that it really could happen – in fact he begins to believe that it probably will.

'One of the reasons why I was looking so greatly forward to the 1989 Salzburg production of *Ballo* was the fact that Karajan, who had not conducted it since his early days as a Kapellmeister at Ulm, was approaching it with intense enthusiasm and verve. Both as a singer and as a conductor, I found his rehearsals with the Vienna Philharmonic riveting! While he repeated certain passages – such as the chords in the opening of the scene with Madame Arvidson – endlessly, to get the rhythms right, in passages where the conductor is not needed, he wouldn't interfere at all. He just let the whole thing flow as if by itself . . . I am deeply sad I was not able to do more things with him and that this very special occasion should have come so late in our careers. Perhaps we were both enclosed in two separate worlds of our own – each one too big, maybe – and it wasn't possible to bring them together until that fatal summer . . .

'The production, by John Schlesinger, went ahead under Sir Georg Solti. The most interesting thing about it, as far as I am concerned, was the fact that the opera was done in its original Swedish setting instead of the usual Boston setting, I was now Gustavus III, King of Sweden, instead of Riccardo, Governor of New England, and this opened up many new possibilities. Because let's face it, this was the character who, with his enthusiastic, creative nature and love for the arts, fired Verdi's imagination. And in John's production, we actually saw Gustavus working on the building of his famous theater, Drottningholm.

'I have an intense love of Verdi, this giant whose creative output spans almost the entire nineteenth century. He starts off rooted in the bel canto school of Bellini and, to a lesser extent, of Donizetti and by the time of *Don Carlos* he is almost ushering in verismo. But he had been conceiving a new kind of opera as early as the time he composed *Luisa Miller* [1849] and *Rigoletto* [1851], and by the time of *Don Carlos*, he has discarded the established pattern of recitative-aria-cabaletta. In fact, the seeds of his future development are contained even in his earliest works such as *Nabucco* [1842] and *Ernani* [1844]: a new identity is immediately apparent in the terse, virile, muscular style, and Verdi's development reaches its apogee in *Otello* and *Falstaff* where he achieves the complete fulfilment of his creative genius.

'From a singer's point of view, anything connected with Verdi is damn serious. Any Verdi role is the most difficult singing you'll ever be called to deliver. Even though Puccini and the other verismo composers can destroy your voice more easily, they are easier to sing. Even inexperienced young singers can manage them. But no inexperienced young singer can hope to make any sort of impact in a Verdi role, because he demands everything you have, both as a human being and as a singer. His music has feeling, it has pulse, it has red blood and most of all, it has heart. Therefore the sound has to be not only beautiful but generous: it has to have light and, last but not least, it has to be sustained by a very good technique. Without any of those things, you just cannot sing Verdi.

'The operas of Verdi's early and middle period are more difficult, both in terms of singing and of conducting. From a conductor's point of view, the hardest of them all are definitely the earliest, such as *Nabucco*, *Ernani* and *Attila* because there are a good many fluctuations of tempo around and the conductor is responsible for setting every new tempo and creating the right atmosphere for the drama with the kind of accompaniments Verdi was such a genius at inventing. And if he doesn't manage to create excitement with his first downbeat, he will have missed the point altogether. This is why the earlier works are more difficult to conduct than the more poised later operas such as *Aida*, *Don Carlos*, *Otello* and *Falstaff*. You've got to feel this kind of Verdian rhythm and excitement. You've got to have them in your blood.'

TITLE ROLE

Lohengrin

Domingo originally sang his first Wagnerian role, Lohengrin, on 14 January 1968 at the Hamburg State Opera. But, as he explains in the following pages, the experience convinced him that he was not yet ready for Wagner and he decided to wait until he had reached full vocal maturity. Fifteen years later he felt the time had come to return to Wagner and have another go at Lohengrin, this time at the Metropolitan Opera on 27 September 1983, under James Levine, with Anna Tomowa Sintow as Elsa and Eva Marton as Ortrud.

The attempt was hugely successful and, heartened by the public and critical applause, he sang it again at the Vienna State Opera in January 1985, to an end-less standing ovation. Naturally, for a mature tenor in his forties the dangers in singing Wagner are much reduced. They no longer lie in the possibility that the voice might crack – which, as he explains, is what happened after those early performances in Hamburg – but in the possible loss of some of his Italian and French roles. This is why, although after singing Lohengrin he felt ready for Parsifal right away and for Siegmund within two years, he nevertheless de-cided to be cautious and wait nearly another decade before taking them on.

Vocally, as Eugene Kohn who has been a great help preparing Domingo's Wagnerian roles points out, 'the

Wagner roles require some different shaping (or turning) of the passaggio notes (those between the middle and top ranges of the voice), and Plácido's magnificent breath support reflexes allow him to make the differences in coloration, moving from one style to the other without changing his vocal technique.'

'*Lohengrin* and *Der Fliegende Holländer* are Wagner's most "Italian" operas, along with *Rienzi* which is totally Italian! And the role of Lohengrin, although not exactly a bel canto part, is nevertheless a very Italianate part in terms of the amount of light you have to let into your voice. It needs a superb legato line and great sweetness of tone. But there are certain passages – such as the moment where he talks to Ortrud, "*Du Fürchterliches Weib*," where you need that special sort of Wagnerian "bite" in the way you enunciate and sing the words and also a little bit of anger: the anger of the kind of people who are so holy and so clean that anything sneaky or underhand revolts them.

'I first sang it quite early in my career, at the Hamburg State Opera in 1968 a few days before my 27th birthday, and it was really quite an extraordinary experience because it was my first contact with Wagner and his world. I prepared it with great anticipation and wonder and also with a sense of mystery, in approaching a composer whose work I was as yet unfamiliar with and did not have in my repertoire, which then consisted almost exclusively of French and Italian roles.

'I think that one of the chief characteristics of *Lohengrin* is that 80 per cent of the music is very much in the line of a Verdi opera, even in the style of the ensembles – both at the Finale of Act I and the Finale of Act II. The same is true of Lohengrin's duet with Elsa and of his two arias "*Mein lieber Schwan*" and "*In fernem Land*," which are very lyrical

moments. The only part where you have a recitative typical
of the Wagnerian style is the scene in Act III where after his
scene with Elsa, Lohengrin talks to the King, with great
sadness and, in a long introduction to "*In fernem Land,*"
explains everything that has happened. This recitative is very
difficult indeed, both musically and from the point of view
of diction, sort of biting into the consonants the way you
have to in a great deal of German singing. This is where I
first got a glimpse of what I would have to deal with later,
in Parsifal and Siegmund: all those alliterations, where you
have to repeat certain consonants – w, w, w or l, l, l – several times within one sentence.

'This is where I also understood for the first time why
the Wagnerian repertoire is considered dangerous. Firstly,
because it's written for a special kind of tenor, the
Heldentenor. You need a lot of power and, most important,
you need pacing so that you can keep the beauty of your
sound and the freshness in the voice for the ending, where
you have to produce beautiful lyrical singing in "*In fernem
Land*" and "*Mein lieber Schwan,*" which is the hardest thing
in the whole opera. There are also moments of great difficulty in the duet with Elsa, around the point where he sings
"*Höchster Traum,*" where you have about four pages of
very hard singing. This has to do both with the words and
the tessitura which is high and very difficult. This moment
was quite a challenge for me.

'I was altogether very happy and relieved that my first
experience of Wagner was in an opera so close in style to
the Italian repertoire. Nevertheless I decided to leave Wagner
alone for a long, long time, because I had to recognize that
it was too early for me to be singing this repertoire. I think
it hurt me, hurt my throat a little bit. I sang it in January
1968 and I was experiencing problems until May, such as a
little tightness in the throat. And for several months I was

cracking here and there. I would attack a note, think it was secure and then the voice could go "click" and break, even in the middle of an F. Clearly the strain of Wagner's vocal writing was too much for a young tenor under 30. Thinking about it now, I don't think it was the performances that caused the damage, but the very long period of preparation that I put into it, with a coach. My throat was not used to working with a coach. Indeed one of the reasons for my vocal longevity, and the condition of my voice after so many years of hard singing, is precisely the fact that I never use my throat or go to a coach while preparing a role. I prepare almost all my operas – with the exception of Wagner and Gherman in *The Queen of Spades* – alone. Most singers tend to use their voice twice as much as I do, just in preparing their operas, whereas I prepare silently. Then I sit down at the piano and try out certain passages which I feel need to be tried out. This is in stark contrast to most singers, who sing out every time they go to a coach. But the singing I have saved by not going to a coach may be the reason why I have clocked up more performances than anybody! Yet for that first Lohengrin I did go to a coach and that overstretched my throat. And although on the evening itself my performance was considered a success, I have to admit that I was not ready, my throat was not ready, for it yet. So I left it alone for 15 years.

'By the time I came back to it, in 1983 at the Metropolitan Opera, I had 15 years' experience behind me. I had also started my collaboration with pianist and coach Eugene Kohn who sang the part through most of the time while we were coaching, to show me how it should sound. This enabled me to save a lot of voice. But that said, quite apart from the amount of voice you do or don't save there is something inherently dangerous for young voices in Wagnerian singing, which has to do with the pushing you have to do at certain moments. Unless, of course, you are a born Heldentenor – in which case, Lohengrin is one of the Wagner roles that will hurt you least.

'It's a role I would still be happy to sing again today, because I love this opera and its otherworldly dimension. It's a very beautiful and sad fairy tale with an incandescant character coming from other spheres of life, from heaven. It's also one of the most beautiful platonic love stories in existence. And it's ruined by this persistent, relentless curiosity of Elsa's, this poison in her soul which makes her so ungrateful. It is infuriating. For what more could she want? She has the love of a prince, a wonderful prince who comes to rescue her and is such a positive character. And knowing, as she does, after the fight with Telramund, that it's someone who came from above, someone mystical. So why does she have to know his name? But she becomes riddled with doubt and Ortrud and Telramund, who perceive this, proceed to work on it, especially Telramund who is tremendously jealous of Elsa . . . Scenically, Lohengrin is a very straightforward, very "still" character to portray. You have to exude nobility, pride and a sort of illumined aura that comes from Lohengrin's father, Parsifal – my next Wagnerian role – who is also an illumined character.'

DES GRIEUX

Manon Lescaut

Domingo sang his first Puccini Des Grieux with Renata Tebaldi in Hartford, Connecticut, on 15 February 1968, followed a month later by two at Fort Worth. His next performances, two years later at the Arena in Verona, were with another legendary operatic Grande Dame: Magda Olivero, whose 'youth' on stage Domingo found utterly convincing, and who was so impressed by her young partner that she announced that Domingo encapsulated 'a superior vocal civilization.'

As he makes abundantly clear in his comments, Domingo is passionate about this Des Grieux and rightly considers the role among his very best achievements. He has performed it 45 times – hardly enough when one considers that he has sung Loris Ipanov in Fedora, for instance, over 60 times – in Barcelona, Madrid, La Scala, Hamburg, Munich, the Metropolitan Opera, Covent Garden and the Teatro San Carlo for his Neapolitan debut, under Oliviero de Fabritiis with the Greek maverick Elena Suliotis in the title role. In May 1972 he sang the Des Grieux–Manon duet with Montserrat Caballé in Rudolf Bing's Farewell Gala at the Met, an evening in which Corelli, Pavarotti, Price, Siepi, Sutherland, Nilsson, Vickers, Rysanek and Richard Tucker also participated.

Just as historic as this and those first performances

140

with the two great divas of the past was Domingo's performance at the Met in March 1980, directed by Gian Carlo Menotti and conducted by James Levine, with Renata Scotto in the title role. This was the first live telecast from the Met to Europe and it created a justified sensation. Domingo's singing of this impassioned youth remains unsurpassed in our day and the dramatic involvement of both artists was such that, as with Domingo's Otello, the performance could have stood even as straight theater. There is another video recording, of the 1983 Covent Garden production of the work, with Dame Kiri Te Kanawa in the title role, but the former is more riveting dramatically.

'Des Grieux, which I first sang in 1968 in Hartford, Connecticut, is a role I grew to love passionately. In retrospect, I greatly regret not performing it more often, because I consider it one of my best portrayals. I missed out almost a decade – from the early Eighties to the Nineties – the decade when I could sing it well and enjoy singing it. I suppose other commitments must have got in the way . . . Yet this saddens me because it is one of the roles I love most. It also happens to be the most difficult of all the Puccini parts, chiefly because of its length – Des Grieux has more to sing than any other Puccini tenor character – and the tessitura, which is demanding.

'With *Manon Lescaut*, you also get the feeling that Puccini was trying very, very hard to write the best music he was capable of. He had to have a success because his first two operas, *Edgar* and *Le Villi*, were only modest successes. So he really put everything he had, all his heart, into this opera. And he succeeded in creating two characters who are very dramatic, very powerful – and vocally, very, very difficult. People are always pointing out to me that

141

Massenet's *Manon* is more authentic because it's written in the French style and so on. Okay, it may have the impeccable French style but it doesn't have even half the power and emotion of *Manon Lescaut*, which are extraordinary. (In spite of "location" mistakes such as describing Louisiana as a desert.)

'Every one of the opera's four acts contains some of the most beautiful and difficult music ever written for the tenor. In Act I you have two arias *"Tra voi, belle, brune e bionde"* and *"Donna non vidi mai"* and two duets with Manon, *"Cortese damigella"* and *"O come gravi le vostre parole,"* which goes up to A. In the second act you have the big duet "Ah, Manon" and the trio. In the third act you have two big duets – one with Lescaut and one with Manon – a big ensemble and then the fabulous aria *"Guardate, pazzo son."* He says he wants to fight the guards, fight Geronte, it's very, very powerful. In the last act, you have the very extended scene between Manon and Des Grieux, which is full of tremendously difficult phrases at the end of a long evening of very hard singing. Yet these have to be delivered with maximum temperament, feeling and passion. All this makes Des Grieux not only the most difficult Puccini role – even more so than Calaf – but one of the most difficult in the tenor repertoire.

'Dramatically *Manon Lescaut* is one of the world's great love stories. It ends so tragically because of her stupidity. It's very sad, the story of this girl whose worldly ambitions override her love for Des Grieux. This aspect of worldly greed is more obvious in Massenet's *Manon* but it's also present in *Manon Lescaut*. But one of the paradoxes here is the fact that although the characters are very young, they cannot be sung by very young singers because they would lack the vocal power and sheer stamina demanded by both parts. As it happens I was only 27 when I first sang Des

Grieux in Hartford, Connecticut – much too young for the part. I don't think there are many tenors who have sung the Puccini Des Grieux at that age. Basically, it's a mature role, ideal for tenors in their late thirties and forties. After those early performances in Hartford, I sang it again two years later, in 1970, at the Verona Arena, aged 29. Then I went through almost all my thirties without singing Des Grieux. When I came back to it in 1978, at La Scala, I was almost 38 and found it much, much easier not only musically, but physically. Oddly enough, I could accommodate myself into the character's youth much more comfortably.

'Do I feel different when performing the Puccini Des Grieux than I do when singing Massenet's? The answer is yes. The Puccini character has much more temperament and "abandon," both musically and dramatically. Massenet's Des Grieux is more naïve, more of an innocent boy. Even in the second act, when the bass, De Bretigny, appears with Lescaut, Des Grieux is blithely unaware of what's going on and still fascinated by Lescaut. He sings "*Ah, Lescaut, il sait que je l'adore*" while De Bretigny is practically propositioning Manon and asking her to go with him that very minute! But Des Grieux doesn't realize what's going on under his nose. So, he's a very naïve, romantic and unworldly youth who goes to St Sulpice to become a priest. These are aspects which, even though we are dealing with the same character, you don't find in Puccini, whose Des Grieux is both a much more manly character and a far more dramatic and important tenor role than Massenet's.'

MANRICO

Il Trovatore

Domingo first sang Manrico on 14 March 1968 in New Orleans and went on to sing 50 performances in Hamburg, Vienna, New York, Philadelphia, San Francisco, Fort Worth, Paris, Madrid, Munich, Zurich and Frankfurt over the next 21 years. He sang it for the last time in Piero Faggioni's Covent Garden production in June 1989. Among the 50 he rates the one in Frankfurt as the best of his life.

Although he is the first to admit that he is not a high note tenor par excellence, Domingo sang the high C at the end of 'Di quella pira' on many of those occasions, while on some he transposed it down a semitone. As far as the interpolation of 'traditional' high notes, not written by Verdi himself, into his operas, especially Rigoletto *and* Il Trovatore, *Domingo finds himself poised between the views of the purist camp, headed by conductor Riccardo Muti, to whom scores are sacrosanct and the interpolation of any extraneous notes anathema, and the free-for-all camp numbering many singers as its spokespersons, who think nothing of manipulating scores to the greater glory of their particular vocal virtuosity.*

Domingo recognizes that a performance of Rigoletto *without the B naturals at the end of 'La donna è mobile' would fall flat on its face and the tenor in question would be skinned alive. Similarly he*

*knows better than anyone that the monster of a high
C interpolated by tradition at the end of 'Di quella
pira,' in place of Verdi's G, turns a comfortable, central role into a terror for most tenors – even high tenors sweat blood and tears over it. But the public love,
expect and will not easily forgo the visceral satisfaction it affords them if well sung.*

*So, in his recording of the role, Domingo was de-
termined to sing it and sing it well. As Sherrill Milnes
recalls, he did six or eight takes, keeping his energies
going higher and higher until he got it right and then
chose between the two that worked. 'He just stood
there and forced it out, he made it work by doing as
many takes as he needed of the end of the aria, until
he nailed it! It took courage to do that, to stand in
front of all those people, with a towel around your
neck and will it out.'*

*The recording Milnes refers to was made in the
Seventies, by which time Domingo's formidable technique enabled him to do what he liked with his voice
– including the manufacture of high notes he did not
possess by nature.*

'Il Trovatore is the second of Verdi's "Spanish" operas and
Manrico, my fourth major Verdi role, is the most romantic
and beautiful of his Spanish heroes: a man who finds himself in extraordinary circumstances. For he is a nobleman
who has been abducted and brought up by a gypsy, Azucena,
in place of her own son whom she mistakenly threw onto a
burning pyre as a baby. The real intended victim, though,
was none other than Manrico himself, to whom she has
since been an apparently loving mother. He, of course, senses
there is something wrong in this whole schizophrenic situation, the craziness originating from his "mother" who is

always crying for revenge. He is also an artistic soul, a professional singer, a troubadour, who met the heroine, Leonora, when she crowned him winner at a singing tournament. This means that he must also be a sort of nomad, travelling to such events, then rushing back to the gypsy camp and moving about backwards and forwards, with them.

'In the first half of the opera, his first three scenes, Manrico has to sing a romantic serenade to Leonora, then a trio with her and his rival (an unknown brother), the Count di Luna. Like her namesake in *Forza*, this Leonora is also a beautiful Spanish noblewoman with a strong personality and a mind of her own. (As we see not only in her determination to have Manrico but also in her decision to kill herself at the end, in order to save him but without having to fulfil her promise to give herself to Luna in exchange.) But, unlike her namesake in *Forza*, although she too is of high rank and a lady-in-waiting to the Princess of Aragon, she appears to be her own mistress, with no father or brother to interfere with her decisions. The only impediment to her union with Manrico is the rivalry of Count di Luna. In her opening scene we see her waiting for Manrico and mistaking the Count di Luna for him. The scene ends with Manrico's timely arrival and the two men rushing off to fight a duel.

'In the next act, we learn the outcome of this duel. Back at the gypsy camp, Manrico narrates the whole episode to his mother: how, even though he has been slightly wounded, he got the best of his rival and held him at his mercy. Meanwhile Azucena keeps singing *"Mi vendica, mi vendica"* (Avenge me, avenge me), and, in a momentary lapse, sort of insinuates that she has killed her own son. Manrico's immediate response, "Then who am I?" forces her to try to cover her tracks. But this casts doubts in his mind and he responds with the aria *"Mal reggendo all'aspro assalto"* in

146

which he explains that, although his enemy lay at his mercy, a mysterious instinct, a voice from Heaven, prevented him from killing him. While Azucena marvels at this "strange mercy," a note arrives warning Manrico that Leonora, fearing him dead, is about to enter a convent. Despite Azucena's protestations, Manrico rushes off to rescue her.

'The second half is the meaty part of *Il Trovatore*, which has the best music – many, many moments of vintage Verdi! First comes Manrico's aria *"Ah, si ben mio"* and his famous cabaletta *"Di quella pira"* (with its much awaited high C not written by Verdi but interpolated later), which I was very happy to sing in Vienna but not quite so happy to sing in London. The reason is that in Vienna I got at least four minutes' applause after *"Ah si ben mio"* which allowed me to recover my breath and prepare myself for *"Di quella pira."* But the London public, although warm and appreciative, didn't want to interrupt the scene and saved its applause for the end of *"Di quella pira."* Yet not getting my moment's respite made the latter even more difficult . . .

'But whatever the circumstances, singing this wonderful music, and singing it well, is an incomparable sensation, one of the greatest and most thrilling moments you can experience on stage. And in the next act comes some of the most beautiful music you're ever called on to sing: first, that gorgeous, nostalgic duet *"Ai nostri monti"* followed by soft singing in *"Riposa, madre."* Then you have that more dramatic duet with Leonora, *"Ha quest'infame l'amor venduto"* which I love singing. In fact I love all of Manrico and *Il Trovatore* passionately.

'Yet I have sung it comparatively little – a total of about 50 performances, not enough to satisfy or satiate my appetite for it. The reason is that confounded, interpolated high C. But for this, Manrico is not a high role. It's quite central, much, much easier than the Duke of Mantua, easier than

Alvaro, and ideal for my voice. But the insertion of that high C makes it virtually unsingable for someone like me who is not a high note tenor par excellence. So, much to my regret, I have had to limit my appearances as Manrico and eventually to drop it from my repertoire. Yet, apart from the top C, I could sing it even now! In fact I'm longing to do so again. I might just say, "Hell, I'll do it minus the high C" – however much the public have come to expect and look forward to it – as I did in London in Piero Faggioni's production in 1989. Some of the public will understand and some won't, but that will be just too bad!'

DUKE OF MANTUA

Rigoletto

The Duke of Mantua, one of Verdi's best loved and most famous roles, is written essentially for a light lyric tenor. Yet as Domingo wisely points out below, no tenor worth the name can afford not to include it in his repertoire. Domingo first performed it on 2 January 1969 at the Hamburg State Opera during its golden Liebermann Years, where he also sang his first Radames and Alvaro. But it never became one of his signature roles. He has sung it only on twelve occasions which, apart from the four in Hamburg, included one in San Antonio, one in Vienna (both in the early Seventies) and six in a new production at the Metropolitan Opera in November 1977.

Since then he has not sung it again in public. But he recorded it for Deutsche Grammophon two years later, in 1979, with Piero Cappuccilli in the title role and Ileana Cotrubas as Gilda under Carlo Maria Giulini, whose way of working with the strings fascinated the conductor in Domingo, especially in the first Rigoletto–Gilda Scene. He found Giulini's way of obtaining beautiful sound quality, little accents and so many other refined touches, amazing. At the beginning of the opera, Giulini didn't want the Duke's recitative, which is sung over the off-stage band's accompaniment, to be sung with metronomic precision. He wanted Domingo to sing 'Della mia bella incog-

nita borghese' *and the words that follow as naturally as if he were speaking, but without disturbing the tempo. The words had to just press forward without undue emphasis on the beginning or the middle of every bar. Giulini explained that the band automatically emphasizes those beats and if the tenor makes the same accentuation, the text would not be heard. 'There are thousands of such details to be learnt in the operatic repertoire and they can indeed be learnt from the special people I'm fortunate enough to work with. Ten or twelve musician-conductors stand at the top of their world, and it's no accident that they are there,' he remarked in his autobiography.*

What is remarkable about Domingo's own portrayal of the Duke in this recording is the way he manages to lighten his heavy lirico spinto voice for Act I, where his 'Questa o quella' *really sounds as if it's being sung by a carefree, debonair youth. And the force of the carnal desire he infuses into the Duke's vocally straining duettino with the Countess of Ceprano, '*Partite, crudele' *– while keeping the voice itself as light as possible – makes the urgency of the Duke's demands on her almost palpable.*

Domingo has plenty to say about the crucial importance of the ability to lighten the voice at will and keep it fresh and youthful sounding – which he considers a sine qua non of a tenor's technique – in the chapters on Count Almaviva and Gabriele Adorno. But Act I of this recording is an admirable example of this skill.

Gramophone's verdict on Domingo's remarkable achievement as the Duke of Mantua was 'lighter and more flexible than one could possibly expect from a tenor who is also the leading Otello of the day.'

150

'The Duke of Mantua is not one of the Verdi parts roles I have been closely associated with. It was never an easy role for me and I have sung maybe a total of about 12 performances in my whole career. Yet it is such an important role for a tenor that I couldn't afford not to have it in my repertoire. Vocally, it is one of the top, top tenor roles. His music and the music of the entire opera is fabulous. The fact that *Rigoletto*, one of Verdi's best loved operas, was composed relatively early in his career is yet another pointer to the scale of this giant's genius.

'Vocally speaking, every time the Duke steps on stage he has some very beautiful yet very difficult music to sing! In Act I, he starts off with *"Questa o quella,"* which is much, much harder to sing than people think. It sounds deceptively easy, but requires a light sound and agility at the very beginning of the evening, before you've had a chance to warm up. This is followed by the equally deceptively easy-sounding duettino with the Countess of Ceprano, written entirely in the passaggio zone. It must be sung rather softly, which is always difficult in this area of the voice and can play tricks with intonation.' (Interestingly enough, Pavarotti also singles out this duettino as exceptionally difficult.) 'Then in Act II he has the beautiful, romantic aria: *"E inseparabile d'amor il Dio,"* followed by his duet with Gilda which culminates in *"Addio, addio speranza ed anima."*

'Then, in Act III, comes the recitative *"Ella mi fu rapita"* followed by *"Parmi veder le lagrime,"* the Duke's best aria because of its beauty of line and those modulations, those turns Verdi has written into it. But, despite its beauty, unfortunately this aria lies a little too high for me. I was never able to sing it quite as beautifully as I would have liked to, because I was always worried about the tessitura. I tried my best but it was never easy for me. On top of that there is a B flat which was not written by Verdi but which every tenor likes to include as a showpiece. And if you sing it with the cabaletta – and I did so both with and without – it becomes even more difficult. But the hardest aria of them all comes in Act IV. It is "*La donna è mobile,*" one of the best known and loved pieces of the operatic repertoire. It ends in B flat and God help the tenor who fails to make an impact with it! This is followed by that exquisite quartet "*Bella figlia dell'amore*" after which you have to repeat "*La donna è mobile.*" And the second time round is even harder, culminating in B natural . . .

'Yet in this role your singing should be excellent throughout, because the Duke of Mantua is a role that depends entirely on vocalism, plus charm and a certain kind of light-hearted, debonair demeanor. There is no character development during the course of the opera. The Duke is and remains a cynic through and through, a really negative character who is not just a compulsive womanizer. He is also mean and totally selfish. He is not nice to Rigoletto, he is not nice to Ceprano, he is not nice to Monterone or Maddalena or Sparafucile. Verdi gives him a line that shows that he doesn't give a damn about anybody other than himself. Momentarily, I think, he cares for Gilda. In "*Parmi veder le lagrime*" we see that he is capable of some feeling and sympathize with him for a moment. But when, in the middle of the aria, the chorus of courtiers bursts in and informs him that Gilda has been abducted and brought to the palace, he forgets his romantic feelings and reverts to his true form, rejoicing at the prospect of making love to her. So, although he was sorry that she has been kidnapped, he is ready to take advantage of her as soon as he knows she is at his mercy. He doesn't even think of the possibility that she might have been raped by some of the courtiers on the way to the palace! So there is no redeeming quality in the Duke of Mantua.

'The only positive thing about him is his charm, which is reflected in all his music, and must also be reflected in your portrayal, along with elegance and lightness of touch. You could, if you like, ignore his most serious negative side and put him across merely as a fickle extrovert. Yet even so, there should always be this implicit streak of cruelty. In my portrayal, I always tried to take away a little bit of this cruelty, and make a joke of some of the meanest things the Duke says.

'But I don't think that there is anything any interpreter can do to make the Duke come across as anything but a negative character. He is a terrible man and, in the end, Rigoletto cannot take it. He has been seconding the Duke in all his iniquities and playing the *buffone* – perhaps not agreeing with him inwardly but nevertheless going along with him. But when his own daughter is involved, he cannot accept it and we have this great tragedy. He pays Sparafucile to murder the Duke, only to find that his daughter has sacrificed herself so that he can be spared. But I don't think Gilda kills herself for the Duke. I think she kills herself for love, the ideal of love she has lost and cannot live without.'

ALVARO

La Forza del Destino

Alvaro is another of Domingo's vintage Verdi portrayals. Vocally state-of-the-art and dramatically hauntingly moving. He first sang this sad, unfortunate hero at the Hamburg State Opera on 18 January 1969. Three months earlier, when his second son was born on 11 October 1968, he and his wife had chosen to name him Alvaro. The reason is that years ago, in Mexico, Marta's first positive feelings towards Domingo had been stirred when she heard him singing the famous tenor/baritone duet from Forza, *'Solenne in quest'ora.' Until then she had considered him somewhat lightweight and superficial. But this duet convinced her that there was something unusual, something special about this young man. Anyone listening to Domingo singing this duet on record or video – the incomparable way in which he bites, hurls, and charges the words with feeling – will know exactly what she means.*

Alvaro was also the role in which Domingo made his debut at the Teatro Colon in Buenos Aires on 14 July 1972. This was his first contact with the knowledgeable, ultra-demonstrative, appreciative Argentinean public. All in all, he sang Alvaro 40 times in, apart from the places mentioned, Vienna, Frankfurt, Paris and the Metropolitan Opera (on two occasions), in March 1977 and February/March 1996. He

154

*also sang it once in Valencia in 1974. Having heard
that the famous 'high note' tenor Giacomo Lauri Volpi
had retired to this Spanish coastal city, he was eager
to meet him. So he invited him to the performance
and at the end even introduced him to the public who
gave him a standing ovation. This appeared to move
him very much. Domingo then visited him at home a
couple of times and Lauri Volpi demonstrated his famous high notes, which he could still produce apparently effortlessly. (The middle of the voice had gone,
of course.) He was 82 at the time and this had the
effect of goading Domingo to perfect his own technique and production of high notes even more. Yet
unbeknownst to him at the time, this encounter would
haunt Domingo for the rest of his life and not in a
positive way, either. Obviously the curse of* Forza *must
have been surreptitiously at work.*

'My next big Verdi role, after the Duke of Mantua, was
Alvaro in *La Forza del Destino*, the third of Verdi's "Spanish" operas which I sang also in 1969 in Hamburg. Alvaro
is a very particular role, in the sense that he is one of the
unluckiest, most tortured and complex characters in my
repertoire and also has some of the most difficult tenor music
Verdi ever wrote! It's high from start to finish. His Act I
duet with Leonora is already high and, despite this tough
tessitura, requires great vocal ease. The trio that follows it,
with her and the father, is also tough and requires some
very "charged" singing on your part.

'After this opening scene, Alvaro disappears for a very
long time, the whole of Act II, which gives you a marvellous
chance to rest! But the very minute he reappears in Act III
he has to sing his famous aria *"Oh, tu che in seno agl'angeli"*
which, as all my colleagues agree, is one of the most beauti-

155

ful yet treacherous in all Verdi. It begins with a long recitative that is almost unique in Verdi, in which Alvaro summarizes all his past life. The words are especially important and must be given the most meaningful inflection. But the big difficulty comes in the aria, where Alvaro reflects on Leonora, his lost love. The orchestra is going plump, plump, plump, plump and you have to sing a gorgeous but terribly exposed phrase climbing up to A flat, which has to be injected with the right feeling and atmosphere. Ideally that A flat should be sung piano – softly. The moment he finishes this, comes his important duet with the baritone Don Carlo, "*Solenne in quest'ora.*" And in most productions I did we also included the ensuing, even more impassioned duet with Carlo in the Battlefield Scene, which culminates in the fabulous phrase "*Al chiostro, all'eremo, ai santi altari.*" Then, in the last act, you have the duet with Carlo in the monastery, the trio and the short duet with Leonora, all of which have a consistently tough tessitura.

'As a character, Alvaro is very proud but at the same time has a slight complex, a chip on his shoulder, about his ancestry. He is proud of being an Inca, yet when somebody throws this back at him, he takes offence and gets mad. This is something I don't understand about him. If you're proud of who you are, what does it matter what other people think? But at the same time I love Alvaro precisely because he gives me the opportunity to express anger, all that pent-up anger, and also because of how much he suffers. I have often said that the part of performing I enjoy most is suffering onstage! I love it! It gives you the possibility to sing better, with more passion. Okay, there are also moments of joy which give me pleasure because the voice may sound beautiful. But the most dramatic moments, the moments of tragedy and unhappiness are the best. *Forza*, of course, is brimming with both. In fact in this opera you don't get the satisfaction of even one moment's joy. The two protagonists suffer from beginning to end. And when, after so much anguish and separation, they find each other again at the finale and one hopes at last that they might have earned their happiness, Carlo, Leonora's brother, bursts in and stabs her.

'Leonora is a very typical Verdi heroine, a very deep-feeling woman whose passion is left unconsummated. In this sense Verdi's heroines – with the exception of Violetta, Desdemona and Lina in *Stiffelio* who have "done it," to put it bluntly, and Amelia in *Simon Boccanegra* who soon will – differ diametrically from Puccini's, whose passions are physically fulfilled. Therefore when facing a Verdi heroine I feel very different than when confronted by a Puccini lady. The passion in Verdi is less carnal.

'This doesn't mean that Verdi ladies are not sensual. Desdemona and Leonora in *Forza* are both very sensual. And just like Desdemona, Leonora is an interesting lady who has great strength of character. Again, like Desdemona whose passion for Otello was fired by the stories about his past that he used to tell her father, so Leonora is intrigued and fascinated by this strange, exotic foreigner whose past she barely knows . . . We don't know how or where she and Alvaro first set eyes on each other, or how their relationship would have developed if his request for her hand had been accepted. But when her father decides that a suitor with Inca blood is unworthy of his daughter, Alvaro asks her to elope and she agrees. And the fact that she, a typical Spanish noble girl very much controlled by and fond of her father, agrees to follow a foreigner into exile despite her doubts and regrets about leaving behind her family, home and country, shows how determined and how very much in love she is . . . I imagine her as a very attractive, sensual Andaluza with an absolutely unbelievable smile, beautiful teeth, beau-

157

tiful black eyes, black hair and a skin that is neither too dark nor too pale. In short, a typical Andaluza, guaranteed to drive him crazy! Of course we don't know if they would have lived happily ever after or whether they would have been pursued furiously by an avenging father or brother because, just as they are about to elope, destiny steps in and the story changes altogether.

'Destiny is depicted by that haunting musical theme which I have also conducted many, many times. And having done so, I must say that *Forza* is almost as difficult to conduct as to sing. Its style of composition is poised between early and late Verdi. It has beautiful, long scenes but they need to be well paced by a keen awareness of tempi which must not be allowed to slacken. They must sound vigorous and exciting, otherwise the opera can seem too long and too boring with so many extraneous characters such as Preziosilla and Melitone around to dilute the dramatic tension. The conductor must, therefore, compensate for this by ensuring that, musically at least, the tension doesn't flag.

'In theater lore *Forza* is supposed to be as unlucky for its performers as it is for the characters in its story. Like *Macbeth* in the straight theater which has the jinx on it, something often tends to go wrong with performances of *Forza*. Well, I must say that in one way at least it also proved unlucky for me. After Hamburg I also sang in Vienna and, in 1971, in Valencia, where the famous tenor of the past, Giacomo Lauri Volpi, chanced to be present at one of the performances. I was just 30 at the time but, after hearing my performance, Lauri Volpi declared that "someone who sings Alvaro so well cannot be 30 years old!" He then spread the rumor that I must be at least five or six years older. And this started the whole controversy about my age which goes on to this day. It's simply ridiculous! All you have to do is check out not just my birth certificate – because people might claim I could fake that – but the register in the church I was baptized in. There, sandwiched between the names of other children baptized around the same time, in 1941, you will find mine . . . But the whole saga began just because I sang so well in that performance of *Forza* in Valencia! . . . As soon as I was informed he was at the performance I announced to the audience who applauded and cheered him. So I don't think I deserved this behavior on his part . . . And, as a result of the rumor started by him, in his book *Voci Parallele* Rodolfo Celletti, the famous Italian musicologist, wrote that I was born in 1934! And since then, there has always been this doubt in people's minds. They think, Okay, Plácido says he's 59, but is he? So, in a way, the proverbial jinx that attaches to *Forza* also rubbed off on me, a little bit.'

DES GRIEUX

Massenet's Manon

This has not been an important role in Domingo's ca-reer. He sang it only twice – at NYCO and Vancouver – in 1969 and has not recorded the complete opera (there are some extracts – arias and duets – in live and commercial recordings). In fact the Massenet Des Grieux is one of the only two parts in Domingo's rep-ertoire (the other is Enzo Grimaldo in La Gioconda*) of which we, and posterity, have no record.*

Be that as it may, Des Grieux was Domingo's first Massenet part and it sowed the seed of his great love for this French composer which later culminated in his searing portrayals of Werther, Rodrigue in Le Cid *and Jean in* Hérodiade*. Intuitive and accomplished musician that the 28-year-old Domingo already was, he soon pinpointed the fact that those recitatives of Massenet's that precede his great arias are key mo-ments that must be infused with maximum tension and drama and that they offer cues as to the kind of atmosphere the singer is called to create in the follow-ing aria through the right choice of vocal colors.*

As Domingo rightly points out in his comparative analysis of Massenet's and Puccini's Des Grieux, the former is more lightweight and naïve and the heroine more starkly mercenary in Massenet than in Puccini. Manon *is one of Massenet's early operas – fifth of his 25 – written as a crowd-pleaser for his 'dear public'*

*and dramatically much weaker than his later works
or the novel by Abbé Prévost on which it is based. Yet
two scenes – the Cours-la-reine, and the scene where
the old Count comes to St Sulpice to dissuade his son
from taking holy orders – are vintage Massenet, sure
pointers to the composer he would soon become. The
characterization of both principals is also very vivid
and it is a great shame that we have no record or any
means of witnessing what an artist such as Domingo
could do with the role.*

'This is a role I sang very little – perhaps a total of seven or
eight performances in my career, at NYCO and Vancouver
in 1969. In retrospect I regret it because parts of this role,
and this opera as a whole, are really very moving. But somehow I wasn't obviously identified with it in the minds of
opera planners worldwide.

'In a way I see why, because the Massenet Des Grieux
was always a very hard part for me. "*Ah, fuyez douce image*" in particular which is very, very high, was always a
great challenge for me. But of course it's glorious. And the
recitative "*Ah, je suis seul, c'est le moment suprême*" that
precedes this aria is one of those moments which, as we will
discuss apropos of *Le Cid*, I call "oracles" because they
reveal the exact mood you should set with your voice in the
aria that follows. I love Massenet's music passionately. I
think he has to be one of the most exciting composers
around, even if slightly underestimated. I think he is to the
operatic world what Tchaikovsky is to the symphonic: a
giant whose apparent ease and prolific gift for dishing out a
seemingly endless flow of melodies causes some to depre-
cate his gifts. Massenet was a particularly grandiose composer for the tenor and the soprano. Des Grieux's second-
act aria "The Dream," for instance, is one of the most beau-

tiful in the French repertoire.

'As I explain in my discussion of his counterpart in Puccini's *Manon Lescaut*, as a character Massenet's Des Grieux is young, naïve and unwordly [see pp. 141-143]. A romantic hero par excellence who lacks the manliness and sheer passion of Puccini's character.'

CALAF

Turandot

As Domingo explains in the discussion that follows, he sang his first Calaf – one of the most daunting tenor roles, with an atrociously exposed B natural at the end of 'Nessun dorma' – right in the horse's mouth: on 16 July 1969 at the Arena in Verona, which boasts one of the most spoilt, knowledgeable and rowdy publics in Italy – which is to say in the world! He was also singing next to the greatest Turandot of the day, Birgit Nilsson.

As well as being as nervous as he describes in his recollection that follows, unbeknownst to him he also had a cold. 'He didn't know it and I didn't know it either,' recalls Birgit Nilsson, 'until a few days later, after he gave it to me! His kiss at the finale was so long that the public started to make a joke of it and yell, "Eee, basta, basta" (Hey, enough, enough). And a week later I had tonsillitis! But I must say it was worth it, in order to sing with Plácido Domingo! For he was born not just with a stunning voice but also the great, rare gift of musicality, which you either have or you don't, and was also a charming, fantastic person. And, yes, all the high notes were in place!'

A few months later, on February 1970, Domingo sang Calaf again with Nilsson at the Met. Subsequent performances include a run in Cologne in December 1981, Franco Zeffirelli's visually stunning productions

163

at La Scala in December 1983 with Ghena Dimitrova in the title role, and conducted by Lorin Maazel, his even more phantasmagoric production at the Met in 1997 and Andrei Serban's colorful staging at Covent Garden in September 1984, with Gwyneth Jones in the title role, who comments: 'There is only one thing more exciting than singing high Cs and that is singing them with a gorgeous tenor! You can't believe the sensation when soaring up there in the stratosphere with a tenor like Plácido Domingo!'

Domingo was already familiar with Turandot, *having sung the parts of Altoum (in Mexico City) and Pang (in Monterrey) in 1960. In his biography,* My First Forty Years, *he vividly recalls the impact the wonderful music of this opera, which he had never heard before, had on him. 'Although the Emperor has practically nothing to sing, I was given a beautiful costume for the production and Marta, whom I was getting to know better in those days, now enjoys reminding me of how proud I was to be so beautifully clad despite having such a small role. When I was engaged to sing the Emperor, I had never even heard of* Turandot *and I shall never forget coming into the rehearsal hall at the very moment when the chorus and the orchestra were working on* "Perché tarda la luna," *the chorus to the moon. Perhaps if I were to hear them today I would notice that they were playing flat or not singing so well. But at that moment the music had the most profound effect on me. It was one of the most moving experiences of my life, the most beautiful thing I had ever heard.'*

'If ever there was a difficult moment, a nervous moment in my career, it was singing Calaf for the first time, at the Verona Arena in 1969! I was still in my twenties and not only was I singing opposite the legendary Birgit Nilsson, the great Turandot of the day, but I was also making both my Italian debut and my debut at the Arena! You just can't imagine how I felt.

'Nevertheless, I loved singing Calaf! I like this character very much. He is one of those obsessional, almost suicidal types who gets so fixated on this woman that he doesn't care what he does in order to win her. He is playing Russian roulette and risks everything. In fact he loves taking risks. He doesn't only gamble once but three times. He is different, stubborn as a mule and very intriguing. But I like him! What sets him apart from all the other suitors is the fact that while, like them, he falls under Turandot's spell, unlike them he is not in awe of her. He barges in and appears so secure and confident of winning that he puzzles even her. He is intelligent enough to instantly sense the passion behind this woman who is supposed to be so cold, and astute enough to notice right away that she likes him, too. You can see that in the last riddle, when he's convinced he's on the point of being defeated, she helps him. She doesn't want him to be defeated. She sort of wills him to win. The subtext here is, "It's me, it's me, don't you realize? It's me!" She wants him to win even though this means that her "glory is finished."

'I always liked to make my Calaf very, very dashing, very daring, very superior, very arrogant, stubborn and extremely, recklessly bold! His obsession with Turandot, and with the challenge facing him, is such that he is prepared to go to extremes. This trait also shows the negative side of his character: the fact that he displays little humanity or concern for his father, who would almost certainly be tortured and killed in the effort to discover Calaf's name. But he is so focused on his own obsession that he is oblivious to everything else. He loves challenges to the point of addiction. Even winning the riddles and his prize, Turandot, is not enough for him. He doesn't want to possess her against her will. He wants her to want him. So he sets himself another challenge by saying, "Now I have a riddle for you!" I think it's a fascinating situation! But I hope Turandot does not become too subservient, because then who knows . . .

'All in all, I think *Turandot* is the opera in which I always had the most fun! And this despite the fact that, apart from Act I which is comfortable and enjoyable, Calaf is certainly very difficult vocally. And I'm not just talking about the famous B natural at the end of "*Nessun dorma,*" the toughest moment, which of course everyone is waiting for, but also the fact that all the time you are battling against a very heavy orchestration which your voice must pierce through in order to project. Both his and Turandot's tessitura is not only extremely high but very strained, as if their voices, as well as their characters, are being stretched to extremes. I wonder whether Puccini, who at that stage in his life had problems and pain in his own throat, was unconsciously, maybe even deliberately, passing this strain on to his hero and heroine by giving them such tough, difficult music . . .

'Yet even on that first evening in Verona, after mastering my nerves, I had fun with this opera. And I remember a funny incident involving my children. The stage in Verona is, of course, vast and the scenery was very realistic. Every time I answered a riddle, I had to climb about 30 steps up a very wide staircase. I was wearing a cape which swayed and billowed in the evening breeze so that Placi and Alvaro, who were very little at the time, whispered to Marta: "Mami, look, Papi is flying!"'

TITLE ROLE

Ernani

I think I should start my introduction to this wonderful Domingo portrayal with a piece of very good news: the fact that Domingo is seriously thinking of singing Ernani again at the Vienna State Opera in the near future. The very thought of seeing Domingo again in this major Verdi part in which he made his debut at La Scala on 7 December 1969 is enough to set the imagination alight with possibilities: new details and subtle colorings that he is sure to bring to this part which he last sang for the opening of the 1982–83 season at La Scala, 13 years after his debut. In between he only sang two performances of the part: one at the Metropolitan Opera on 19 January 1971 and one in concert in Amsterdam on 15 January 1972.

As Domingo goes on to explain, Ernani is one of the very difficult roles in the tenor repertoire. So much so, that before the 1982 opening at La Scala, he decided to try a different system of warming up the voice. As he explains in his autobiography, the most important thing for him when he begins to warm up is not the extension of the voice – the high and low notes – but the quality of the sound in the middle. He begins by singing C-D-E-D, C-D-E-D, C-D-E-D-C with vowel sounds. Then up a semitone: D flat-E flat-F-E flat-D flat-E flat-F-E flat-D flat, and so on. He also finds singing semitones a help: C-C sharp-D-D sharp-

167

E-E flat-D-D flat-C; then the same beginning on C sharp, etc. By doing these simple exercises, which require a smooth, legato sound that can only be produced by proper support, he makes his diaphragm work. He doesn't go higher than about G. When the middle register is ready, he begins to sing extended arpeggios. For instance, starting on his low C, he sings upwards C-E-G-C-E-G and then back downwards F-D-B-G-F-D-C. Then some scales which he extends by one note each time, from C up to the D a ninth above it and down. Then from C to E, C to F and so on, always adding European vowel sounds – first 'i', then 'e', 'a', 'o', 'u'. The next step is to sing because adding the text brings another dimension to his work.

Until the Ernani *at La Scala, he used to sing fragments of various arias during his warm-ups. But in this case he was so worried about the tessitura of his aria, which comes right at the beginning of Act I, that he asked one of La Scala's musical assistants to come to his dressing room and play through the whole aria, which he sang in full voice. 'As a result, when I walked onstage I was completely ready and able to sing at my best.' The video recording of the 1982 premiere – which also featured Mirella Freni, Renato Bruson and Nicolai Ghiaurov, under the baton of Riccardo Muti – certainly bears out his claim.*

'Ernani is the first of Verdi's four "Spanish" operas – set in Spain – which also include *Il Trovatore*, *La Forza del Destino* and *Don Carlos*. The role of Ernani is a very special part for me. It's the part with which I made my debut at La Scala in 1969, with a wonderful cast consisting of Raina Kabaivanska as Elvira, Piero Cappuccilli as the King and Nicolai Ghiaurov as Silva under the baton of Antonino

Votto. For a 28-year-old singer to make his Scala debut in such an important role and with such a cast was an extraordinary opportunity.

'But what also makes Ernani special is the fact that it is Verdi's first great tenor role. Although chronologically *Nabucco* is an earlier opera, the tenor role in it, Ismaele, is not big or important and he is certainly not a protagonist. But Ernani heralds the beginning of a series of glorious tenor roles which lead right up to Otello, and stretch through most of Verdi's life as well as a vast chunk of the nineteenth century. And I have sung most of them! Ismaele [*Nabucco*], Macduff [*Macbeth*], Carlo III in *Giovanna D'Arco*, Oronte [*I Lombardi nella prima crociata*] on record and Arrigo [*La battaglia di Legnano*] in concert. But from Stiffelio on I have sung all Verdi's heroes on stage: Rodolfo [*Luisa Miller*], Gabriele Adorno [*Simon Boccanegra*], the Duke of Mantua [*Rigoletto*], Alfredo [*La Traviata*], Manrico [*Il Trovatore*], Riccardo [*Un Ballo in Maschera*] Alvaro [*La Forza del Destino*], Arrigo [*I Vespri Siciliani*], Radames [*Aida*] and the title roles in *Don Carlos* and *Otello*. The only omission is Fenton in *Falstaff*.

'Ernani's music is very, very difficult to sing. But it's sensational! The ensemble, the aria, the cabaletta, the duet with Silva, the trio with the King and Elvira, the trio with Silva and finally the last trio with Silva and Elvira which is quite magisterial. Ernani's aria and cabaletta "*Come rugiada al cespite*" and "*Oh tu chel'alma adora*" is difficult, the ensembles are difficult, because you have to be heard above all the mêlée but hardest of all is the last trio. All in all Ernani is one of the great Verdi tenor roles.

'The character is fantastic! I love the idea of this outlaw who steals from the rich to give to the poor, a little bit like Robin Hood or Fra Diavolo. In reality, of course, Ernani is a nobleman, who has spent years living among and leading his bandits. But his love for Elvira forces him to return to his past and, through his involvement with the King and the Count (Silva), to find himself back at his roots and forced to reveal his true name: Giovanni d'Aragona, Duke of Segorbia and Cardona, a very noble and tragic character, who dies because of loyalty to his oath to Silva. In those days, people considered themselves bound by their oaths. It was a matter of honor. Nowadays, of course, one is amazed that Ernani should consider a commitment such as the one he made to Silva, binding. For the bass Silva, Ernani's enemy, is one of the most terrible, unrelenting characters I can think of in the entire repertoire. Unlike Fiesco in *Simon Boccanegra*, another terrifying character Verdi gives to the bass who at least relents, understands and forgives in the end (even though this is too late for Simone), Silva does not. Absolutely not. He is made of pure, unadulterated steel. A really nasty man. Ernani finds himself in the unenviable situation of having to fight against not just him, not just one, but two super-powerful people at the same time: Silva and the King.'

ENZO

La Gioconda

Enzo has not been a particularly important part in Domingo's career even though his portrayal was scenically dashing and vocally thrilling. He has sung only 17 performances of the role, but what makes Enzo extra special for him is the fact that it was the part in which he made his debut in his native Madrid, on 14 May 1970. Not surprisingly, he recalls the occasion vividly as one of the most moving of his career.

'When the audience of my native city began to applaud me after I had sung one of Enzo's arias, I was unable to continue singing. I spent the next few minutes weeping and trying to overcome my tears. I don't know how I managed to sing the following duet with Laura, which is one of the most difficult parts of the opera. It's a very emotional memory.'

Domingo went on to sing Enzo in Berlin eleven years later, in May 1981, at the Metropolitan Opera in September 1982 and February 1983, and the Vienna State Opera in May 1986 with Eva Marton in the title role. There is a commercial video recording available of the latter occasion.

Domingo made a commercial recording of the role for EMI in summer 2002.

'Enzo, along with the Massenet Des Grieux, is one of the two major tenor roles I have not recorded. I hope to put

171

this right in 2001! It is a wonderful role, which I sang first in Madrid on 14 May 1970. Enzo's music is extraordinary! His arias "*Cielo e mar!*" and the duet with Laura, "*Laggiù, nelle nebbie remote*" are marvellous and so is the great ensemble "*Già ti veggo immota e smorta*" and his tremendously dramatic duet with Barnaba. Of these, the most difficult are the aria, which is so well known and loved, but tougher still is the duet with Laura which has an ongoing momentum that doesn't allow you any space to breathe. And after those galloping phrases, you have to sing a very difficult B flat together with Laura and then continue along more lyrical lines. The third act ensemble is also very beautiful with some truly wonderful melodies.

'Dramatically speaking, the characters are not very complex. They are all very basic, "up front" characters to be enjoyed more for their music than any hidden depths. Enzo finds himself in the peculiar situation of being loved by Gioconda, whom he is merely fond of in a friendly way, and the passion he feels for Laura whom he hoped to marry before he was proscribed but who was forced by her family to marry a much older man, Alvise. I would say that this opera is purely about vocal enjoyment.'

TITLE ROLE

Roberto Devereux

*NYCO's production of Donizetti's seldom staged op-
era, with Beverly Sills as Queen Elizabeth I and
Domingo in the title role was, in the words of the
New York Post, 'Unquestionably the most exciting
event of the fall 1970 musical season.' This wonderful, underrated opera had not been staged in New York
since 1851, and NYCO pulled out all the stops to make
this staging, by Tito Capobianco, and conducted by
NYCO's Artistic Director, Julius Rudel, a success.*

*Domingo's performances, which drew ecstatic ova-
tions and high critical praise, were sandwiched between* Ballo *at the Met, where he was performing
Gustavus III in the opera's Swedish setting opposite
Montserrat Caballé. He did both his leading ladies
proud: 'Singing opposite Sills, tenors sound pale and
superfluous,' wrote* Time. *'But Sills and Domingo
made an Elizabeth and Essex any opera director might
be tempted to swap a* Ring *cycle for. Bending to one
knee in supplication, baring his chest with soldierly
bravado, singing with graceful, silver mastery,
Domingo made their touching Act I duet a true meet-
ing of romantic equals.'*

*Domingo was already riding high in New York
where, the magazine went on to remark, he was already acquiring a public willing to jostle its way into
the opera any night he chose to sing. His magnificent*

173

performance in this unjustly underrated work makes one regret he didn't perform more bel canto roles in his career. It also belies his own over-modest remark that he is far from being an ideal bel canto singer. While this might be true of his post-Otello years, it was certainly not true in October 1970 when, after the premiere, on the 15th, Harold Schönberg wrote in the New York Times: 'Mr Domingo is as smooth a tenor as one can find, and the role of Roberto was perfectly in his range. Such easy, long-phrased, accurate singing, backed by a sound that is pure velvet, is to be treasured.'

It makes one ache not to have seen those vintage performances in an area of the repertoire that one has hardly had a chance to sample Domingo's artistry. Those lucky enough to have been present at those five performances should treasure their memories forever.

'My second major bel canto role, eight years after I sang Edgardo in *Lucia*, was the Earl of Essex in Donizetti's *Roberto Devereux*. It was a momentous occasion, at NYCO in 1970, because Beverly Sills was singing Queen Elizabeth, under the baton of Julius Rudel. As you can imagine, singing as interesting a character as Essex with such a partner as Beverly was both challenging and tremendously exciting.

'The reason why I find Essex interesting is that he is a man who finds himself in an unenviable love – or infatuation – situation with a very powerful woman, the Queen of England. And as Radames also found to his cost, this is always hopeless because whatever you do, she has you at her mercy, she can do anything she likes with you. By the end, you get the feeling that Essex is getting a little tired of the whole situation, all those intrigues and power games that invariably take place around figures of power, to the point where he tries to take his own life.

'From the vocal point of view, I was really surprised to discover what a fascinating opera this is! Not just Essex's own music but also Elizabeth's, which is fabulous! Frankly, you don't expect to come across such music in works that are seldom performed. You think there must be a good reason why they are rarely heard. But I suspect that, in this case, the main reason is that this opera requires four top singers of the calibre of a Joan Sutherland, Montserrat Caballé, Beverly Sills or Leyla Gencer . . . Essex's own music is very difficult, especially his duets with the Queen and with Sara, Countess of Nottingham, the other main character: "*Ah, quest'addio fatale.*" There is also some exceptional music in his duet with the baritone and in his final aria and cabaletta ("*A morte*") before he goes to the scaffold. It was a very rewarding role to sing and I don't understand why I never did so again. But I suppose that, with so much repertoire, theaters tended to engage me for more important and popular parts.'

RODOLFO

Luisa Miller

Domingo sang Rodolfo for the first time on 4 No-
vember 1971 at the Metropolitan Opera, where he
also performed it again eight years later, in January
1979. In June 1979 he sang five equally memorable
performances at Covent Garden and, while in Lon-
don, also recorded the role for Deutsche
Grammophon, with a cast including Katia Ricciarelli,
Renato Bruson and Elena Obraztsova, under the ba-
ton of Lorin Maazel. At the time, all the recording
companies seemed to have gone wild about Luisa
Miller, *or simply didn't wish to miss out on its sudden*
popularity, and the other two of the Three Tenors also
recorded the part: Pavarotti for Decca and Carreras
for Philips.

Three years later, Domingo sang his last two per-
formances of Rodolfo in Hamburg in January and June
1982. All in all, he sang 16 performances of this role
in his career. But although this is not a great deal,
nonetheless Domingo made a big impact in this opera
where his concept of Verdi as a Bel canto composer
with a capital 'B' was put to excellent effect. The ob-
vious example is Rodolfo's 'showpiece' Act II aria
'Quando le sere al placido,' which brought the house
down both in New York and London and which was
delivered in a way that highlighted all Domingo's art-
istry: first the vibrant, passionate delivery of the words

176

which made the pathos of the lover's ardor and the tension contained in his outburst even more poignant; then the change of vocal color to soft, plangent lyric sound for the aria's melancholy ending. What makes Domingo's delivery of what Charles Osborne, the distinguished Verdi specialist, calls 'a lyrical bel canto melody of great beauty' so special is the fact that although he imbues it with every quality one can hope for in bel canto singing, he also infuses it with throbbing underlying tension and excitement that makes of it something more than just a beautiful lyrical melody. This 'goccia di verismo' (drop of verismo) into this quintessentially lyric part – and not just in the aria – is what made Domingo's interpretation, both on stage and disc, the most outstanding in my memory.

'In my mind I always associate Rodolfo in *Luisa* with Arrigo in *I Vespri Siciliani*. The two roles have several musical and dramatic similarities. Both are very high – although Rodolfo is not so extreme or quite as demanding as Arrigo – and both are rebellious sons. In fact in some ways Rodolfo reminds me a bit of some rebellious juniors of our own day.

'He is in love with this precious, innocent girl who is the victim of destiny. For the only thing these two have done wrong is being born into the wrong family. Like Romeo's and Juliet's, their two families are at loggerheads, and out of self-interest, Rodolfo's father, Count Walter, wants him to marry the mezzo, Federica. Luisa loves Rodolfo deeply regardless of the fact that – as her own father and the man he wishes her to marry, Wurm, make a point of telling her – she realizes he's probably going to marry Federica. But Rodolfo is equally passionately in love with Luisa and at the finale of Act I threatens and blackmails his father that, unless he relents and lets him marry her, he will reveal the

Count's guilty past, the criminal way in which he became Count Walter, to everyone.

'Vocally Rodolfo is a very satisfying, yet far from easy role to sing. At the very beginning of Act I he already has some hard music. His opening phrase *"Ah mi amor che sprimere"* has a bit of coloratura, as does his whole duet with Luisa. Then comes the even more difficult duet with Federica which is high yet has to be sung lightly, with a spring to the voice. And, at the end of the first act, you have the ensemble in which he threatens his father that he will kill the girl unless he relents.

'Then, mercifully, the tenor disappears for a while. But when you return you have to plunge into the famous aria *"Quando le sere al placido,"* which has always been one of my favorites. Rodolfo has received a letter from Luisa, informing him that she has been seeing Wurm – what a name for an operatic character, Wurm! So he bursts into this aria in which he reminisces about their lovely times together and expresses his pain at being betrayed. He challenges Wurm to a duel. But the latter doesn't accept his challenge because he is a coward, fires a shot in the air and escapes. Rodolfo's father arrives and while he's trying to console him, Rodolfo sings a glorious cabaletta.

'In the last act, Rodolfo is slightly reminiscent of Otello. His entry is accompanied by some sombre tones and musical phrases, which are not dissimilar to those in Otello's last-act entry. He administers poison to Luisa and then takes some himself. He doesn't ask any questions. He just forces the poison on her, and only after they have both taken it, does she reveal that she had written that letter only because she was forced to, and that she loves him alone. Rodolfo then kills Wurm and he and Luisa die together. This scene also has the most exciting music: a tremendous duet with Luisa and a great trio with the father.

178

'So this is a very black opera, black through and through. Of course, it's based on Schiller's great play *Kabale und Liebe*. Yet Rodolfo is a very rewarding role to sing and I'm sad that I cannot do so any more because of its consistently high tessitura which I can no longer sustain through a whole evening.'

VASCO DA GAMA

L'Africaine

Domingo first sang Vasco in San Francisco in a major new production that included Shirley Verrett as Selika on 3 November 1972, then in Barcelona and, six years later at Covent Garden. Then he let it go for a decade until 1988, when the San Francisco production was revived. On all three occasions it proved a very good part for him, both vocally and scenically, despite the fact that psychologically the part is rather 'up-front' and uncomplicated.

In the six years between those initial performances in San Francisco and the 1978 Covent Garden production, Domingo was already becoming the leading singer-actor of our day. Grace Bumbry who sang Amneris in some performances of Aida *at the Vienna State Opera in 1973, the year after the San Francisco production of* L'Africaine, *had (as she explains in the introduction to Radames) found him vocally splendid but not particularly distinguished scenically. 'But when I met him again for* L'Africaine, *I noticed a big difference. A totally different calibre of singing-actor, or actor-singer, had come to the fore and was already in full fruition. I remember that his rendition of "O Paradis" was wonderful, and not just for its vocal bravura but also because of the way the action had developed to that point. He was very inspiring to everyone else in the cast because an artist of Plácido's calibre*

180

*does have that effect on people. He makes you want
to do your best, too.'*

'I first sang Vasco da Gama at the San Francisco Opera in
1972, when I persuaded Kurt Herbert Adler to mount a
production of this rarity with Shirley Verrett as Selika, later
in an improvised production at the Liceo in Barcelona, and
finally at Covent Garden in 1978, this time with Grace
Bumbry in the title role.

'I wouldn't say that *L'Africaine* is a masterpiece, but I
think that it contains Meyerbeer's best music. As far as the
drama is concerned, the story is very far-fetched. Vasco himself is not particularly interesting and doesn't develop at all
during the course of the action. His most powerful moment
is in Act I, where he challenges the Royal Council in Lisbon
and persuades them to let him undertake the long voyage to
India. This much is historical truth. So off he sets and during this journey he meets the beautiful, exotic African slave
girl, Selika.

'Vocally it's a very enjoyable part despite some moments
of considerable vocal difficulty. The tessitura is extremely
demanding. Not only do you have the very beautiful and
famous aria "*O Paradis*" – a tenor showpiece if there ever
was one, which everyone is waiting for and by which they
will judge your performance – but phrases strewn with A
flats all over. So, although an enjoyable sing it's far from
being a walkover.

'One of the distinct disadvantages is the fact that Vasco
disappears before the end of the opera, for no good reason.
This means that, dramatically speaking, the part is a little
flat. But the singing is anything but flat. It's fantastic and I
consider Vasco to be among my best portrayals. I'm also
very proud to have brought him, and this opera, out of rela-
tive oblivion.'

181

ARRIGO

I Vespri Siciliani

Arrigo has been one of the proudest achievements in Domingo's career. It is the most difficult Verdi role after Otello. Yet if one were to look at Otello purely from the vocal point of view and remove the immense, draining emotional commitment it demands from its interpreters, one might be tempted to say it is easier than Arrigo, especially for a tenor like Domingo who has never been a high note tenor par excellence.

Domingo sang it for the first time in Paris on 9 April 1974, nine months before his first Otello. Two months later he performed it in Hamburg, in the following September and October at the Metropolitan Opera and at the end of the year at the Liceo in Barcelona: a total of 13 performances. (Fourteen if one counts the open dress rehearsal in Paris.) What makes Arrigo such a near-impossible part to sing and cast is its consistently stratospherically high tessitura. It is noteworthy that, as he points out, none of Domingo's illustrious predecessors ever had a go at this part and of his contemporaries, neither has Pavarotti who is a high note tenor par excellence. This makes Domingo's technical mastery that made such a feat possible even more remarkable. For being able, through the technical manipulation of his vocal resources, to manufacture B naturals and even high Cs is one thing: being able to sing an entire evening at a

*tessitura as murderous as Arrigo's, which includes a
D flat, and make a resounding success of it is a posi-
tively Herculean dare!*

*All the more reason to regret that there is no video
recording of any of Domingo's performances of Vespri.
One has to make do with an audio recording from
RCA featuring Martina Arroyo as Elena, Ruggero
Raimondi as Procida and Sherrill Milnes as Montforte
under the baton of James Levine. Domingo, who is
particularly fond of this opera, despite the difficulties
of its tenor role, is now planning to conduct the work
in Verona in 2002 with Sylvie Valayre as Elena and,
again, Ruggero Raimondi as Procida – a vintage cast
if ever there was one!*

'Without doubt Arrigo is one of the two most difficult roles
in my entire repertoire. He is also a very interesting character: very rough, very, very aggressive, fanatical and, above
all, extremely difficult vocally. My only other role which,
because of the enormous emotional commitment it involves,
is even more demanding and wearing is Otello. But I am
very proud to have included Arrigo in my repertoire because very few of the great tenors of the past did so. Caruso
never sang it and neither did Bjoerling or Di Stefano. The
role is stratospherically high – it includes a D flat towards
the end, and the opera itself is rarely put on and difficult to
stage. It requires a quartet of great singers – soprano, tenor,
baritone and bass – and most theaters who can get hold of
such a group tend to prefer to put on *Don Carlos*.

'I sang Arrigo in three productions – in Paris, Hamburg
and the Met in 1974 – and all three were by Joseph Svoboda.
I don't know why, but in my mind I tend to associate Arrigo
a little bit with Rodolfo in *Luisa Miller*, because both parts
are vocally very high and both characters are rebellious sons:

Rodolfo for personal reasons while Arrigo is quite a different story. He is a phenomenal character, a revolutionary who is rebellious because he is caught up in the fight to free his country from its French oppressors. This fact generates enormous tension in him because it involves his passionate enmity against a man who, as he discovers halfway through the plot, is his own father: Guy de Montfort, Sicily's French governor. This tension is heightened by his impassioned love for Elena, who is deeply implicated in the plot against the French and who becomes his enemy as soon as it becomes clear that Arrigo is incapable of killing his father, although later she relents.

'Vocally this high tension is reflected in Arrigo's tessitura, which is truly murderous – one of the toughest in all opera. In the first act, he has a wonderful ensemble followed by a tense duet with his father. In Act II comes an important duet with Elena and another big duet with his father, which contains a beautiful melody first heard in the overture. In Act III comes the crucial, tremendously dramatic duet in which the baritone, Guy de Montfort, reveals that Arrigo is his own son – the reason why his life has been spared and he has been let out of prison. Arrigo is dumbfounded and appalled. He suffers deeply at this amazing revelation. For he agreed to participate in the plot with the express purpose of killing the governor, who now turns out to be the father who, he believes, had caused his mother's death by abandoning her. He says, how can you possibly be my father, I hate being your son.

'Yet Act III also contains two of the best tenor/baritone duets in all Verdi. All Verdi tenor/baritone duets are masterpieces, whether you pick the ones in *I Masnadieri*, *La Forza del Destino*, *Don Carlos* or *Otello*. But I think that two duets between Arrigo and Montforte in *Vespri* are among the most beautiful Verdi ever wrote, especially the second one which has the theme of the overture. His duet with Elena is also great. His famous Act IV aria *"Un giorno di pianto"* is really difficult for, although it's a very dramatic and splendid aria, its tessitura is a killer. Yet equally difficult are the trio and the quartet. And, of course, right at the end, in Act V after the Wedding Duet and after you have been singing at this exhausting tessitura all evening, there comes this arietta, so short but so tough, which contains a high D! I am happy to say that, in the recording, I sang it with the high D in place. Arrigo is a part which, despite its difficulties and murderous tessitura, I wish I had sung more. Now, I'm looking forward to conducting *Vespri* instead.'

TITLE ROLE

Roméo et Juliette

Domingo has only sung this legendary romantic hero once in his career, in a run of six performances at the Metropolitan Opera in October 1974, with Judith Blegen as Juliette. As all tenors who undertake this role confirm, he found it very difficult indeed, especially for a voice like his, which is a lirico spinto rather than the light-lyric to lyric voices one usually associates with the role.

His next and only contact with the work came 12 years later, in 1986, when he was asked to conduct it at the Metropolitan Opera with a star cast that included Alfredo Kraus and Cecilia Gasdia, in her Met debut, in the title roles.

Those Met Roméos were sandwiched between performances of Menotti's Goya at Washington Opera in which he was singing the title role, which meant shuttling between the two cities on alternate days – typical Domingo scheduling! In this case he had no choice because the Goya dates came after the Roméos had been booked and there was no way the Met would change them or release him. In the event, his conducting effort was well received and the combination of one great Spanish tenor conducting another made this an extra special occasion.

'Roméo, which I first sang at the Metropolitan Opera, is, along with Hoffmann, one of the longest and most difficult parts in the repertoire, a long, long, and a very high part. But I love them both and played them with the greatest care and love. Of course, the Met performances were a great challenge for me because I came in the wake of Franco Corelli's enormous success in this part, when the production was new.

'But I was very happy with the result. Not only is the music very beautiful – in spots even more beautiful than *Faust* – but it was also my first role based on a Shakespeare character and I relished the experience. Although this was a revival and not a new production by then, I worked a great deal on the characterization with Marta, even down to the way I should walk: in a special, "Renaissance" sort of way, almost on tiptoe, with a light, youthful spring.

'Vocally, its great length renders Roméo very difficult. It's high, but in this case it's not just a question of the tessitura but also of some very exposed high notes in his aria and the duets. Of course, you could say that the entire opera is a continuous duet – I don't know of any other operas that have so many duets for soprano and tenor – so that it's hard to know which one you can single out and love most, as an item. Maybe the Bedroom Duet, which is so exceptional that I still include in concerts, just in order to savor its beauty once again.

'I was only 33 when I sang Roméo. It was the right age, the right time and the right place and I had a lovely time with it. In retrospect, I regret doing it just this once. I wish I had also sung it in Paris!'

DICK JOHNSON (OR RAMERREZ)

La Fanciulla del West

Dick Johnson is one of Domingo's most popular roles; he performed it no fewer than 80 times in 25 years. The first time was on 26 November 1974 in Turin and the last on 15 December 1995 in Bonn. In between, he sang it in Miami and Covent Garden in April and May 1977 respectively, again at Covent Garden in 1978 and 1982, Vienna, Buenos Aires and San Francisco in 1979, Madrid in 1983, Barcelona in 1984, Vienna in 1988, Berlin in 1989, Chicago in 1990, and La Scala, Los Angeles and the Metropolitan Opera in 1991 and 1992.

He is particularly fond of this role which is far from easy to sing but terrific fun to perform. The atmosphere of the Wild West in the nineteenth century delights him, and evokes memories of children's comics and westerns. His joy in performing Dick Johnson was infectious. Indeed, it was the only role, among the 60-plus we discussed for the purposes of this book, at which he spontaneously exclaimed: 'What can I tell you? Now we are going through all my roles, one by one, I realize how much I miss them!'

Among the many productions of Fanciulla he appeared in were three by Piero Faggioni whom, as he has already stated in the chapter on Don José, he rightly considers among the most brilliant directors on the operatic circuit. (But regrets that his extreme

188

perfectionism and irascible nature have prevented him from dominating the operatic world to the extent that his talent deserves.) As a former actor, Faggioni has an acute gift for getting under the characters' skin, understanding the motivations behind each of their utterances and 'acting them out' to the singer's lasting benefit. Domingo states that he owes a considerable slice of his insights into Don José, Cavaradossi, Des Grieux, Paolo and Otello as well as Dick Johnson, to Faggioni. His favorite of the three Faggioni productions of Fanciulla *he appeared in was Covent Garden's, with spectacular sets by Ken Adam (of James Bond fame). There is an excellent commercial video recording available, enabling both Domingo's current fans and posterity to sample his vintage portrayal, which also features Carol Neblett as Minnie and Silvano Carroli as Jack Rance, under the baton of Nello Santi.*

There are also three recordings – one CD and one video by Deutsche Grammophon and one by Sony – the former two with Sherrill Milnes and the latter with Juan Pons as Jack Rance, and Carol Neblett, Barbara Daniels and Mara Zampieri as Minnie respectively, under the batons of Zubin Mehta, Lorin Maazel and Nello Santi.

'This is another wonderful Puccini part and what can I tell you? Now that I'm going through all my roles with you, one by one, so many of which I don't sing any longer, I realize how much I miss them! Ramerrez in particular is very dear to me and I have very fond memories of several productions of *Fanciulla*, the best of which was Piero Faggioni's at Covent Garden in 1977, with sets by Ken Adam and Zubin Mehta in the pit. Only the fact that I'll be singing the part again in Los Angeles in 2002, with Catherine

Malfitano as Minnie, stops me from wallowing in a fit of nostalgia!

'But although highly enjoyable, Ramerrez, or Dick Johnson, is not an easy role to sing. Quite the opposite. The first act presents some difficulties in the shape of the phrase "*Amai la vita e l'amo*" which is very high and culminates in a B natural. What can I tell you? I have never been a tenor with great ease at the top. Maybe other tenors might tell you that this kind of high note is what they enjoy most. I don't. In Act II, he has the aria "*Or son sei mesi*" which is one of the most difficult Puccini arias, with a line of sustained B flats at the end, which are very tough indeed – "*La mia vergogna, a-himè, a-himè, a-himè vergogna mia*" – because by then you are quite tired. But although my technique, breath support and control enabled me to sing this line without breathing between those B flats, eventually I came to the conclusion that, for the sake of expression, it was better to breathe before each one, each "*a-himè*". Even if this breath took the shape of a gasp, it gave the phrase extra impetus.

'Dramatically this opera is great fun, almost like a Western, and boasts one of the greatest of all Puccini heroines, Minnie. No composer – not even Strauss – loved his girls as much as Puccini and he gives this particular girl, Minnie, one of the greatest entrances an operatic heroine can hope for! Not only is she the only female character in the opera (with the exception of Wowkle, her squaw, who has but a few lines to sing), but she also has a spectacular first entry, into a bar full of adoring men! Everyone, all the miners and the bartender, loves her so much and, in the end, their love prevails. Even though they are very jealous of Minnie's love for Ramerrez, and want to have him executed, they find themselves unable to do such a thing to this angel of a girl who has done so much for them. It's a very human reaction.

'Again here we have a heroine and a situation typical of Puccini. I cannot make up my mind whether I prefer Puccini's ladies to Verdi's, about whom we know a lot less than we do about Puccini's. When singing Des Grieux or Ramerrez in a performance that's going well, I can't say whom I prefer! In a sense Puccini's ladies are far more modern. Puccini's ladies are usually the ones who go to bed! When we first encounter her, Minnie is a virgin, but I believe that in Act II, when Jack Rance, the sheriff, leaves Minnie's hut after he has lost his bet at cards, she and Ramerrez certainly make love. There is almost tangible proof of the consummation of their passion in the music! And by the third act, he and Minnie have already been living together for a while. Minnie has found love, and she goes to save Ramerrez like a lioness. And in this rare instance of an opera that doesn't end in tragedy, she is allowed to keep her love.' (*Turandot* has a happy ending, but it is marred by the previous tragedy of Liu's death.)

TITLE ROLE

Otello

If one were forced to name one single role as Domingo's signature part, one which he has made uniquely his own during the past quarter century, it would have to be Otello. He first sang it in 1975, aged 34, at the Hamburg State Opera, against everybody's advice. Voice experts, critics, managements and Rolf Liebermann himself were convinced it would prove his undoing! The only dissenting voice – apart from his own calm inner conviction that the part was right for him and he for it – was Birgit Nilsson:

'The moment I first heard Plácido sing, which was as Don Rodrigo at NYCO in 1966, a good three years before we actually sang together, I thought to myself, this man is going to be a great Otello one day! People laughed at me and said, "But his voice is so lyrical, how could it possibly ever stretch to such a dramatic role?" But I could already hear Otello in it. And I was deeply gratified when he justified my prediction!'

Justify it he did, right from that first Otello in 1975. As he is the first to admit, the Hamburg State Opera, whose Intendant, August Everding, directed the production, pulled out all the stops to make the preparation period as close to ideal as possible: Domingo and the rest of the cast – which was also as near-ideal as one could hope for, with Katia Ricciarelli as Desdemona, Sherrill Milnes as Iago, and star billing even for the minor roles with Werner Hollweg as Cassio, Hans Sotin as Lodovico and Hannah Schwarz as Emilia under the baton of James Levine – were given maximum rehearsal time. Domingo states he had 150 hours of rehearsal!

'*I couldn't tell if Plácido was nervous or not,*' *says Sherrill Milnes.* '*He's very good at keeping these things inside and always managing to present a calm, affable front. What I can tell you was that he was already a splendid Otello. What makes Plácido's Otello so special in the history of the role is the fact that, although he is very strong, you also feel his vulnerability. The fact that he doesn't possess the amount of vocal power of a Del Monaco or a Vickers works for him. You love his Otello, you weep for him, much more than you ever did for those of the past. And, again, he loves his words, he spits them, he bites them, he caresses them, he feels every one of them.*

'*There were 58 curtain calls but believe it or not, this is not the most we ever got after an* Otello. *That record goes to the last of a run of performances at the Vienna State Opera in 1989, which also happened to be the last performance of the season. Again, Katia was Desdemona and the conductor was Michael Schoenwandt. Right from the start we felt a sort of electricity in the air, the feeling that tonight, the stars are in the right place – a* Sternstunde *as it's rightly called in German – and by the end of our Act II Otello–Iago duet the place exploded! It went berserk! And at the end, we took our bows, the* soli, *the* tutti, *and half an hour or 40 to 50 curtain calls after, we were still there. By then we were all getting tired of smiling, the way that you do at wedding receptions, and finally an hour-and-a-half and 101 curtain calls later, we got away!'*

Since then Domingo has sung the part all over the world. I have been lucky enough to attend a great many of those performances over the years, starting with those vintage evenings under Carlos Kleiber at Covent Garden and La Scala in 1980, and later in New York, Vienna and again in London, in Elijah Moshinsky's production.

Yet nothing had prepared me for what I was to witness and experience at the Metropolitan Opera last autumn, on 12 October 1999, the last of a run of four performances. ('You were convinced it was going be my last, weren't you?' Domingo winked wryly over dinner afterwards. 'All of you who came tonight thought the same!') This was simply the greatest of all Domingo's Otellos ever, perhaps even the single greatest performance of anything I have seen in my life. One was no longer watching a performance of Otello, or hearing Domingo singing Otello. One was watching Otello, a great and noble spirit slowly crucifying itself. One forgot to feel sorry for Desdemona. For, every word uttered sounded like another nail being hammered into this almost visible cross of pain. At the end, there was a deadly silence for a few moments. Then a howl, an explosion of applause. Yet what was unique about this ovation – something I had never witnessed anywhere in all my opera-going years – was that after God knows how many curtain calls (I wasn't counting) I noticed that the cheering crowds were no longer shouting DO-MIN-GO but O-TEL-LO, O-TEL-LO, O-TEL-LO. They knew that had they not just seen Domingo as Otello. They had seen Otello. It was the most moving verdict any artist could hope for.

It was endorsed by Anthony Tommasini, who

*wrote in the New York Times: 'I have heard him per-
form Otello many times, but have never been more
moved by the impassioned vocality and dramatic fer-
vor.' Elijah Moshinsky, who has collaborated with
Domingo on two productions of the work, concludes
that 'Domingo's Otello is unsurpassed in the history
of the role. The creation of this part has been a lifetime's
work. Like a Rembrandt self-portrait, it got deeper
and darker.'*

'This was the role everyone was so afraid of and said I
shouldn't do because it would harm my voice! But I always
felt confident that I could do it, that it would be a good role
for me, even though I was very young, barely 34, when I
did my first one in 1975, at the Hamburg State Opera. And
I think that first Otello was a great performance, with Katia
[Ricciarelli] as Desdemona and Sherrill [Milnes] as Iago,
Jimmy [Levine] conducting, and August Everding directing.
There was a great stir and commotion with the international press and managements, and everybody came from
everywhere! Of course, when I compare those first performances with those of 20 and now 25 years later, I realize
how much better I could do the part, how much stronger
the characterization could be. But this doesn't mean that
the first ones were bad!

'After Hamburg, my next Otello was at the Paris Opèra,
in a production directed by Terry Hands; next came
Zeffirelli's at La Scala, Ponnelle's in Munich, Faggioni's in
Bregenz and Madrid, Moshinsky's in London, Olmi's in
Salzburg. But the single thing that has remained with me,
through all these stagings, and which is central to my portrayal is the "African" element that Zeffirelli gave me. In
fact, I could say that my portrayal of Otello is based largely
on Zeffirelli's ideas, which had in turn been influenced by

Lord Olivier's monumental, yet controversial, "African" rather than "Moorish" interpretation of the role in Shakespeare's play at the Old Vic. I, too, think of Otello as a man deeply rooted in his African origins, despite his great military career and the universal respect he enjoyed in Venice. He is a Moor, he cannot change his blood. He carries within him all the beliefs inherent in his religion, as well as social insecurities, while at the same time he is the proudest of warriors. He doesn't start to think about his color until the quartet, where he sings: "*Forse perché ho sul viso quest'atro tenebroz.*" And the more rejected he feels by what he loves most in the world, the more he retreats into those roots, the only thing left for him to cling to. Scenically, the most poignant and effective way of communicating this retreat is to have Otello appear in Act IV dressed in completely different, African clothes including an earring, which I don't use in the first three acts, where he wears Venetian costume. The native clothes symbolize his return to the rituals and religious beliefs of his race. Because from the moment he enters Desdemona's bed-chamber, his every utterance has something to do with religion. His first question is whether she has said her prayers. He wants her prepared for death, which he sees as a ritual punishment for the terrible wrong he thinks she has committed . . . but with the underlying hope that after killing himself, too, they might meet in another life where, perhaps, everything will be better. And for me the most poignant thing in the whole opera is that he kills himself far from Desdemona's body, at least far enough for him not to be able to reach her. He tries, he crawls towards her, thinking about the love duet "*Un bacio, un bacio, ancora un bacio*" but he doesn't make it, he doesn't kiss her again . . . and I find this devastating. For Verdi has written not only tremendous pathos into this scene, but also an incredible, plastic sort of beauty, if one can talk of beauty in connection with death.

'Another key factor to bear in mind when interpreting this role is Otello's relationship with Iago – and I have been lucky enough to have had a variety of great Iagos of our day as my partners. Some were sensational, because they were so subtle, while others were so obvious as to be hardly believable! Those who were subtle, I looked in the eye. Those who were not, I merely listened to, without ever looking at them. It is difficult to imagine how anyone would believe a man like Iago, which is why, throughout the opera, I never look him in the eyes. If I did, I would be tempted to react in the way I would myself in such a situation, challenge him to stop insinuating things and come out with the whole truth – something Otello doesn't do. So I avoid Iago's eyes and let his voice do it all, like the sirens who beguiled Ulysses with their voices. And, like theirs, Iago's voice should have a very special kind of sound: a caressing, almost hypnotic quality that makes you dizzy so you cannot react in a fully rational way but only hear what you want to hear, what comes out of your own subconscious fears and self-doubts.

'After performing Otello many times, I have come to the conclusion that for reasons of pacing – because in Verdi's opera everything happens faster than in Shakespeare's play – it is better to delay the outburst for as long as possible, by ignoring Iago's insinuations and treating them as unimportant. Of course, the turning point, the thing that pushes Otello over the brink and causes his collapse, is the handkerchief. That's when he crumbles and is totally destroyed. And this half conversation of Iago's with Cassio, the way he can play with and manipulate this giant of a man is really very hard to believe . . . But of course, the higher your position, the greater the destruction once an operatic character, or a real person, a human being, starts to fall . . . And Otello's act of self-destruction is truly horrible.

'From both the dramatic and the vocal point of view, Otello is the most demanding of all my roles, largely because of the enormously demanding second act, which is almost an opera in itself, the equivalent of *Pagliacci* – tremendously intense. You start off with the tense and vocally demanding scene with Iago. This is followed by what I consider the most difficult section of the entire opera: the quartet, which has a hideously taxing tessitura with a top line of B flats, requires a "covering" kind of sound, never a forte, and has almost an a capella ending. I can assure you that without this quartet *Otello* would be a much, much easier opera to sing! At the end of it, you have the exclamation *"Tu fuggi, m'hai legato alla croce,"* and from that moment on until the end of Act II you are constantly involved without any chance to rest: first Otello's intensely moving aria *"Ora e per sempre addio"* and then the highly dramatic duet with Iago, *"Sì, pel ciel."* Otello is the most demanding of all my Verdi roles, along with Arrigo in *I Vespri Siciliani* which I first sang in Paris in 1974 and which has a murderous tessitura stretching up to a high D.

'Throughout the opera, it is crucial to remember to alter your vocal colors according to the dramatic situation and Otello's inner state. After the celli solo at the end of Act I, for instance, the atmosphere is set for us so perfectly that we have to color our voice like a cello, the perfect instrument for expressing a long, flowing, seamless legato line. If we failed to do this and came out with a slightly "white" voice instead, we would instantly ruin the rapturous mood that should prevail throughout the duet. At the beginning of our career, this vocal response to the instrumentation has to be self-conscious. But, given time and experience, it becomes almost automatic and an immensely creative and rewarding part of our craft.

'Looking at my entire repertoire, I have to say Otello is

198

the most demanding of all my roles. The combination of the singing and the drama is so, so intense that it drains you completely . . . And oddly enough what I'm thinking about is the last act, when you have all the vocal difficulties of the role behind you and can just give, abandon yourself to it completely and feel it . . . You (Otello) are going back to your roots and you are the punisher. You come to your wife's bedroom to punish, you have to punish. Yet because you are very concerned with the afterlife, the beyond, you also ask whether she had said her prayers. He comes to punish now, because he is blind. He says you have been a sinner and I have to punish you. This is part of his religion, the part of him he cannot shed. Yet in another world, things may be different. But for here and now, this is it. Experiencing all of this with every fibre of your being is very, very intense and exhausting.

'Of course, with the years and maturity, you grow and do certain things in the role differently. Vocally speaking, as time went by, for instance, I have been able to darken the color because the voice itself has grown darker with the years. Also, I have learnt to save more voice through expression and characterization. And even as far as the latter is concerned, to do less in terms of acting and more in terms of sheer presence. The deeper you get into the character, the more you can put him across by sheer emanation, and by doing this you get even deeper under the character's skin. But ultimately Otello is the kind of role about which you never feel you have really found everything that is there . . . I don't know if it's too late but if it's not, despite clocking up 213 performances of the role, I would still like to work on a new production, with a totally new director with fresh ideas, especially as next year, 2001, will be my 25th anniversary with this role.'

LORIS IPANOV

Fedora

Loris Ipanov is one of the roles Domingo has put firmly back on the operatic map. He sang it first at the Liceo in Barcelona on 15 February 1977 and has since clocked up 64 performances worldwide – with Renata Scotto, Mirella Freni, Agnes Baltsa, Maria Guleghina among his leading ladies – in Modena for Freni's 40th anniversary on stage, the Liceo in 1988, Madrid, La Scala, Zurich, Chicago, Vienna, London, the Metropolitan Opera, Los Angeles, Buenos Aires, Washington, Mexico City and Rome. Surprisingly enough those Rome performances, with Daniella Dessi in the title role, were Domingo's stage debut in Rome, where up to then he had only sung concerts including the first appearance of The Three Tenors and the film of Tosca, televised live in the actual locations where the events in the story took place.

Vocally Loris is a tenor showpiece – he has a famous aria and is every bit as important in the opera as the heroine of the title role. It was first sung by Caruso at its world premiere at the Teatro Lirico in Milan and gave that legendary tenor his first great success. Gigli also sang it a lot with Maria Caniglia but it had not been heard in Rome since 1968 when Antonietta Stella had performed the title role with Mario Del Monaco as Loris.

One can confidently state that the current burst of

Fedora *productions is due almost entirely to Domingo for whom Loris – another of those suffering characters he is so fond of – is an ideal vehicle at this stage of his career. And in this sense it is, perhaps, significant that Domingo was pronounced a tenor, and hired by the Mexican National Opera, after being given Loris's famous aria 'Amor ti vieta' to sight-read during his audition at that theater back in 1960, having first sung two baritone arias. So, his championing of this work could be seen as a case of 'noblesse oblige.'*

'Along with Siegmund in *Die Walküre* and Alvaro in *La Forza del Destino* Loris is one of the three operatic heroes in my repertoire who suffers most. Which is to say that he is a great favorite of mine! The situation in which he finds himself is truly pitiful. He is passionately in love with this woman Fedora Romanov, who is his deadly enemy because she thinks he is the murderer of her fiancé. Of course, she is acting out of ignorance. But even when she discovers the truth it is too late for her to prevent the train of events she has set in motion. Loris's brother has been arrested in Russia and dies a horrible death by drowning in his prison cell. This breaks their mother's heart and she dies without ever seeing the exiled Loris again.

'The question I always ask myself is: How can he, knowing all this tragedy she has brought to his family as well as the plot she has hatched against himself, forgive her in her dying moments, when she takes poison and dies in his arms? It's a great dilemma. But I think that because she is dying, he can say, "I forgive you. Die in peace."

'Vocally, although very dramatic, it's not a difficult part. It's short, but you have to be in very good physical shape for it. Loris has one of the most famous arias in the tenor repertoire, "*Amor ti vieta*," and another beautiful passage

"Mia madre, la mia vecchia madre" in Act II. The reason why you need to be in good shape is that sometimes the voice has to ride over a very heavy orchestra – usually these are passages where the tessitura is also high. But, overall, Loris is not a difficult part.

'You ask how one copes on evenings when one is not in very good physical shape – as, in my case, an evening during a run of *Un Ballo in Maschera* in Los Angeles and the opening night of my latest run of *Otello* at the Met. What you do on such occasions is summon all your technique. You have to be very careful and use more technique and less abandon. You can't let yourself go or throw yourself into the part because you have to control everything technically and dose the sound much more carefully. Usually you have to give less volume. But the most frustrating thing of all is that you cannot abandon yourself to the character or sing spontaneously. You have to think, think technically about exactly where to place the voice, whereas when you are feeling well, all this comes spontaneously.'

TITLE ROLE

Werther

Werther is a role that Domingo has sung very little, just 12 performances in his entire career: seven at the Bavarian State Opera in December 1977 and 1979 and five at the Metropolitan Opera in October 1978. In Munich his Charlotte was Brigitte Fassbaender and the production, specially mounted for him, was by Kurt Horres.

It was a dark and sombre production which arguably overstated the atmosphere of death that permeates this melancholy hero to the point of overkill. Domingo felt at the time that its intentions were revealed too early, in the second act, which was set in a graveyard – thus leaving the dénouement dramatically nowhere to go. But he loved the staging in Act III with its abstract motifs: the snowy wastes of Charlotte's room with a table, an unsupported door, the pistols.

The Munich production gave Domingo the opportunity to explore the masochistic bent and inherent death wish of the character, which he developed even further in New York. He has often said that he doesn't believe he really possesses a role until he has sung it 20 times, so one can assume that his portrayal in Werther *would have mellowed and become even more haunting had he gone on singing it. On record, although Alfredo Kraus is arguably more idiomatic in his French singing and projects the character's melan-*

choly accurately in his choice of vocal color, nothing can beat the passion and intensity of Werther's pain as expressed in Domingo's outburst in 'O souffle du printemps' both in the Orfeo and the Deutsche Grammophon recordings that feature Brigitte Fassbaender and Elena Obraztsova as Charlotte.

'I love the role of Werther so much that I'm sure that singing it is the secret or avowed dream of every tenor. The beauty of its music, the romanticism, the temperament and feeling of this character are things I very much associate myself with. But sadly I only sang it a handful of times, first at the Bavarian State Opera at the end of 1977, and a year later at the Met. Incredibly enough I prepared myself as thoroughly and wholeheartedly for Werther as I did for Otello, vocally, emotionally and physically – to the point of losing 10 lbs.

'I see the character very much as the product of his times, when suicides and suicidal types were very much in fashion. Of course, he suffers. But he is almost a masochist who makes a tragedy out of everything he sees. He sees the children, "*Ah, les enfants*," and instantly conjures up a tragedy. He sees a beautiful landscape and again, it evokes only pain. When he first meets Charlotte, after Albert's entry, he already knows that he will kill himself. He sings, "*Moi, je mourrais.*" It's as if he is looking for an excuse for suicide! And if it weren't Charlotte, then someone else would have triggered off this suicidal streak of his.

'Vocally it's very difficult. Not the first act, that's relatively easy. But in the second act comes this very, very dramatic and exciting aria "*Un autre est son époux*," which you should always endeavour to sing very well. In his next aria, "*Lorsque l'enfant revient d'un voyage*," already he's talking about death . . . In Act III, just before his big aria,

204

comes the typical Massenet "oracle" moment, in the shape of the single phrase, "*Tout mon âme est là*," that immediately precedes his big, wonderful aria "*Pourquoi me reveiller, O souffle du printemps*," both very romantic and melancholy yet also very dramatic in its climax . . . The last scene is relaxed, but you have to deliver it very beautifully and your control over your voice must be very, very acute because Werther's singing at this point is soft, but soft with a great deal of underlying power and intensity . . . The color of death should also be there, in your voice. The public always responds very strongly to this scene . . . All in all Werther is one of the most beautiful roles to portray.'

JOSÉ DE ESPRONCEDA

El Poeta

El Poeta, *the only opera by Federico Moreno Torroba, the famous Spanish composer of some of the most popular* zarzuelas *(Spanish operettas), including* Luisa Fernanda, *was composed especially for Domingo. It was premiered in Madrid on 19 June 1980, to mixed reviews. But although, as Domingo points out, it contains some beautiful music – Espronceda's Monologue in Act II, his duet with Teresa and her aria in Act III – the libretto was so shallow and insubstantial that it failed both to inspire the composer to produce the best music he was capable of, and to do justice to its subject matter, the very interesting nineteenth-century Spanish romantic poet José de Espronceda.*

Espronceda (1808–42) the scion of a military family, received a liberal, humanistic education and embraced progressive, reformist causes throughout his life. Briefly exiled in his youth for his membership of the young secret liberal society 'Los Numantinos,' *on his return to Madrid he decided to emigrate first to Portugal and, after his expulsion thence to London, the center for Liberal Spanish exiles. There he met and fell in love with Teresa Mancha who, during this restless, peripatetic soul's brief sojourn in Paris, married a wealthy merchant, only to abandon her husband and elope to Paris as soon as Espronceda reappeared on the scene. Eventually they settled in Madrid,*

206

where the social climate was not such as to accept their relationship, despite her giving birth to a daughter. Teresa abandoned Espronceda in 1836 and died in abject poverty two years later. Eventually he married Carmen de Osorio to whom he dedicated his first volume of poems. Soon he became a very famous and popular poet as well as Spain's envoy to The Hague after the progressive revolution of 1840. When he died suddenly in 1842 of croup his funeral was a popular apotheosis.

The general consensus in Spain after the premiere of El Poeta *was that the librettist, José Mendez Herrera, totally failed to capture the complexity and originality of this very popular national poet and, after the three performances at Madrid's Teatro de la Zarzuela (Madrid's opera house before the opening of the Teatro Real in 1997), it was never staged again.*

Domingo's own performance, though, was highly praised as was that of Angeles Gulin as Carmen de Osorio. In retrospect he is happy to have given a close family friend such as Moreno Torroba, who died in 1999, the joy of composing an opera for him and hearing it performed by such a good cast.

'El Poeta came about because Federico Moreno Torroba, one of Spain's most famous composers of *zarzuelas*, as well as outstanding pieces for the guitar, and who was a great family friend and had worked closely with my parents, had never written an opera before. He felt it was time he tried and decided to write one specifically with me in mind. So we started discussing possible subjects. I suggested Goya, who had always fascinated me – and who ended up being the subject of the next opera composed for me. But he came up with this idea of *El Poeta*, based on the life of José

Espronceda, a Spanish poet who had led a very interesting life and was exiled for his political beliefs.

'But the problem with *El Poeta* was that this fascinating life of Espronceda's was never reflected in the libretto, which was very weak and superficial. This is a problem with many Spanish librettists in our day. They seldom bother to probe deeply into their subjects and end up barely skimming the surface. When I eventually read about Espronceda's life, I was amazed to discover how profound a man he was and how riveting his life had been. There was plenty of material there for a great libretto. The fact that we didn't have such a thing was a great pity because some of Moreno Torroba's music was very beautiful.

'But this was not enough to sustain the weak libretto. So, although *El Poeta* was well received by the public, it has not been performed since then and appears to have fallen into oblivion.'

POLLIONE

Norma

Along with Edgardo in Lucia, *Pollione is Domingo's most important bel canto role, even though he has sung only seven performances in his career, all at the Metropolitan Opera, firstly with Renata Scotto in the title role on 21 September 1981. It is a typical Bel canto-with-a-capital-'B' role and requires more substance in the sound and a more burnished vocal color than the average bel canto part. This makes it a good vehicle for Domingo and he made a big impact in it.*

'There was Plácido Domingo as Pollione, an ardently sung performance of a role most tenors find ungrateful. Domingo did everything necessary to bring the part to life. His rich, firm, expressively pliant voice sounds more impressive each season' wrote Opera News, *while the New York Post added that 'Plácido Domingo's burnished tenor was in a fine state for Pollione, and he cut a handsome figure. I wish he'd been brave enough to tackle that first-act high C, however.'*

This brings us to the issue for and against transposition which has cropped up on several occasions in Domingo's career and which is discussed by him in detail in the chapters on Manrico and Aeneas. It boils down to whether a singer is entitled to transpose the odd few notes, or even a few bars of music down a semitone to make them fit his voice comfortably and blend credibly with the rest of this performance or not. In some cases the high notes in question are not even written by the composers themselves but interpolated later by performing tradition. We do know that the composers themselves were – and are – always ready to adjust sections of their music to accommodate individual voices. So the answer to the whole question of transposition must be yes, especially when this gives the public – and in some cases, through video recordings, posterity – the chance to see a great, world-class artist in a part he might otherwise avoid.

It is definitely to be regretted that no videotape exists of those performances or of any of Domingo's other two bel canto parts, to capture the unique combination of good taste with ardor and intensity in the sound as well as the dramatic portrayal that he, like Callas, brought to those heroes and heroines. This made them live and make a vibrant, relevant link with us at the end of the 20th and now the beginning of the 21st century in a way seldom achieved by so-called bel canto experts. (With the exception of Leyla Gencer, the great Turkish soprano who never received the full recognition she deserves.)

'As you know, I'm always looking for new repertoire. So when the Met offered me five performances of Pollione in *Norma* in the autumn of 1981, I jumped at the chance to have a go at this plum part! And I must say it proved a real treat, because we had a great cast headed by Renata Scotto as Norma and Tatiana Troyanos as Adalgisa, with Jimmy [Levine] conducting. So the experience was highly enjoyable.

'Basically, Pollione is one of the most gratifying bel canto heroes, because it's much meatier than the usual bel canto role. In fact the whole of *Norma* has more meat than the average bel canto opera. Pollione's first aria and cabaletta *"Meco all'altar"* and *"Me protegge, me difende un poter maggior di loro"* which are very difficult, require almost a lirico spinto, dramatic kind of sound. This is why Pollione has always been sung by tenors with some heft in them, such as Corelli. The rest of Pollione's music, especially his duet with Adalgisa, needs a fantastic technique, because it contains quite long and quite demanding coloratura passages. Then Pollione has a substantial trio, a very intense duet with Norma and that glorious final ensemble, before he and Norma walk into the pyre.

'As a character, I find Pollione difficult to understand. Of course, we don't know his whole story, because the libretto doesn't give us any hints of his background or any indication of how happy he was with Norma during their relationship. They produced two children, so it must have been a very strong relationship for a while. But we never see any of this, for at the beginning of the opera Pollione is already in love with Adalgisa. And by the end, he is totally repentant and ready to die with Norma. Of course, this is the kind of situation that could happen to any human being.

'The music in the whole of *Norma* is so breathtakingly beautiful – along with *Lucia*, it's the most beautiful bel canto opera – that it makes one realize even more what a tragedy it was that both Bellini and Donizetti died so young. In fact Bellini, who was tremendously handsome, is supposed to have been poisoned by a woman – a very operatic death, one could say. I feel that with his gift for melody, had he lived and written more operas, he would have proved himself an even greater musician.'

AENEAS

Les Troyens

Domingo has only attempted Aeneas once, in a new production by Fabrizio Melano at the Metropolitan Opera in September 1983, mounted for the Met's centenary. Although he had originally been scheduled to sing six performances, he ended up withdrawing after the fourth. Two months before the opening, he asked to be released from his contract, because he began to harbor doubts about the suitability of the role for his voice.

This was the first role he had doubts about in 20 years, he told the New York Times the week before the premiere, and he felt it was his duty to tell the Met to look for a replacement, stressing that it wasn't the high notes that bothered him in this part but the overall high tessitura, which he feared might cause vocal problems for some time afterwards. Yet he stipulated that he would 'go all the way with Jimmy' (Levine) if no replacement could be found.

He received a tumultuous ovation and his relief at having risen to this mammoth challenge must have been immense. It is within this context of stress and self-doubt followed by relief that one must view his otherwise inexplicable sense of disappointment at what he considered a lukewarm critical reception: the fact that some of the critics carped about transposition. Yet most of the main reviews were favorable. Some

212

critics took pains to point out to their readers that these transpositions involved some eight pages of music in a score as long as Tristan und Isolde. 'Even with these concessions,' wrote the New York Times, 'the part of Aeneas made tremendous demands on Mr Domingo's voice, but he handled them with much success.' The critic went on to add that Domingo and Troyanos 'spun out their great love duet "Nuit d'ivresse" in exquisite fashion.'

The New York Daily News went even further in praising him: 'Although it was reported that Plácido Domingo had wished to be relieved of his assignment as Aeneas, the role happily turned out to be a very good one for him. He looked absolutely wonderful as the noble Trojan hero, the uniquely visceral impact of his voice was a perfect fit and, though he had occasional problems with the French text, he at least delivered the basic sense of it with panache. Only two brief sections – his entrance and a portion of his last-act aria – were transposed downward while the rest of the role, including the cruelly high love duet, was sung confidently in key.' The prestigious Village Voice added, 'Yes, Domingo came through his first Aeneas endeavor with his reputation intact . . . he turned in a genuine star performance.'

In view of this very favorable general consensus Domingo's sense of hurt at the time doesn't appear justified. It could be that the immense and, in him rare, strain of preparing for a role about which he didn't feel fully confident took a disproportionate toll on his nervous system, for once. But with the equanimity that comes with the passage of time, he now views his single foray into this part as what it truly was: a colossal success.

'Aeneas, or Enée in French, was a hugely challenging role, one of the biggest challenges in my career. It was a special role for a special occasion, the centenary of the Met in 1983. I decided to do it and although I harbored some doubts until the last moment, I am very happy with the result. It is my only Berlioz role on stage, despite the fact that the French repertoire has been central to my career.

'The reason why this part is considered one of the sacred monsters of the tenor repertoire is its length and its tessitura. The latter is consistently high and often hovers on the passaggio. You also have some very strenuous high notes to sing. But it was a great, great satisfaction. And if you listen to the last aria you will see that it brought the house down!

'Like some of my "mystical" roles – Samson, Parsifal and Jean in *Hérodiade* – Aeneas is a character who experiences a clash between his duty and his love for a woman, Didon. In his case, of course, the clash is between a woman and patriotism rather than religious duty. This makes him both a very exciting and a very moving hero. Both dramatically and vocally, it is an extraordinary role. Aeneas's big aria, the wonderful, protracted duet *"Nuit d'ivresse et d'estase infinie"* – which was fabulous with Tatiana (Troyanos) as Didon – and some of the battle music are all exceptional. The most difficult part is undoubtedly *"Nuit d'ivresse."* The tessitura is tough and requires meticulous control because it's all soft singing, along a big, flowing, seamless line, with Berlioz's endless imagination leading from one thought, one phrase, to another . . .

'*Les Troyens* is such a monumentally difficult piece to stage that it tends to be mounted only on special occasions. In our case, almost everyone was satisfied, except for some critics who carped at the fact that I transposed the high C and the last few bars of Aeneas's last aria, the Farewell Aria ("*Debout, Troyens!*"). Of course, there are traditional, universally accepted transpositions in Rodolfo, Edgardo, Faust, Manrico and Chénier. But whenever a singer with a big name does it, they see fit to attack. Personally, I consider the premiere of *Les Troyens* among the greatest performances I've given in my life. But the fact that that's all they found to say about it made me sick. So I thought, if that's all they feel I have to offer, let them have other tenors! So I sang a few more performances and then withdrew.

'But although I have not sung it since, I love this work deeply and plan to go and see it when the Met revives it next season, to renew my contact with the piece. Ben Heppner, who will sing Aeneas, will be phenomenal!'

PAOLO

Francesca da Rimini

Domingo sang this handsome hero in Zandonai's rarely performed work on two occasions: once in concert at Carnegie Hall in March 1973 and in a new production at the Metropolitan Opera in March 1984, with Renata Scotto in the title role, which after its run in New York was taken on tour to Washington, Atlanta, Memphis, Minneapolis, Detroit, Toronto and Cleveland.

It was a lavish staging, with atmospheric sets by Ezio Frigerio, which vividly evoked both the magnificence and austerity of mediaeval Rimini and Ravenna, and the Battle Scene between the Guelphs and Ghibellines – in which crossbows and fireballs were thrown across the stage – was worthy of a Hollywood movie. Faggioni was trying to compensate, by making the staging very lavish, for an undistinguished score that lacks not only originality but even a single memorable aria – the saving grace of several other less than great operas. The only really beautiful passage is the extended love duet to which Domingo refers below.

Both the staging and Domingo's performance won high praise: 'Plácido Domingo, though largely wasted in this part, made a stalwart Paolo. His appearance and tenorial efforts provided some of the evening's more satisfying moments,' wrote the New York Times while the New York Post added that, 'Domingo's voice

216

was free, passionate, and consistently on a high level.
His highest notes had a vibrantly useful ring.' The Wall
Street Journal concluded, 'Paolo's music fitted the tenor
as splendidly as Franca Squarciapino's costumes.'

'*Francesca da Rimini* is an opera I have sung very little, but
enjoyed tremendously. It is seldom put on, because it is very
elaborate to stage. But I was lucky enough to sing it in a
wonderful production by Piero Faggioni at the Metropolitan Opera, with magnificent sets by Ezio Frigerio, which
instantly created the right atmosphere. I would very much
like to bring this production to Los Angeles in the coming
years, and have to look for a good cast.

'For this work is not only very difficult to stage, but also
difficult to cast. You need a superb lirico spinto or dramatic
soprano – in the production I sang we had Renata Scotto –
a first-rate baritone and another tenor for the part of the
third Malatesta brother, Malatestino. The love duet between
Paolo and Francesca in Act III, for a start, is one of the most
beautiful pieces of music ever written. It's a long, long duet
– Paolo and Francesca are reading the love story of Lancelot
and Guinevere and through it end up expressing their own
passion – and charged with so much sensual feeling that
you can actually experience and feel their passion when singing it. And I am proud to say that the video of the Met
performance we did with Renata is really fabulous!

'As a character Paolo is very complicated and the situation in which he finds himself even more so! Because of the
plot hatched by his brother Giovanni (or Gianciotto) the
Lame in Act I, in which he does not appear at all, he finds
himself in the atrociously embarrassing situation of having
to trick Francesca into thinking that he, Paolo the Handsome, to whom she is introduced and falls instantly in love
with – as does he – is her intended husband. In reality she

finds herself married to his lame brother! Paolo's and Francesca's dream of love is shattered, and after a series of convoluted developments they are killed together by her jealous husband.

'The libretto is based on a play by D'Annuzio and the opera was premiered in Turin in 1914. It is the only one of Zandonai's operas that is still in the repertoire.'

Title role in *Samson et Dalila*: 'As with Jean in *Herodiate* and *Parsifal*, in this opera the fight is between a woman and God.' Domingo with Denyce Graves as Dalila at the Metropolitan Opera in 1990.

Don José in *Carmen*: Domingo with Teresa Berganza in Piero Faggioni's historic production of *Carmen* in Hamburg, 1977.

The title role in *Les Contes d'Hoffmann*: One of Domingo's greatest achievements, a role 'both difficult to act and to sing'. CLIVE BARDA/ARENA PAL

With Leona Mitchell as Antonia at Covent Garden in John Schlesinger's production. This is Domingo's favourite staging of *Hoffmann* that he has performed the role in. ZOE DOMINIC

As Hoffmann in the Olympia Act holding fragments of the broken doll. FOTO FAYER

Canio in *Pagliacci*: Another of Domingo's most popular portrayals, 'a character you can play in several different ways: as a bit of a brute; a drunkard; the paterfamilias of the travelling troupe of players; as a man suspicious of his wife because he feels older or as a straightforward man, a good man who becomes so profoundly shocked and disappointed by his wife's infidelity, that he cracks – it is this last interpretation I prefer.' WINNIE KLOTZ/METROPOLITAN OPERA

Count Almaviva in *Il Barbiere di Siviglia*: Domingo's only Rossini role which he sang only once, in Guadalajara in 1966. A part that 'requires all your technique because it's very high and demands great agility and lightness of touch.' But he also performed the famous 'Duetto del metallo' in *Hommage to Sevilla*, a sensational video by the late Jean Pierre Ponnelle devoted to operatic heroes hailing from the Andalusian capital. Domingo played both the parts of Almaviva and Figaro with immense aplomb and distinction. He is pictured here as Almaviva being shaved by himself as Figaro!

Domingo as Radames in *Aida* in Sonia Frizell's production at the Metropolitan Opera: As near-perfect a role as you can hope to get, because Aida is an opera about two ladies fighting over the same man — you!' © BETH BERGMAN

Alvaro in *La forza del destino* at the Metropolitan Opera: 'One of the unhappiest, unluckiest, most complex and most tortured characters in my repertoire as well as having some of the most difficult music Verdi wrote for the tenor.'
WINNIE KLOTZ/METROPOLITAN OPERA

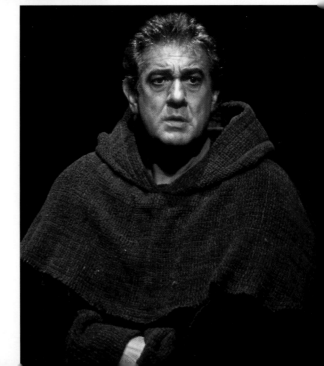

Lohengrin: Domingo's first Wagnerian role, which triggered off his ongoing love-affair with Wagner. © ROBERT CAHEN

'Lohengrin is a beautiful character and comes from another sphere of life; from heaven.' Pictured at the Metropolitan Opera in 1984. © BETH BERGMAN

Title role in *Lohengrin* at the Vienna State Opera in 1985: A part Domingo loves, most especially because of its 'otherworldly dimension.' © FOTO FAYER

As Manrico in *Il Trovatore* at Covent Garden in 1989: 'The most romantic of Verdi's "Spanish" heroes.' CLIVE BARDA/ARENA PAL

Title Role in *Ernani*: The opera in which Domingo made his debut at La Scala in December 1969. LELLI & MASOTTI/TEATRO ALLA SCALA

Calaf in *Turandot*: The role in which Domingo made his debut in Verona in 1969 and which he always enjoyed singing: 'He is an obsessional, almost suicidal type, who gets so fixated on this woman that he plays Russian roulette in order to win her.' ROBERT CAHEN

Vasco da Gama in *L'Africaine*: 'A vocally very enjoyable part yet far from being a walkover . . . you have the famous aria "O Paradis" which everyone is waiting for and by which they will judge your whole performance.' With Grace Bumbry as Selika, at Covent Garden. ZOE DOMINIC

Domingo as Dick Johnson in *La fanciulla del West*: 'Dramatically the whole opera is great fun, almost like a Western movie, and boasts one of the greatest of all Puccini heroines, Minnie.' Here with Barbara Daniels as Minnie at the Met. © BETH BERGMAN

Domingo as Otello, perhaps his greatest role: 'The creation of this role has been a lifetimes' work, like a Rembrandt self-portrait. It just got darker and deeper.' ZOE DOMINIC

Lucero in *Divinas Palabras* at the Teatro Real, Madrid in 1997: 'A character who is a kind of gypsy, a bit of a profiteer, a bit of a conquistador and really rather unpleasant.' © ASTRID KESSLER

Jose de Espronceda in *El Poeta* at Teatro de la Zarzuela in Madrid: 'Some of his music is very beautiful but sadly the libretto did not reflect the tremendously interesting and eventful life of this famous and colourful Spanish romantic poet.'
© TEATRO DE LA ZARZUELA

Opposite: Plácido in *Parsifal*, here with Jessye Norman as Kundry: 'A unique character, one of those illuminated beings whose mystical dimension is very hard to put across on stage.' 'The finale of this opera is such a mystical moment that I cannot find the words to describe it. I feel as if God is about to descend and come on stage to bless and lift us all higher.'
WINNIE KLOTZ/METROPOLITAN OPERA

Paolo in Zandonai's *Francesca da Rimini*: 'Paolo's music contains one of the most beautiful love duets in the repertoire'. Here with Renata Scotto as Francesca in Piero Faggioni's phantasmagoric Metropolitan Opera production. © BETH BERGMAN

Siegmünd in *Die Walküre* in Vienna: 'He and Sieglinde are the most lovable and magnificent characters in the whole *Ring*. I hate the fact that these two supremely lovable characters disappear from the Tetralogy at the end of *Die Walküre*.'
VIENNA STATE OPERA

Title role in *Stiffelio* at the
Metropolitan Opera:
Domingo's penultimate Verdi
role on stage and 'a phenomenal
surprise for me to discover this
work and this wonderful
character so late in my career.'
WINNIE KLOTZ/METROPOLITAN
OPERA

Pery in *Il Guarany* in Bonn 1994: 'I chose to do this work first in Bonn and later in Washington because
I wanted to inaugurate my term as Artistic Director there with something beautiful, exotic, different
and *new*!' ASTRID KESSLER

Title role in *Idomeneo* at the Metropolitan Opera: 'A fantastic role with everything you could ask for: he has a lot of great singing and is a marvellous character to portray. He suffers from the opening Scene and goes on doing so until the finale in the last Act!' ROBERT CAHEN

Jean in *Hérodiade* in Vienna: 'A holy man who is not allowed to indulge his carnal passions even though in this opera, unlike Strauss's *Salome*, the Baptist reciprocates Salome's feelings.' FOTO FAYER

Gabriele Adorno in *Simon Boccanegra* at the Metropolitan Opera: Domingo's last Verdi role on stage which he admits, 'should have been one of my first as it's usually sung by young tenors at the beginning of their career' but to which he brought amazing vocal freshness and youthfulness. With Kiri Te Kanawa as Amelia at the Metropolitan Opera in 1992. WINNIE KLOTZ/METROPOLITAN OPERA

Jean de Leyden in *Le Prophète*: 'A very, very long and excruciatingly hard role and a character who is considered as a sort of god by his sect. It reminds me of some of those weird cults that keep springing up in the States in our own day.' (With Agnes Baltsa as Fides at the Vienna State Opera in 1998.) AXEL ZEININGER, VIENNA STATE OPERA

One of Domingo's greatest achievements 40 years into his career – Gherman in *The Queen of Spades* in June 1999 at the Vienna State Opera: 'The Otello of the Russian repertoire which I was finally convinced I should sing even though I speak no Russian. For how could I let a great meaty role such as this pass me by without tasting it?'
FOTO FAYER

Below left: Domingo in Elijah Moshinsky's Metropolitan Opera production in March 1999, with Galina Gorchakova as Lisa. WINNIE KLOTZ/METROPOLITAN OPERA

Below right: Domingo as Gherman with Elisabeth Söderström as the Countess.
© BETH BERGMAN

Title role in *Le Cid* at the Teatro de la Maestranza, Seville: 'As a patriotic Spaniard, it was wonderful to perform a role that gives you the opportunity to sing about the greatness, the grandeur, the freedom and the glory of Spain and its king.' ASTRID KESSLER

Last plate: Don Juan in *Margarita la Tornera*, Domingo's last role in the twentieth century: 'Like Mozart's Don Giovanni, a professional seducer of women for whom seducing a nun is the ultimate challenge and ecstasy . . . but a hero whose soul, unlike that of Mozart's hero, is saved in the end.' At the Teatro Real, Madrid in December 1999. ASTRID KESSLER

TITLE ROLE

Goya

Goya *by Gian Carlo Menotti, the distinguished Italian composer who has lived most of his life in America and writes his own libretti in English, was the second opera composed especially for Plácido Domingo, who first suggested the idea to Menotti in 1983. As he explains in his discussion of Moreno Torroba's* El Poeta, *Domingo had had* Goya *on the brain for a long time, having always been fascinated by the great artist who dominated Spanish painting at the turn of the nineteenth century. But when Torroba appeared unresponsive to his suggestion of Goya as a subject for an opera, Domingo put the idea on ice and bided his time until the right composer came his way.*

Menotti is as great an admirer of Goya as Domingo and leapt to the suggestion with alacrity. He produced a musically attractive and dramatically very interesting work, with pertinent psychological probes into an artist's world: the nature of an artist's involvement with the world around him, and the way an artist experiences love, which were as relevant to Menotti as to Goya and which, personally, I found very moving. The central theme of the story was Goya's hypothetical passionate love affair with the Duchess of Alba, Spain's most fearless, unconventional and democratic aristocrat, and contrasted her courageous stance on social issues with Goya's reticence on such matters, due to his social ambitions and burning desire to be a court painter.

The opera was premiered in Washington on 15 November 1986 in the presence of the Queen of Spain, and ran for a further four performances. The Washington public and press were enthusiastic: 'Goya is intensive theater, comic, probing, visually spectacular and sometimes emotionally harrowing. In its first production, it works effectively in almost all dimensions. One dimension is music, which is helpful and used with considerable skill. The score was properly lyric and superbly functional, as Menotti's music always is.' The critic went on to add that, unlike most operas, in this work the music was not really what the show was all about, the dominant attraction, and neither was the plot, which was only loosely founded on historic accuracy. 'The crux of this work is the intense, sometimes anguished psychological exploration of the dynamics of love and the significance of an artist's life – which have more to do with the composer-librettist's personal self-questioning than with anything known about Goya.'

Domingo's performance was highly praised, as was Victoria Vergara's as the Duchess: 'Domingo has several passionate arias, he sings and acts very well and is onstage almost constantly,' wrote the Washington Post while the Washington Times commented that 'Mr Domingo's characterization was as touching as his singing was splendid.'

But, as Domingo remarks below, the vitriolic review of one critic unjustly ruined the chances of this opera being taken up by other theaters.

'Six years after *El Poeta*, I made contact with Goya whose life, as I already mentioned, has always fascinated me. That's when I sang the title role in Giancarlo Menotti's eponymous opera, which was composed for me and premiered in Washington in the presence of the Queen of Spain. *Goya* is a beautifully melodic piece which I enjoyed singing and I look forward to doing so again. Menotti and I worked very closely together. Yet although he is also a great man of the theater, I don't feel that we really went far enough in exploring and plumbing the depth of this character. In fact we agreed that if we ever revive the opera, we will work on that.

'Unfortunately so far this has not been possible because even though there were plans to take it to Los Angeles, Geneva and Covent Garden, the piece was so viciously and, in my view, unjustifiably attacked by the critics that all three theaters took fright and cried off. One reviewer in particular was so vitriolic that, with a few words, he managed to destroy a work written by a well known and respected composer. People are always accusing Menotti of trying to be a latter-day Puccini. My answer to that is why not? Musically, Acts I and II of *Goya* were very melodic. Then Menotti did something very clever. Because by the third act *Goya* has lost his ear, he made the music of this act much more atonal.

'*Goya* was revived in Spoleto, this time in Italian, and well received. In fact I have been asked by the Theater an der Wien to sing it there, also in Italian, in 2004. Well, I don't know. It's difficult to tell, at this stage in my career. Of course I know that, in operatic terms, four years ahead is just right for making future plans so I might just end up saying "yes" because I believe in the piece and because, fortunately, Gian Carlo is still with us, capable of making any necessary changes and adjustments and making out of *Goya* something really beautiful and lasting.'

TITLE ROLE

Parsifal

Domingo had felt ready for this very special role since the mid-Eighties. The only reason why he didn't attempt it right away was that he did not wish to endanger some of his Italian lyric roles. Six years later he felt the time was right. His first Parsifal was at the Metropolitan Opera in March 1991 and the following September he also sang it in Vienna before opening the 1991–92 season at La Scala, to great public and critical acclaim. In summer 1993 he had the ultimate satisfaction – even greater for a non-Wagnerian singer – of repeating his triumph at the Bayreuth Festival, where he returned in summer 1995. His latest Parsifals were concert performances in Rome, London and Salzburg in 1998, and so far he has totalled 35 performances.

Seeing Domingo perform this part is an experience so profound and affecting that one feels privileged, blessed, to be present at such a spiritually charged occasion. There is little I wish to add to his own analysis of the role. It speaks mountains, not just about Parsifal, but also about Domingo himself, artist and man, and allows a glimpse into his innermost center – the sanctum from which he derives strength and inspiration for his art and the source also of that profound, all-pervasive humanity so characteristic of him which shines through every character he inter-

prets and which, on a personal level, never ceases to affect those who know him.

'*Parsifal* is a unique work. The connection with the Holy Grail bestows a very special atmosphere on this opera. I don't agree with those who maintain that it is not a sacred work. It is a sacred work. Its deeply religious, mystical content is very closely linked with Christianity. We are talking about the Holy Grail, the Eucharist, the very essence of our religion. Of course, you could go on analyzing its inner, mystical meaning forever and some people do. But I fear that in over-intellectualizing it you could miss the simplicity of its message.

'As a character, Parsifal is equally unique – one of those illumined beings like Lohengrin and John the Baptist in *Hérodiade* – whose mystical dimension is very hard to put across on stage. Yet something about the sheer otherworldliness of these characters connects to my own innermost center. There is a little bit of me in them, in the sense that you can have a worldly, sophisticated side but also retain a certain childlike innocence inside you – a quality which is also very much part and parcel of these characters.

'For when we first encounter Parsifal, he is a complete innocent: a wild boy out of the woods who doesn't know anything. He is lost in the woods and the only thing he knows is how to hunt for his food. And during the whole opera we watch his learning process – through love and especially compassion, pain and sadness – from total innocence to initiation. Parsifal grows gradually to know and understand everything. Even in Act I, where he knows nothing, the heart of this pure fool, this "*reiner Tor*" resounds to the sufferings of others. He responds first to the suffering of the swan he killed in ignorance – and feels shame when it

223

is pointed out to him that he has done something wrong. Then he reacts to the suffering of Amfortas. He sees what in his ignorance appears to him as tremendous selfishness on the part of all the knights who follow the Grail yet push Amfortas to the limits of his endurance, and also of Titurel whose intolerance pushes his son knowing the tremendous pain and anguish that uncovering the Grail causes him. Without really understanding what he has seen, Parsifal's heart resounds. He feels for Amfortas, his heart center is activated, and this is the first step towards his spiritual awakening.

'In Act II we see Parsifal discovering the beauty and joy of life, with all those beautiful women Klingsor places at his disposal in his garden. It is the most entrancing time of his life. And in the middle of this rapture he hears Kundry's voice for the first time calling him by his name. Then, through her narration, he learns everything about himself and his parents: his father's death, his mother and his own unthinking abandonment of her and, finally, of her death. Throughout this scene we see Parsifal growing more and more deeply and experiencing pain for the first time until he reaches the climax: Kundry's kiss, the focal point of this act. Until then, Parsifal is only half-aware, half-awake. But with this kiss everything becomes clear to him. It is the last test and through it he becomes a man. Now he understands the suffering of Amfortas, and realizes exactly what happened to him. And this new maturity must be reflected in your voice. From here on you sing with a totally different vocal color. This should start right after the kiss, where you sing "*Amfortas, die Wunde*," which is followed by the passage in which Parsifal narrates what he witnessed at the temple – one of the most sublime moments in any work. It's difficult vocally and the text is really tremendous. Very few scenes in opera can compare with this monumental Parsifal–

Kundry duet. I can think only of the Tristan–Isolde love duet, Siegmund and Sieglinde's love duet in Act I of *Die Walküre* and the Amelia–Riccardo duet in *Un Ballo in Maschera* that come close but don't quite match this scene in *Parsifal* – one of the supreme dramatic moments of the operatic repertoire. Through it, Parsifal realizes what he has to do, where his duty lies and how important it is. He realizes he has to liberate Amfortas by healing him with the same weapon that wounded him – the Holy Spear – and restore the blessing of the Grail on the knights.

'Parallel to Parsifal's growth to understanding we have Kundry's despair: her initial conflict with Klingsor for forcing her to seduce Parsifal and her eventual failure to do so. For, during their encounter, Kundry really falls in love with Parsifal. Whether it's real love or an intuitive realization that he holds the key to her redemption is unclear. The talk is about redemption and Kundry, rejected, insists that they should share at least an hour of love. Parsifal replies that this one hour would spell eternal damnation for both of them and for the knights who also await redemption. Kundry then summons Klingsor to wound Parsifal with the holy spear, the same spear that wounded Amfortas. But Parsifal triumphs: a triumph of a stronger will, faith, sense of higher duty. He destroys Klingsor's castle and, almost with great sadness, departs from Kundry. For my feeling is that, because of all she has revealed and awakened in him, Parsifal has also kind of fallen in love with Kundry. But he realizes this is impossible because he now has another mission. As he leaves, he looks back and says, "You know where you can find me again if you wish to be redeemed."

'Then comes this great Prelude to Act III which is musically a very complicated orchestral piece because it has to sound so clean – all the orchestral colors and the intervals are there to prepare us for the most sublime scene in all opera: the Good Friday Scene, which starts with two big surprises. First, the transformation of Kundry from the seductress of the previous act into this penitent who wanders around saying *"dienen, dienen"* (to serve, to serve). The second is Gurnemanz's initial failure to recognize Parsifal, which shows how much Parsifal has grown and changed in the intervening years. And after Parsifal explains about his travels, all the years of wandering in order to return here and restore the Holy Spear, Gurnemanz responds in a way I find psychologically significant: Whereas at the end of Act I he referred to Parsifal as *"verrücktes Knabe"* (a mad boy), he now addresses him as *"O Herr."* And for Parsifal, this moment feels like a great personal triumph. Because he remembers how he was treated before – being thrown out, called a *"Tor"* and told he was only good enough for the company of geese! So being addressed as *"Herr"* and feeling the compassion and recognition of this man represents a big triumph for him.

'Gurnemanz then tells Parsifal, in his narration, everything that has happened to Amfortas and the knights since he left them, how they can no longer partake of Holy Communion, the blessing of the Grail, and that Titurel is dead, which causes Parsifal to blame himself for not returning sooner. Then we have the ritual purification, the washing of the feet and anointing of Parsifal as Keeper of the Grail, followed by the baptism of Kundry. All of this – the orchestration, the melody, the words – is so beautiful that it moves me almost to tears. The genius of Wagner reached such heights in this work that you think, God, had he lived longer what more could he have done? Everything he had, he put into this opera.

'As for the finale of this act, where Parsifal brings back the Spear to the knights, heals Amfortas and is able to unveil the Grail and once more bestow its blessing on the knights, it is such a mystical moment that I don't know that I can find words to describe it. I feel as if God is about to come on stage, to bless and lift us all up higher, to a kind of Resurrection. I feel the presence of God coming down to touch us for a moment. And at the moment Parsifal bestows this blessing I find myself wishing it could reach out, embrace and bring peace to everyone, the audience and the whole world. It's a profoundly emotional experience.

'Technically, Parsifal is one of those roles where you have a young character, who at the beginning has to sing with a youthful voice but yet cannot be sung by a young singer. Vocally, it is not very difficult. You don't have that much singing to do. There are a couple of moments for which your voice should be well rested because it has to sound fresh, but which are so exposed that you could easily get stuck. One is just after Kundry's kiss, where Parsifal sings "*Amfortas die Wunde*" and especially a few phrases on, "*O Klage, O Klage, furchtbare Klage*" which is very very open, exposed singing. The second moment of difficulty lies in two or three pages in Parsifal's duet with Kundry which begins with "*Auf Ewigkeit wärst du verdämmt*" etc. But the main vocal point about Parsifal is that you have to use two voices: one for the youthful "pure fool" and one for the mature Parsifal. Then, in the third act you have to lighten the voice in the Good Friday Scene so that it sounds luminous and casts the right kind of spell.

'But although it is not difficult vocally, Parsifal is difficult musically and especially because of the immense concentration it demands. Even when you are not singing, you are on stage for long periods, silent. But during those silent moments your concentration should be total and extreme, so that you can emanate this special mystical dimension of the character. The moments in Act I, for instance, when Parsifal is standing silent in the temple are very important, because he is learning and absorbing so much that you cannot just stand there, emanating nothing! I have heard that some tenors use the cover of darkness that usually prevails in this scene to creep offstage for a while. I simply don't understand how anyone can do such a thing. For you have to experience, to feel and silently react to everything you see and hear. Because this is a crucial moment, it is where Parsifal's heart is awakened for the first time.

'I must say that participating in this work – one of the greatest, if not the greatest ever written – in any way is a privilege. It brings you so close to God, to our faith and beliefs . . . I am deeply happy to know I have so many *Parsifal*s ahead of me in 2001!'

RAFAEL RUIZ

El Gato Montes

Domingo first sang this dashing, chivalrous matador at the Teatro de la Maestranza in Seville – which happens to be situated a stone's throw from this magical city's famous eponymous bullring – within the context of the cultural celebrations that accompanied Expo '92. There is little doubt that it was thanks to Domingo's clout and enthusiastic championship that the theater was persuaded to put on this work and find the necessary sponsorship from international sources. Domingo also convinced, or cajoled, Deutsche Grammophon to record it.

At the time, Domingo explained his love for El Gato Montes, *which he considers the Spanish answer to Bizet's* Carmen, *by pointing out that it is brimming with the exuberance and musical colors of Spain. It's certainly a highly enjoyable work which aroused warm responses in the public both in Seville and Washington, when it was transferred there, with some significant changes and additions to the score which Domingo describes below.*

Yet some of the most biting comments about its essential merit and qualifications to be considered an opera, and a desirable cultural export at that, came not from America but from Spain's most influential paper, El Pais. Its critic voiced doubts about the right of El Gato Montes *to be called an opera, preferring the term 'zarzuellon' (a big, substantial zarzuela). But he acknowledged that Domingo as the torrero Rafael Ruiz, Veronica Villaroel as Soledad, and Juan Pons in the title role gave excellent accounts of their parts.*

'*El Gato Montes*, by Manuel Penella, is a piece I had known all my life, because it was included in my parents' repertoire. After first singing Rafael in Seville for the celebrations around the Expo and the centenary of the Discovery of America, I took it to Washington, Los Angeles and Madrid (although I didn't actually sing in the Washington staging).

'The reason why I wanted to do it is because it has some beautiful music, a lot of drama and pathos in the first act and a duet which is one of the most popular pieces of Spanish music. It's played in every bullring before every bullfight – by the way, yes, I do enjoy bullfights – so that it's in the ears of every Spaniard. But although the first act, which is 50 minutes long, is very powerful, with the drama developing in a satisfying way, I don't know what happened to Penella after that! He wrote a second act which still has some very beautiful passages, but which is very short. Then he decided to kill off both the tenor and the soprano!!! The tenor, who is a bullfighter, is killed in a corrida and on hearing the news the heroine, Soledad, dies of a heart attack! So after that we are left with the baritone – the Gato Montes of the title – who is an outlaw, also in love with Soledad. Penella had just the right sort of typically operatic triangle there, but chose to make nothing of it. All we have is the baritone who then takes Soledad's body to his hide-away in the mountains of the Sierra Morena. Finally, the police turn up to capture him. But he tells them that he doesn't wish to be killed by them but by one of his own men. So, dramatically at least, things get very, very flat.

'When we decided to bring the work to Washington, I

230

took the liberty of interfering with the plot a little bit and adding some more music, always by the same composer. What we did was to have only the tenor die at the end of the second act. So the Gato Montes took Soledad alive to the mountains, where we gave them a beautiful duet, using Penella's own music, in which she sings of her love for this outlaw who in fact became an outlaw when he killed a man while defending her! The torrero then became her protector, but her true love was the Gato Montes. When, in the finale, the police and the whole village turn up to arrest him, she throws herself in front of him and gets killed instead before he, too, kills himself. This way the piece became much more dramatic and I can't think why Penella himself didn't think of this twist.

'The reason why the *El Gato Montes* is an opera and not a *zarzuela* is because it has no dialogue. Generally, works in which there are more than a few lines of dialogue are considered zarzuelas (or operettas in Austrian or French musical theater) even if the quality of the music is more or less the same. The main difference between zarzuela and Viennese operetta is the style. Otherwise the format is the same – singing, dialogue, some dancing. But operetta is more light-hearted. Most operettas, except for *The Land of Smiles*, are happy-go-lucky while in zarzuelas there is usually a conflict, which is resolved at the end. They are usually rural dramas – set in Galicia, Andalusia or whatever other Spanish region – rather than sophisticated entertainment reflecting city life.'

SIEGMUND

Die Walküre

Siegmund was Domingo's third major Wagner role. After his successful foray into the Wagnerian repertoire with Lohengrin and Parsifal, he sang his first Siegmund at the Vienna State Opera on 19 December 1992 – a night no one lucky enough to have been present is ever likely to forget. The rest of the cast, under the baton of Christoph von Dohnanyi, included Waltraud Meier as Sieglinde, Hildegard Behrens as Brünnhilde and Robert Hale as Wotan. As already mentioned, his first attempt at Lohengrin and Parsifal had been in Hamburg at the Metropolitan Opera respectivly. This time he opted to have his baptism of fire right in the horse's mouth: one of the greatest theaters of the German-speaking world!

The result vindicated his daring and surpassed the expectations of even his most ardent admirers. Instead of the barking sort of sound that often passes for Wagnerian singing, we had exquisite lyrical sound of the kind the composer always yearned for and seldom got: a seamless legato line that enhanced the rapturous ecstasy of the duet at the end of Act I. And the text was delivered in German sufficiently clear for a moderate German speaker such as myself to manage to understand most words – and not a Mediterranean vowel in sight! He was greeted by an ovation that lasted about 25 minutes and even his fellow tenors were impressed: 'To take on Siegmund in German here at the Vienna State Opera, and win – well, I take my hat off to him,' said José Carreras at the time.

Heartened by this successful outcome, Domingo, after some further performances at the VSO, six months later in June 1993 decided to sing the first act of Die Walküre *the coming September in New York for the gala opening of the Metropolitan Opera's 1993–94 season. Since then he has sung several performances of the role at La Scala and in the Met production of* Die Walküre *by Otto Schenk in April 1996 and March/April 2000, and at Bayreuth in July/August 2000.*

Although understandably gratified at the success of his first Siegmunds, Domingo was looking forward to developing and perfecting his portrayal further. By the time he sang it at Covent Garden on 6 December 1996 as part of his 25th Anniversary in this theater, he had become one of the great Siegmunds of our day. 'The part lies perfectly for him, not too high, and exploiting the strength in the middle of his voice. There are precedents – Vickers, Vinay – of Otellos who were also fine Siegmunds. Add the Latin warmth and an Italianate sense of musical line, and you have as beautifully sung a Siegmund as you could hope to hear,' wrote The Times.

'What was startling about Domingo's Siegmund at Covent Garden was that he walked into an existing production and after minimal rehearsal – two or three days at most – and regardless of whether he liked it or not, nevertheless followed it minutely and managed to energize it. He infused life, power and vitality into what had been the weakest link in this Ring *production,' says Peter Katona, Casting Director of the Royal*

233

Opera, Covent Garden. 'It was one of those miracles
you sometimes get in operatic performances. Although
I'm a supporter of proper rehearsal periods, I have to
admit that sometimes miracles can happen with mini-
mum, or even without, rehearsal. I suspect they may
have happened more often to Plácido than to anyone
else because he is a great musician. His musicianship
to me is stronger and more remarkable than his much-
talked-about acting ability. For he seems to take the
music from within and sort of fill it out, the way you
blow up a balloon. In this case we saw something that
had been wilting suddenly bloom again.'

'By the time I sang my first Siegmund, in 1992, the Wagnerian repertoire was becoming very important to me. I was
in the middle of a love affair with Wagner – a love affair
that continues unabated! As a musician, I find his music
supremely fulfilling, because no other composer has worked
so carefully with the text and the orchestration. He was
fanatical about his texts and blends them into the music in
a unique way. He knows exactly how to set the rhythms of
a spoken phrase into music and always writes the right notes
for both short and long syllables.

'I know some people were surprised by the lyricism I
bring to my Wagnerian singing. But, as far as I am concerned, the most important and lucky thing is precisely the
fact that I'm not a Heldentenor! Because most tenors who
usually sing Siegmund tend to be vocally punished from a
steady diet of Siegfried, Tannhäuser and even Tristan whereas
my own experience of Wagner has been limited to Lohengrin
– a very italianate part – and Parsifal. These two roles enabled me to familiarize myself with Wagnerian singing without harming my voice.

'From the textual point of view, even for a quick learner

like me, Siegmund was extremely difficult. I had to cope with a very complex text in a language I'm familiar with but don't possess in the way I do French and Italian. Basically I learnt it between performances of other works, days and nights of study, often into the early morning hours. Sometimes I even woke up in the middle of the night, wondering how this or that phrase should go. And what you learn in the middle of the night you never forget!

'As a character, Siegmund is one of the greatest heroes in operatic literature because of everything we know about his past sufferings and everything that happens to him during the first two acts of the opera. He is a really heroic character fighting to survive first against Hunding and his kinsmen and then against destiny itself. He wins the first battle, against Hunding, but he cannot win the second one, against destiny in the person of Wotan and Fricka who, because of the power politics governing the world of the gods, decide otherwise.

'When I first approached the role, my first guideline was to think about the character and what happens to him during the action, rather than the vocal approach, which should stem from the music. Of course Act I of *Die Walküre* is a marathon race! It involves 65 minutes – more than an hour of more than 100 per cent involved concentration and a hell of a lot of singing! The action centers around four salient points. The first comes when, in relating his story to Hunding, the latter identifies him as the enemy that he and his kinsmen have been hunting and states that, because of the sanctity of the laws of hospitality, he will fight him in the morning, and he had better get hold of some mighty weapon. The second salient point is the moment Siegmund talks about the sword his father promised him: "*Ein Schwert verhiess mir der Vater,*" and wonders where this sword is now and becomes increasingly obsessed by this sword.'

(Domingo always uses the word 'obstinated' and 'obstination' where he means obsessed and obsession.) 'The third point is Sieglinde's story: "*Der manner Sippe sass hier im Saal*," which culminates in "*Winterstürme*," the Spring Scene, this beautiful, romantic moment when light pours into the hut and is also a hint for you also to change and let light into the color of your voice. Of course, the "*Winterstürme*" is so well known and loved that everyone is waiting for it – just as, I suspect, they are also waiting for the cries of "*Wälse, Wälse*" in the previous section, where Siegmund sings of the sword his father promised him, in order to see how long you can hold your G flat and G natural! Then comes the fourth salient point when, after the continuation of his glorious love duet with Sieglinde, Siegmund extracts the sword, Nothung, from the tree and the two flee together in the climax of the act which, incidentally, ends with an A natural. Although this is the only A natural in a role that does not contain any higher notes, the fact that it comes at the end of this very long act which has a very taxing overall tessitura, makes it feel like a B natural or even a high C! Practically all of Siegmund's singing in Act I hovers around the passaggio and this means that, by the time to reach up to this A natural, you are so exhausted that you really have to push the voice. This constant use of the middle voice and the passaggio zone, which forces one to push the voice, is one of the main reasons why Wagner is considered dangerous for the voice and especially for young voices.

'Needless to say, Siegmund is also one of the most wonderful characters to portray. Wagner's genius enables him to pour every kind of feeling into this act: despair, exasperation, hope, ecstatsy, looking forward to the future. But what is so sad is that he created this pair of supremely lovable characters – in fact the most lovable and magnificent in the whole *Ring* – only to have them disappear from the Tetralogy altogether at the end of Act II of *Die Walküre*! Siegmund is created only to serve as the father of Siegfried, for the continuation of the *Ring*. And I find this desperately sad because he is such a fabulous character that I would have liked Wagner to continue with his story! Both of them are fabulous characters. What can I tell you? Look at Act II. You see them rushing and fleeing from their home, and you have Sieglinde's sadness, after having found real love, that she had to give herself to Hunding before.

'Then Brünnhilde appears and explains everything. She knows that, after Fricka's bullying intervention, there is no hope for Siegmund. Wotan will no longer protect him. Nevertheless, in the end, Siegmund manages to convince Brünnhilde that he must live. He fights for his new-found happiness with all his might and makes her promise something which, of course, she cannot deliver (because of the ultimate power of the supreme God . . .). So Siegmund must die, and his Death Scene is one of the most unbelievable deaths I've ever been called to perform. While I'm dying – and I die in Wotan's arms – I realize that it is he, my father, who has killed me and my sadness is such that I cannot stop myself from crying. Luckily, I don't have to sing any more because I don't know how I would manage to. The tragic story of Siegmund, of both these noble souls who go through so much suffering only to die and disappear at this point in the opera – the realization that this is the end of them – overwhelms me. I cannot think of any suffering in all opera that can compare to theirs . . . except, perhaps, that of Loris Ipanov who forgives the eponymous heroine in *Fedora*.'

TITLE ROLE

Stiffelio

*'If there is buried treasure in Verdi's output, it's prob-
ably lying there in* Stiffelio,*' wrote the New York Times
after the Metropolitan Opera production in March
1993 which followed the enormous success of the
Royal Opera's staging that propelled this work out of
oblivion.* Stiffelio *immediately preceded* Rigoletto *and
was only performed in heavily censored chunks in
Verdi's time. After 1857 it vanished altogether, as Verdi
transferred most of its music into* Aroldo.

Domingo points out that Stiffelio *is a highly unusual opera as far as the story is concerned – the plot
is almost modern rather than nineteenth century. Faced
with his wife's adultery, the preacher Stiffelio is too
passionate a man to be a complacent husband and
too committed to his faith to be a vengeful one. The
only solution is to forgive – an admirable yet highly
un-operatic reaction.*

*Be that as it may, Domingo's performance won
high praise both at the Met and everywhere else he
has performed the part – 28 times so far, in Madrid,
London and Los Angeles in 1995, Vienna in 1997
and again the Met in 1998. 'The Met revival was remarkable for the central performance by Plácido
Domingo,' wrote the New York Times. 'Mr Domingo
sings the part splendidly. As a man, faced with lying
and prevarication in everyone around him, Stiffelio is*

238

a distant pre-echo of Otello and Mr Domingo's vibrant tone enforced the link. The moment when he discovers the truth about his wife – a shriek of pure melody – is thrilling. The arietta in the third act, which might be well known as an aria if it came in a different opera, is beautifully done, as is the final address from the pulpit, where a radiant assertiveness is given to the expression of emptiness and dejection.'

It is important to stress the fact that Domingo was 52 when he first undertook this challenge during this decade of self-renewal, which makes the vocal bravura he brings to the part even more remarkable.

'*Stiffelio* is my penultimate Verdi role. Although I knew some of the music because Mario Del Monaco had performed it, I didn't really know the whole opera well until the Nineties, when I came to study it. And I must say, it was a phenomenal surprise for me to discover this work and find this character so late in my career. It's a wonderful role, both vocally and dramatically. I love the drama – which is very unusual in operatic terms – and the vocal side, which is quite demanding.

'I am glad to have performed Verdi's original version of the work rather than his subsequent revised edition, entitled *Aroldo*, in which the hero becomes an Englishman returning from the Crusades, and which is less believable. *Stiffelio* rings truer and is more poignant because, as in the original play the libretto is based on, the hero is a priest whose wife, in a moment of weakness, gets involved with that terrible character Raffaele. One of the many unusual features in this opera is the fact that the villain, Raffaele, is also a tenor! This goes very much against the grain because in most operatic plots the villain is usually a baritone or a bass. But there the baritone, Lina's father, is a good guy and so is the

239

bass, another priest.

'Stiffelio himself is a very noble, upright character who goes through a lot and develops very much through the action. But his integrity is obvious from the beginning. When he is initially confronted by the report that a man has been seen climbing out of the window of his house, it never even crosses his mind that he was visiting his wife Lina. He thinks he probably came to see his cousin who also lives with them. And when he is presented with an item that can furnish proof, one way or another, in the shape of a wallet dropped while the man was escaping, he decides to burn it. But of course it was his wife and Raffaele, whom he considered a friend, who betrayed him.

'Vocally, the part is demanding right from the beginning: you start off with quite a difficult aria, an ensemble and a duet. It's a little bit like *"Celeste Aida."* Okay, it doesn't have such an exposed ending but it does have a very high tessitura. Then right away you have another one: a duet with Lina which is not really a duet but like an aria most of the time. So you have two big, important moments in quick succession and at the very beginning of the opera. After that, you have the big scene where you confront Lina with the fact that inside her locked prayer book there is a letter hidden. He demands that she open it and when she refuses he forces it open, and the letter is dropped on the floor. Lina's father, who knew that something was going on, picks it up. It's very dramatic, this scene. It culminates in a monumental ensemble which starts off as an aria and then develops into an ensemble.

'Act II is also wonderful. The tessitura is very, very high throughout. To my mind, its most exceptional feature is that fantastic quartet, which is reminiscent of the great quartet in *Rigoletto*. This kind of quartet – in this case a dialogue between Stiffelio and Lina, accompanied by observations from her father and Raffaele – later found its apotheosis in *"Bella figlia dell'amore"* in *Rigoletto*. This is not surprising because *Stiffelio* immediately preceded *Rigoletto* and Verdi's other two romantic operas *Il Trovatore* and *La Traviata*. The act ends in a rather low-key way, with Stiffelio almost fainting from the pain and shock of discovering that a man whom he considered a friend turns out to be his wife's lover.

'Act III is one of the most riveting and unprecedented in the repertoire. Stiffelio asks Lina for a divorce – a rare enough feature in any operatic plot – and hands her the divorce papers to sign. She agrees and after she signs them, she asks him to hear her confession as a priest – a terrible and highly unusual situation for a husband, or even an ex-husband, to find himself in! And this is one of Verdi's most inspired moments, a really divine duet in a scene that is unique, totally unprecedented in opera! A divorce followed by a confession, it's really unbelievable! And even stranger and more unusual is his next move. He mounts his pulpit to preach a sermon, alludes to Christ's treatment of Maria Maddalena and says that the woman is forgiven: *"Perdonata, perdonata."* It's very dramatic and very, very touching.

'But then this opera full-of-surprises was also a surprise for all of us. It proved a great success everywhere I sang it, be it the Met, Covent Garden, Vienna or Los Angeles – in retrospect, it feels very satisfying to know that we resurrected this work from oblivion and that, thanks to our efforts, *Stiffelio* now has a place in the repertoire.'

PERY

Il Guarany

Pery was one of the most imaginative additions to Domingo's repertoire during the Nineties, when he learnt more new operas than he had since the beginning of his career. He sang it first on 5 June 1994 in Bonn as part of a co-production between the Bonn State Theater and Washington Opera, a total of eleven performances. (During the following 1994–95 season he sang three more new parts: Jean in Hérodiade, *Idomeneo, and Gabriele Adorno in* Simon Boccanegra.*)*

Il Guarany, *by the Brazilian composer Carlos Gomes, a pupil of Ponchielli, is based on the romantic novel* O Guarani *by José de Alencar and had its world premiere at La Scala in 1870. It was admired by Verdi and soon became a national symbol for Brazilians, whose country had recently become independent from Portugal. In fact the hero and heroine of* Il Guarany – Pery and Ceci, short for Cecilia – who dared cross the racial divide, are the Brazilian equivalent of Romeo and Juliet.

Musically, as well as some Verdian overtones, the work has echoes of Gomes's teacher Ponchielli, Meyerbeer and Wagner, with practically no references to native Indian music.

Within a few years of its premiere,* Il Guarany – *basically an Italian opera that happens to have been*

242

written by a Brazilian – was performed in most major international theaters, including Covent Garden in 1872 and the Metropolitan Opera in 1884. Then it gradually vanished from the repertoire, possibly because it is so difficult both to stage and to cast. Had Gomes dared imagine the success of this opera, both with the Milanese public and his own countrymen, surely he would not have been so nervous before the premiere as to take refuge in La Scala's fly tower, in case of a fiasco!

The Bonn–Washington co-production provided a formula that ensured a budget that could set an inspired director's imagination free – and did the work proud. Giancarlo Del Monaco, the great tenor Mario Del Monaco's director son, the Intendant at Bonn, was a committed champion of this work that his father had performed and loved, while Domingo was enthusiastic about resurrecting a worthy Latin-American opera. The next step was to choose a director capable of doing the work justice. They convinced Werner Herzog, the inspirational German film director of Fitzcarraldo *(the obvious connection between opera and the Brazilian jungle setting was irresistible) to direct. Herzog more than justified his choice. He used his vast budget to magnificent effect and produced a poetic, visually gripping and dramatically powerful staging. As the lights dimmed, the theater was flooded by two minutes of recorded tropical birdsong. This set the mood for the evocative scenery that placed the work convincingly in context. The scene of Pery's conversion to Christianity, with all its controversial subtext, was powerfully staged and movingly acted by Domingo, and the final scene, where the fortress of the 'baddies', the cannibalistic Indian tribe of*

243

the Aymoré, is blown up, killing everyone inside, ex-
cept the lovers, was so realistic that it seemed almost
apocalyptic.

'Il Guarany, along with several other operas by Antonio
Carlos Gomes – such as *Fosca* – was premiered at La Scala
in 1870. One of the greatest things one can say in its praise
is the fact that it counted Verdi, a known admirer of Gomes's
music, among its fans. Gomes has a beautiful style and a
very good hand for melody. He was a composer very much
in the style of Donizetti, Verdi and Ponchielli, whose pupil
he was. In fact, the big ensemble in *Il Guarany* is quite reminiscent of the ensemble in *La Gioconda*. I suppose it fell
into oblivion because it demands a cluster of first-rate singers, as does *Fosca* and *Salvatore Rossa*. But when managements do get hold of such top singers they tend to go for
Don Carlos, or another of the big Verdi operas instead!

'I chose to do it first in Bonn, in a magnificent production by Werner Herzog, which was a co-production with
Washington Opera because I wanted to inaugurate my term
as Artistic Director in Washington with something beautiful, exotic, different and new! And it proved a huge success
with the public in both places, was televised and turned
into a video.

'Vocally the title role, Pery, is very difficult. For a start
it's very long. You are on stage most of the evening. You
have two duets with Cecilia, one of which is so well known
in Brazil that most Brazilians regard it almost like a national anthem (in fact some Brazilian television stations sign
off with a tune from the overture of *Il Guarany*), one with
Gonzales, and one with Cecilia's father. You also have an
aria at the beginning of Act II, "*Vanto io pur*," where Pery
is contemplating the contrast between Cecilia's background
and his own. He also participates in most of the ensembles.

Throughout the tessitura is very demanding, a lot of it hovering on the passaggio. Dramatically, as with Alvaro in *Forza*, you have to balance his passion for Cecilia with his pride as an Indian, a Guarany.

'All in all I am very happy to have helped resurrect this very attractive work from oblivion.'

TITLE ROLE

Idomeneo

Idomeneo was one of Domingo's new roles, undertaken in the Nineties when he had embarked on a period of new challenges that have kept both his voice and his enthusiasm for his art fresh. One of the few obvious gaps was Mozart, whose operas were absent from Domingo's repertoire since his early days in Mexico and Tel Aviv. The reason is that Domingo is not a Mozart tenor. But there is one Mozart role that non-Mozart tenors can and do undertake: Idomeneo, one of the most beautiful and poignant Mozart ever wrote. It is charged with so much feeling, so many references to Mozart's own feelings about the father–son relationship, that one almost feels the music aching to break away from the corset of the strictly classical form. In some passages it almost ushers in Verdi. This is the reason why Pavarotti (at the 1983 Salzburg Festival) and Domingo have both sung the role with distinction.

After eight performances at the Met in the 1994–95 season – four in October 1994 and four in March 1995 – and one on tour with the Met in Frankfurt in May 1996, Domingo went on to perform the role with equal distinction at the Vienna State Opera in January 1997 and the Chicago Lyric Opera in November 1997. This brings the total to 16 performances of this opera which he has also recorded for Deutsche

246

Grammophon with Carol Vaness, Cecilia Bartoli, Thomas Hampson and Bryn Terfel, under James Levine.

'Idomeneo is my last Mozart role. I came to it late in my career, in the mid-Nineties. It's a mature role and I'm very glad I sang it when I did, for it immediately became one of my favorites. It's a fantastic part, with everything that you could ask for: it has a lot of great singing and the character is wonderful to portray; he suffers from beginning to end! His suffering starts at his first entry – the moment he sets eyes on his son, having promised Neptune to sacrifice the first person he encounters, in return for being saved from drowning – and goes on and on until the last scene. In fact I have never smiled with such joy in any opera as I did at the finale of *Idomeneo*! Because I cannot even bear to think about what it must feel like to know you have to kill your own son. There is no pain in the world that could compare with Idomeneo's in this situation.

'Of course, if you look at it from the spiritual point of view, you could say that he is being punished for his appalling, arrogant selfishness in making that monstrous promise to Neptune. He could have promised to forgive his enemies or, at any rate, offered to make some personal sacrifice in return for his salvation instead of promising to sacrifice the first being he encounters onshore. For even if that person had not happened to be Idamante, it would still have been another innocent human being, somebody else's son (or husband or father). I find his assumption that his life is worth more than another's deeply spiritually flawed . . .

'Vocally, although Idomeneo is not easy, it's wonderful. It feels more like a bel canto rather than a typically Mozartian role, probably because the drama of the situation is so intense that you can feel Mozart breaking away from the con-

247

fines of the strictly "classical" form. In my first aria, "*Vedrommi intorno*," I have just emerged from the sea, I am relieved to be alive but, even before I see that the person approaching me is my son, I grieve for the innocent victim who has to pay for my life with his. Then I have the glorious aria "*Fuor del mar*," which has the most beautiful music, with quite a lot of coloratura, and although difficult, is marvellous to sing. The Prayer is also very beautiful. The last aria I didn't do; I did only the recitative because that aria was cut from the Met production. These recitatives of Mozart's are among the greatest moments in this opera, the key not only to Idomeneo's but to all the characters' innermost feelings and, again, so intense as to seem almost un-Mozartian . . . One of the most breathtaking moments in this work, however, is the response of the Chorus in Act III, after I reveal that, in order to placate the God, I will have to sacrifice my own son. The music of the chorus in "*O voto tremendo*" is quite incredible, with a modulation going to C major which is just so unbearably poignant and beautiful that, at this moment, you think that there is no composer as simple and as great as Mozart.'

JEAN

Hérodiade

*Domingo sang John the Baptist in Massenet's opera
(based on the story by Gustave Flaubert) in two productions: Lotfi Mansouri's in San Francisco in November 1994, with Renée Fleming as Salome, Dolora
Zajick in the title role and Juan Pons as Hérode under
the baton of Valery Gergiev, and Hermann Nitsch's in
Vienna in February 1995 with Nancy Gustavson as
Salome, Agnes Baltsa in the title role and Juan Pons
again as Hérode, under Marcello Viotti.*

*In both cases, Domingo made a superb job of sing-
ing this prophet: at once lyrical and heroic, with impeccable style and utmost vocal beauty throughout.
Thankfully there is an excellent recording, by Sony –
but regrettably no video recording – with the cast of
the San Francisco production.*

'I wouldn't say that *Hérodiade* is among Massenet's greatest works. It's very, very long, about three and a half hours,
and the music is not all on the same, consistently high level.
I have sung Jean on two occasions: once, about six years
ago, in San Francisco and once in Vienna. Dramatically, it's
interesting to compare the very different way in which the
Baptist is portrayed in *Hérodiade* and in Richard Strauss's
Salome, where he is a far, far more important role but, alas,
not a tenor! Yet I was very happy to add John the Baptist to
my roster of French roles and especially to my roster of

Massenet parts which now number four on stage and one – Araquil in *La Navarraise* – on record.

'In *Hérodiade* we get several other significant differences. For a start, Jean reciprocates Salome's feelings for him. But, as a holy man, he cannot allow himself to indulge in carnal passions. Herodias doesn't know until the end that her rival for Herod's affections is her own daughter and Salome doesn't know until the end that Herodias is her mother. She finds out when – far from asking for the Baptist's death – she sees his head on a platter and lunges at Herodias, whom she considers responsible, with a dagger. When the latter reveals that she is Salome's mother, hoping to save herself, Salome stabs herself in horror! So, the Baptist is not the most important role in the opera. He is not that important or that taxing vocally, either. But he does have some beautiful music, especially in his love duet with Salome in Act I, which is very sensual and at the same time very lyrical and in which he asks her to love him "as one loves in dreams." Also wonderful is his last-act aria, sung in prison, "*Adieu, donc, vains objets,*" and the duet with Salome in which he confesses his love for her.

'Singing Jean whetted my appetite for more Massenet parts especially, maybe, Roland in *Esclarmonde*. Another part which, sadly, is no longer possible for me but which I would have enjoyed is Jean in *Le Jongleur de Notre-Dame.*'

GABRIELE ADORNO

Simon Boccanegra

Amazingly enough, Domingo first sang this youthful Verdi role – which most tenors sing at the beginning rather than the peak of their career – in January 1995 at the Metropolitan Opera, in a very good production by Giancarlo Del Monaco with evocative sets by Michael Scott. The rest of the cast included Kiri Te Kanawa as Amelia, Vladimir Chernov in the title role, and Robert Lloyd and Roberto Scandiuzzi sharing the role of Fiesco, under the baton of James Levine.

Domingo's superb portrayal of this young Verdi hero, which he has now sung 14 times, at this stage in his career is the most eloquent vindication of everything his artistry stands for, and a lesson for all young tenors. Every time I heard him sing this part, in New York and London, he sounded younger than almost everyone else in the cast, many of whom were half his age. 'Plácido Domingo makes the stage come alive and reminds us that great opera is an interaction of personality, voice, music, costumes and sets. The vocal fireworks of the evening came from him and one only felt sorry that Verdi had not given his Gabriele Adorno a bigger part,' wrote the New York Times.

After those initial five performances, Domingo went on to sing a further five at Covent Garden with Kallen Esperian as Amelia, Sergei Leiferkus in the title role and Roberto Scandiuzzi as Fiesco in June/July

1997 and four in a revival of the Met production in January/February 1999, of which there is an excellent video recording.

'I admit it's funny that my last Verdi role so far, Gabriele Adorno, should have been one of my first ones! It's usually sung by young tenors quite early in their careers. He is a young, impulsive character very much in love with the heroine, Amelia, very much involved in Genoese politics and convinced of the Doge's complicity in Amelia's kidnap.

'It was a heartening experience for me to attempt this role so late and to have to lighten my voice in a very special way in order to produce a youthful sound. Because one of the most important things for any tenor voice is to preserve its youthfulness. Tenors must always sound youthful since almost all the characters they are called to portray are young. So, no matter how dramatic the role, you shouldn't ever make it sound heavy. You must always infuse lightness into your voice. How much or how little depends on the specific role and how it's written. It's a matter of positioning the voice, thinking youthful and thinking also of the timbre. If, for instance, you hear me sing one of Otello's arias in concert, followed by one of Adorno's arias, you will immediately notice the change of vocal color.

'So, making such a success of this role this late in my career was a great satisfaction. I sang it in both the usual, later edition (at the Met) and the original version, which is a bit more difficult, at Covent Garden. I think I prefer the later, with one exception: Adorno's duet with Fiesco, the Vengeance Duet, which in the earlier version is strong, exciting and imbued by his thirst for revenge against the Doge but which in the later version is very soft and muted; a sort of conversation permeated by religious overtones. So my ideal solution – which we put into practice in Washington –

252

is to perform the later version but substitute the Adorno–Fiesco duet from the earlier edition.

'All in all, Adorno is a rewarding sing and doesn't present any serious difficulties – which is not to say it's easy, for there is no such thing as an easy role in the operatic repertoire. The first duet with Amelia has a problematic tessitura, but it's followed by an ensemble which includes some very noble, beautiful passages for the tenor. In the second act, the most difficult for the tenor, the problem with the aria, the exquisite duet with Amelia and the trio is no longer just one of tessitura but also of endurance, stamina. You have to pace yourself carefully to ensure that the voice sounds youthful throughout. In the last scene, Adorno has a couple of beautiful phrases and ensembles.

'I greatly enjoyed adding this engaging young character to my repertoire. It whetted my appetite for my next new Verdi role: Arrigo in *La Battaglia di Legnano*, which I will sing in concert with the Covent Garden company at London's Festival Hall in June/July 2000. I am also preparing an album of all Verdi's tenor arias for 2001. It will include not only all those I have already sung but those from the few Verdi operas missing from my repertoire: *Oberto, Un Giorno di Regno, Alzira, I Masnadieri, Il Corsaro, I Due Foscari, Attila, Aroldo* and *Falstaff*.'

LUCERO

Divinas Palabras

Garcia Abril's opera Divinas Palabras *was composed for the opening of Madrid's Teatro Real in October 1997 and proved a great success for its composer and for Domingo. The complex libretto, based on a play by Ramon Maria del Valle Inclan, is set among the poor and petty crooks of Galicia – as a critic rightly remarked, the characters could have stepped out of Goya's 'black pictures' – and the sets and costumes by Francisco Leal were atmospheric and served to illumine the production by Carlos Plaza.*

After some initial doubts Domingo gave the project his full support and made himself available for two full weeks of rehearsals which, as the composer again remarked, 'is extraordinary for an artist like him, at the peak of his career. I have nothing but praise and gratitude for him.'

The work also proved a remarkable public and critical success: 'The success of this performance shows that the traditional operagoer is far more open to new music than we imagine, when offered a persuasive, beautiful performance delivered responsibly with care and great skill. This was made possible by Plácido Domingo, Garcia Abril, José Carlos Plaza and the conductor Antonio Ros Marba,' wrote El Pais, Spain's equivalent to The Times.

ABC added: 'What Garcia Abril has created here

for and with Plácido Domingo is certainly not easy to perform or simple to sing. Our great tenor, at the peak of his art, sings with overwhelming conviction, wonderful timbre and abandon and is a fine actor.'

'*Divinas Palabras* is the last of the three operas written for me. Its composer is an enormously talented Spaniard, Antonio Garcia Abril, who had already written some fantastic music for films, musicals as well as symphonic works, but never an opera. The music he produced for *Divinas Palabras* was very good and very powerful. In this case we also had a very good libretto. But the problem was the story, the plot. It's so sordid and so . . . brutal that I wouldn't even dream of bringing it to Washington or Los Angeles.

'The story has to do with a family of farmers fighting among themselves over who will inherit a carriage belonging to a handicapped boy whose mother dies. After her death, a dispute arises between her two surviving brothers and sister over who will have control of this carriage. Once they do get hold of it, they take the boy, who is about 17, to a tavern in Galicia, get him drunk and kill him. The story is so, so disgusting that it puts you off completely. Of course one knows that there is such a sordid, brutal side to life, that such things exist and that it's right that one should know about them. But does one want to hear an opera about them?

'The music, although difficult, was very beautiful and challenging. My character – who is called by several names, chief of which is Lucero – was also challenging. He is a kind of gypsy, a vagabond who lives on the streets, kind of simpatico, a bit of a profiteer, a bit of a conquistador but, really, rather unpleasant. I tried to make him appear a bit better than he is and hope that this came across. His most difficult scene was the first, when he appears with a little dog who had to be trained to respond to Lucero's questions, by raising his tail and his front paw if the answer was "yes." It was an amusing but difficult scene to pull off.

'As I said, I would have liked to take this opera elsewhere. But in the theaters where I wield influence over artistic decisions both I and the piece itself would be crucified. Right or wrong, they would slay the piece. They would never stomach it. And who knows, maybe they would be right. Still, it's a pity because musically, *Divinas Palabras* is a very good, very strong work.'

JEAN DE LEYDEN

Le Prophète

Domingo sang Jean de Leyden in Vienna in May/June 1998 in a production by Hans Neuenfels. In a rumor-laden city such as Vienna, everybody had been antici-pating a great scandal and controversy, but in the event the general reaction was one of disappointment. While Domingo and Agnes Baltsa, in the mammoth role of Fides, gave towering performances, the production was such a shambles and for the most part so hideous that they were totally wasted.

'Any comments on individual performances, whether good or bad, on an otherwise dismal evening, become totally irrelevant,' wrote Merker. 'The real question that needs addressing is: how was such a thing allowed to come about? ... One cannot help wonder-ing, too, why it is necessary to drag certain works from oblivion when they should have been left well alone.' At the time of its Paris premiere, on 16 April 1849, Heinrich Heine had described Le Prophète *as a 'mis-erable work,' but Richard Wagner and Hector Berlioz were reported to have been deeply moved and im-pressed by it.*

But whatever the musical merits or demerits of the work as such, it was certainly not helped by Hans Neuenfels's mess of a production. Yet Domingo's con-tribution in this endlessly long role impressed every-one. 'He was like an Atlas who carried the whole per-

257

formance on his shoulders,' says Agnes Baltsa. 'He just got on his chariot and off he went. He sang with gorgeous beauty of voice, filled the stage and left everyone behind.' The Süddeutsche Zeitung's critic rightly observed, 'However dull or confusing a production, one's eyes are immediately drawn in fascination towards Plácido Domingo the moment he steps on stage. It's quite unbelievable that even the most questionable production gains somewhat in quality from the sheer presence of this artist. His voice sounds both warm and opulent and is reminiscent of his greatest triumphs. One has to ask oneself, though, how such a great artist can derive any pleasure from being associated with such a disaster!'

The answer, as Domingo goes on to affirm, is that he doesn't!

'I was looking forward to *Le Prophète* because I had always had good experiences with Meyerbeer's *L'Africaine*. But I have to say I was disappointed by the production at the Vienna State Opera. I would have liked a production that helped clarify the weird plot of this opera – set among the Anabaptists in the sixteenth century – rather than obscure it even further! As it was, Hans Neuenfels's production, which was highly controversial, rendered it even more incomprehensible.

'There are two versions of *Le Prophète*. The normal version which is tough enough but singable, and the higher version which Gedda used to do and which all high tenors prefer. Needless to say, we opted for the former. In either version, Jean de Leyden is a very, very long and excruciatingly hard role, despite the fact that we trimmed it a bit for the Vienna production, with a number of cuts. Still, Jean certainly has some very beautiful and rousing passages to sing: his aria "*Sous les vastes arceux d'un temple magnifique*" closely followed by "*Pour Berthe moi je soupire,*" a couple of duets, notably with his mother, Fides, trios and the triumphal hymn with the Chorus, "*Roi du ciel et des anges.*"

'As far as the drama is concerned, this is one of those operatic plots which are so unrealistic as to be almost comical. Yet the fact that Jean is considered almost like a god by this sect reminds me of some of those weird sects that seem to have sprung up all over the States in our own day. A plot such as this needs tremendous help from the director. When I arrived for rehearsals in Vienna I made it clear to Neuenfels that I would do whatever he wanted but that I feared that what he was doing was gratuitously controversial and bound to cause an outcry. But he didn't think so and was convinced by his own view of the work, which he professed to love, and worked harder than I've ever seen any director work on every detail, every extra and each member of the chorus. But the result was disappointing. Yet I am glad I did it. It was an experience and yet another role to add to my repertoire!'

GHERMAN

The Queen of Spades

*Domingo first performed this major role – the first
and, so far, the only big Russian part in his repertoire
– in a production by Elijah Moshinsky at the Metropolitan Opera on 18 March 1999 – 40 years into his
career. The rest of the principals, with the exception
of Elizabeth Söderström as the Countess, were entirely
Russian, with Galina Gorchakova as Lisa, Olga
Borodina as Pauline, Dimitri Hvorostovsky as Yeletsky
and Vassily Gerello as Tomsky. The smaller parts were
also mostly sung by Russians and the conductor was
the Metropolitan Opera's Principal Guest Conductor
Valery Gergiev, Artistic Director of the Maryinsky
Theater, St Petersburg.*

*Domingo agreed to undertake this role fully aware
that not only is it enormously demanding from the
vocal and dramatic points of view but that it would
also present a formidable linguistic challenge for a non-
Russian speaker. Watching him rehearse Gherman day
after day for several weeks was seeing a different side
of Plácido Domingo: here was the world's greatest singing actor being visibly nervous and displaying the humility of a beginner, worried about whether everything
would come together for the opening night.*

*'Our first coaching session was a revelation,' re-
calls Yelena Kurdina, the Met's pre-eminent Russian
coach. 'I was expecting this singer I had always ad-*

mired, this superstar, and I found . . . a student! A pupil who was totally open, totally receptive, completely concentrated, focused and motivated, and really there at every minute of our two-hour sessions, which he never allowed anybody to interrupt, never cancelled and for which he was always on time. We started from the very beginning: notes, words, breathings, pronunciation, taking everything apart, phrase by phrase. And when we finally started shaping the part musically, he is such a natural musician, that everything seemed to pour out of his soul. He just knew, instinctively, how the musical line should go. You can't teach that. You can teach stylistic things, but you cannot teach musicality. And one of the reasons why, in my opinion, he is the best Gherman I have seen, was both because of the way he acted it, and the way he held the legato line. It was a treat to hear someone instilling the fabulous Italian legato line in Russian singing, something you never hear in a part like this.'

The critics on both sides of the Atlantic were unanimously enthusiastic. The result exceeded all expectations: 'Domingo looked and sounded like a man reborn,' wrote the Financial Times. 'It is a long while since the voice was as fresh as this and the top notes so free from strain . . . Domingo gave it everything Tchaikovsky could have wanted – power, intensity, romantic grandeur, attention to detail. It is remarkable to think that this is his 30th season at the Met. The occasion was a big success for him and he must have worked hard at it.'

After seven performances at the Metropolitan Opera, Domingo sang Gherman again a few months later, in June 1999, in a revival of Kurt Horres's pro-

*duction at the Vienna State Opera, this time under the
baton of Seiji Ozawa. (Shortly before the latter's ap-
pointment as Music Director of this theater.) Lisa was
again sung by Galina Gorchakova, the Countess by
the veteran Belgian mezzo-soprano Rita Gorr, Yeletsky
by Dimitri Hvorostovsky and Tomsky by Sergei
Leiferkus. In this stark, austere production Domingo
again delivered a gripping account of the obsessed,
self-destructive hero – or rather anti-hero – that dif-
fered subtly from the one he had delivered in the more
opulent, more atmospherically 'Russian' production
at the Metropolitan Opera. He himself explains these
differences in his analysis of the role that follows.*

'My reply to your observation that I keep seeking new challenges at a time in my career when I could be travelling the
world with a handful of "safe" roles, is that I always like
looking for something new. I consider it my duty both as a
musician and a singing actor. Basically it's the only way to
grow. And how could I let a great, meaty role such as
Gherman pass me by without tasting him? I had, of course,
known and loved it from afar for many years and was always being told that it is the Otello of the Russian repertoire. Finally, I was convinced I should sing it, even though
I know no Russian.

'Of course, the effort involved was tremendous. I had
never, ever sung anything in Russian before in my life. My
only other Russian role, Lensky, performed at the beginning of my career in Tel Aviv, with Marta in the role of
Tatiana, had been sung in Hebrew! So learning Gherman in
Russian was one of the hardest things I have ever done.
Because not only did I not know a single word of Russian,
but had no conception of the sound and structure of the
language, either. I was fortunate to work with a wonderful

Russian coach at the Met, Yelena Kurdina, for weeks and weeks, patiently and painstakingly. We started off working phonetically. Then, when the sounds began to make sense to me, I had an exact translation of the libretto and began to match it, word by word, to the phonetic sounds. Only at the end of this long and slow process did I begin to memorize it. I could have taken short cuts, but I didn't want to. If you love your work and career the way I do, then you will take the extra time. And I must say, it was worth it from start to finish in every sense: musically, vocally and dramatically and also from the point of view of personal satisfaction.

'Because through Gherman I was plunged into an entirely new musical world, Tchaikovsky's world, which I had almost forgotten since my early brush with it at the beginning of my career and which is entirely different, both musically and stylistically, from that of any other composer in my repertoire. In fact we should consider ourselves fortunate that Tchaikovsky left such a wonderful operatic legacy. For not only is he one of the greatest symphonic composers of all time – with so many symphonies, concertos, ballets and suites to his credit – but also one of the very few who managed to compose equally great operas. Of course this means that his orchestral virtuosity spills into his operas, which are symphonic masterpieces as well as wonderful vocally and dramatically. Their musical construction is fantastic. The score of *The Queen of Spades*, for instance, has a great deal in common with the Pathétique Symphony. I was lucky to have in the pit Valery Gergiev, who has such total mastery of this repertoire.

'Vocally, the role is one of the most demanding in the tenor repertoire. It is very dramatic and requires not only tremendous reserves of vocal power, but also great stamina and endurance because Gherman is present in every scene.

So you're constantly onstage. Yet at the same time, it is a very grateful role, because it is very well written and thought out. For example, in the finale of Act I, which you could say borders on being a little too dramatic and heavy, the instrumentation is so well thought out that the voice carries over the orchestra. In fact the most difficult moment in Act I is not, as one might think, the finale of Scene 2, but the end of the first scene, and the duet with Lisa in Scene 2. The aria *"Ya neveryn chtoby"* and duet in the last act (Scene 2) and Gherman's last aria, as he lies dying, are also very difficult.

'From the dramatic point of view, Gherman is one of the most interesting characters I have ever played. As I have already mentioned, I have a special liking for characters who suffer. They are invariably more interesting and absorbing, they literally suck you in. Gherman is unique in the sense that, alone among all the suffering characters I have portrayed, he is almost completely negative. In Pushkin he is totally black. But Tchaikovsky, being a quintessentially romantic composer, turns Gherman almost into a romantic hero and invests him with some vestiges of decency. In the opera, the initial motivation for Gherman's obsession with gambling is his love for Lisa, whom he realizes that, as a penniless German officer, he cannot hope to possess, whereas in Pushkin this obsession is a febrile, frenetic passion per se. But even in the opera, the moment he becomes sure of Lisa's love, she becomes secondary to his obsession with gambling, despite her being the initial reason why he wishes to become rich. And this is a great mystery to me . . . this switch from his passion for a woman to a passion for cards . . . Of course in Pushkin things are much clearer. Gherman is brutally cynical and declares that if necessary he will make love to the old Countess in order to obtain the secret of the three cards. But Tchaikovsky suppresses some of the worst things he says, and makes his love for Lisa run parallel to his obsession with gambling.

'When he first appears at the beginning of the opera and Tomsky asks him what is the matter, in his first aria "*Ya imeni yeyo ne znayu*," Gherman says he has seen Lisa and adds, "I want to know who she is and at the same time I don't want to know" – almost a premonition, to my mind – followed by a passionate declaration of his love for this unknown girl. And, because the dramatic plot is so well conceived, at that precise moment Yeletsky arrives by coincidence, and there is this fabulous duet in which he talks about how happy his life is and how well things are going for him at the moment, while Gherman sings exactly the opposite: how wretched his own life is. Lisa then arrives with the old Countess, and we have this wonderful quintet. As soon as the two women depart, Tomsky begins to relate the whole story of the old Countess's past as the "Venus of Moscow" etc., and we get the clues to the whole story. For at this moment Gherman not only finds out who Lisa is, but also that she is engaged to Prince Yeletsky, and that the difference in their social status is such that as a penniless foreign officer he can never hope to have her. At the same moment he hears the story of the three cards and in his despair latches on to it with ever-increasing obsession until the point in the next scene when it takes him over completely and he will be unable to think or see any thing else anymore . . .

'By the next scene (Act II, Scene 2), the grand ball in the Empress's presence, Lisa is already totally taken with him and gives him the key to her house so that he can visit her tomorrow. But he says, no, no, tonight! And in this scene he really sees her world, the world she lives and moves in and realizes, even more than before, the chasm between this glittering world and his own.

'In this scene, for me it is legitimate to assume that when

265

Gherman comes to see Lisa in her apartment and sings that beautiful aria *"Prosti, prelestnoe sozdanye"* he comes to confess his passion and that he genuinely intends to kill himself. But at that moment – in the opera, at least – the old Countess appears, so that this genuine outpouring of feeling is interrupted. And when it is resumed, after the old lady has scolded Lisa for being awake and making so much noise and withdrawn to her bedroom, even though Gherman still repeats the same words to Lisa, *"Krasavitsa boginya, angel,"* they sound somewhat hollow to me, almost like an afterthought to his now imperative need to discover the secret of the three cards from the old Countess. Yes, he loves Lisa, but he also knows that the key to this secret also resides here, in this house. And this is a turning point for him. From this moment on, he becomes increasingly obsessive.

'And from this moment on, he is lost. He hardly thinks of Lisa any more, only of how to get hold of the old lady. This is the reason why, once inside the house, he hides himself and, instead of following Lisa to her bedroom, he stays hidden until all the servants have gone to bed and the old Countess is alone, reminiscing. And what I would like to see one day is a staging in which his reason for staying hidden will be made more obvious by having Gherman hide right behind the Countess and sort of react to everything she is saying. In the Vienna staging, it was possible to make this a little more obvious than in New York.

'And then comes the climax of the tragedy of this opera, the death of the Countess. It is a tragedy because Gherman really has neither the wish nor the intention of killing or even hurting the old lady. Yet he knows from Tomsky's story that the moment she reveals the secret of the cards she will die. He tells her not to be afraid, but if he believes in the whole story then he also has to believe that the moment she reveals the secret of the cards, she is doomed to die. Yet he

266

insists. He begs and coaxes that if she ever had any mater-
nal feelings she should reveal her secret to him for what
good is it to her now, old that she is? Then he starts to get
mean, lose control and abuse her verbally with the worst
kind of language one can use to a lady – especially a lady
who has been, but no longer is, beautiful – in order to hurt
her. At this point she begins to have a heart attack.

'In the next act (Act III, Scene 1) we see Gherman at his
quarters in the barracks, having hallucinations. He is thinking about the corpse, the funeral, everything black, and hears,
or thinks he hears, the funeral music. In the middle of this
hallucination, he thinks he sees the Countess and that she
reveals the three cards to him. In the next scene, which is
different in Tchaikovsky's opera from the corresponding
scene in Pushkin, unbelievably enough Lisa has forgiven
him, comes to him and is prepared to give him a second
chance. But although overjoyed, his immediate reaction is
to say, let's go. She asks go where, and he replies to the
gambling tables. When she recoils and says how can you
possibly be like this he retorts, "But you don't understand,
she [the old lady] has told me the secret of the three cards."
And he is so cynical and insulting that as soon as he leaves,
Lisa throws herself into the Neva.

'The last scene is a moment of coolness for Gherman,
after the feverish, obsessive outpourings of the previous acts.
In the midst of all the animation at the gaming tables, he
appears calm and collected in a way that we haven't seen
him before. And I don't know whether this is because he is
secure in the knowledge that he has the secret of the cards
or what else is going on in his mind. Is he still thinking of
Lisa? Because, of course, he doesn't know that she has killed
herself. Personally, I think she is still part of his thoughts.
Or is this coolness, this one moment of stillness in this febrile character, due to a premonition of destiny, of impend-

ing death? I think the former is more likely. Because he appears totally confident of winning and, of course, he gets the first two cards right. And when he puts down the third card, the ace, he is still sure he has won. But when it turns out to be the Queen of Spades instead, he realizes that "the apparition," the ghost of the old Countess, or whatever one wants to call it, has tricked him and shouts, "What else do you want, you old bitch? My life? Take it!" and proceeds to shoot himself.

'Tchaikovsky has been much criticized for changing the ending and offering a dramatic resolution different from Pushkin's. In Pushkin Gherman doesn't kill himself but ends up in a lunatic asylum. But I can't think what else Tchaikovsky could do. He has to end the opera with a coup de theâtre, and his ending is a wonderful coup. Kurt Horres changed the ending in his production in Vienna and had Gherman die after having a sort of fit himself. But I prefer it when he kills himself, as it says in the libretto.

'Yet I wouldn't mind doing a production where we take Pushkin's idea and start off with Gherman in a lunatic asylum, during the orchestral introduction. Then he starts remembering everything . . . Maybe he tried to kill himself, didn't succeed and ended up in a lunatic asylum . . . So what I'm saying is that I would be open to another, different production, although at the moment I'm very happy with Moshinsky's which was great and made the part work well for me. There was one scene, though, which I felt worked better in the Vienna production: the Hallucination Scene, which I found more effective, more "crazy" in Horres's staging, with the church as the setting for the Countess's funeral, and her images popping out from everywhere rather than having her pop out of the floor of his barrack quarters as in the Met production.'

TITLE ROLE

Le Cid

Domingo had already sung the title role in about a dozen concert performances of Le Cid – one at Carnegie Hall in 1976, three in Hamburg in 1979, one at the Chatelet in Paris in 1981, two in Vienna in 1987, two in Madrid in 1988 and three in Chicago in 1993 – before performing it on stage for the first time at the Teatro de la Maestranza in Seville in May 1999, in a visually stunning production by Ugo de Ana, with the Portuguese soprano Elisabete Matos as Chimene and Ferrucio Furlanetto as Don Diego under the baton of Garcia Navarro. Performing an opera about Spain's national hero in the presence of the King and Queen of Spain, who flew down from Madrid, made the premiere an extra special occasion for him.

It was his fourth Massenet role on stage and he had by now assimilated all the particularities of the great French composer's style, which he explains in detail in his analysis. His performance was so dashing that it made one regret that his first appearance in this role on stage did not happen earlier in his career, when he possessed even greater reserves of power for some of the heroic passages. Yet one wouldn't exchange the insights of the mature Domingo into the private, lonely side of the hero – of all heroes, one could say – even for that!

In November 1999 Domingo sang a further eight

*performances at Washington Opera, making the total
number of performances of* Le Cid *in his career 24:
twelve in concert and twelve on stage.*

'As you know, I had sung Rodrigue in Massenet's *Le Cid*
several times in concert before I came to perform it on stage.
But on each occasion I was left with a feeling of dissatisfac-
tion. I was longing not merely to sing, but also to play
Rodrigue. For there was no doubt in my mind that *Le Cid*
is an opera made for the stage. There is huge dramatic po-
tential in the work, if staged the right way. But at the same
time I was aware that this is both a very expensive and very
difficult work to stage. So, when the Teatro de la Maestranza
first suggested the idea, I was tempted right away. We got
around the first problem – the expense – by my using my
position as Artistic Director of the Washington Opera to
persuade the two theaters to co-operate in a co-production.
Once we overcame that, we had to find a director with valid
ideas that would do the work justice.

'As far as the staging is concerned, the problem is the
fact that *Le Cid* is an "epic" opera. It has to do with the
legendary thirteenth-century Spanish hero who liberated
parts of southern Spain from the Arabs. And like all epic
operas – such as, for instance, *Aida* – it contains battle scenes,
triumph scenes, etc. which require huge choruses. Poised in
between those scenes, where you get a lot of fanfare, are
some intimate, tender, "personal" scenes in which the protagonists find themselves alone, free to give vent to their
innermost feelings. And as always in epic, monumental operas, the best music always accompanies the intimate scenes.
In *Le Cid* the heart of the opera lies equally in Chimene's
aria "*Pleurez, mes yeux*" and my aria "*O souverain.*" There
are also musical highlights in Chimene's duet with the Infanta
and in my duet with my father.

270

'As always, Massenet's music is very special, very individual. A characteristic of his is always to precede the most important moments, the climaxes, by recitatives in which there are a few key words which set the stage and reveal to you the essence of what's to follow. In my mind, I refer to those phrases as "oracles" because they tell me everything I need to know about the mood, the feeling, the color I should bring to this music. In *Manon* the oracle is the phrase "*Je suis seul, seul enfin*" that precedes "*A fuyez, douce image.*" In *Werther* it's the words "*Tout mon âme est là*" that immediately precede his heartbreaking aria, "*Pourquoi me reveiller.*" In both cases, the moment you hear those words, you know something monumentally important is coming. In *Le Cid* the oracle is the phrase "*Ah, tout est fini, tout mon rêve de gloire,*" which hardly feels like singing but more like reciting the principal monologue, a long, reflective monologue, in a Shakespeare or a great French classical play. And this aspect is a special characteristic of Massenet's. Of course, as is evident in the dances, he also appears to like Spanish music a lot. Also interesting is the fact that *Le Cid* was composed ten years after Bizet's *Carmen* and is chronologically very close to *Manon* (it was premiered only a year after the latter) and so combines both styles: the classical and verismo. In fact it is French verismo.

'On the whole, I think that Massenet is an underestimated composer. (And I am proud to have performed five of his big roles: Rodrigue, Des Grieux in *Manon*, the title role in *Werther*, John the Baptist in *Hérodiade* and Araquil in *La Navarraise*.) But I feel that with this production of *Le Cid* we have vindicated his reputation as a composer capable of writing a grand opera in the style of Meyerbeer – which, of course, was all the rage at the time.

'As a Spaniard, it is, of course, wonderful to perform a role which gives you the opportunity to speak about the greatness, the grandeur, the freedom and the glory of Spain and its king. It's very rousing especially if, like me, you have deep feeling for your country.'

DON JUAN

Margarita la Tornera

Don Juan was Domingo's last role in the twentieth century and his first of the new century and millennium. One can hardly think of a more dashing hero with whom to make this landmark transition. A quintessentially Spanish hero par excellence in an opera written by a Spaniard and a symbol of virility and joie de vivre, even though it is an aged Don Juan that we encounter in Chapi's opera, on his last adventure, after the ultimate dare: seducing a nun.

Domingo sang it at Madrid's Teatro Real in December 1999 and January 2000 with Elisabete Matos in the title role, the nun Don Juan is pursuing as the crowning achievement of his career! The music is pleasant enough to the ear – and very difficult to sing in certain passages – but essentially unmemorable. It confirmed the view that most forgotten or seldom performed works are forgotten for a very good reason: that they don't compare favorably with their composer's best and most famous works – which is not to say that it is not interesting to air them from time to time. But undoubtedly Chapi will continue to remain more famous for his zarzuelas than this foray into 'opera seria.'

'*Margarita la Tornera* is by Chapi, one of Spain's best-known composers of *zarzuelas*. The story is from Jose Zorilla, the creator of Don Juan Tenorio, the character on whom the legend of Don Juan is based. The libretto is not very good but the opera has some very beautiful and very difficult music. All the parts, my part, Don Juan, and the title role, Margarita, are very difficult, and so is the other soprano role and the bass part. But I feel a strong zeal about championing Spanish music and works that have been neglected. So I thought we should revive this opera which had not been seen since 1909. This year I also recorded *La Dolores*, a beautiful opera by Bretón, and *Merlin* by Albeniz, one of the greatest Spanish composers. So I'm trying to do all I can for Spanish music and am always looking for suitable works.

'How does the character of Don Juan in this opera compare with the Don Juan or, in operatic terms, the Don Giovanni we know? Basically it's the same sort of character, a professional seducer of women for whom seducing a nun is the ultimate challenge. In fact he tells the character who is the equivalent of Leporello that for a professional seducer this is the ultimate experience, the ultimate ecstasy.

'I must say that, despite the weak libretto, I found this a very rewarding opera. Act I is very difficult vocally, Act II has a kind of Donizetti-like ensemble while Act III is very dramatic and contains some very, very beautiful passages. It is also the most fulfilling dramatically, because in it we see Don Juan's redemption. In the music he sings with Margarita in this act Don Juan repents. Unlike Mozart's Don Giovanni, this Don Juan really repents. He truly loves Margarita and is genuinely sorry about the mess he has made of his life. So, instead of being removed to burn in Hell, he sees the light, metaphorically speaking. And I think our production illustrated this very well through a detail in the staging which, I think, helped clarify the meaning of the work: In Act I, there was a little girl crossing the stage holding a lighted candle. It is a supernatural moment and arouses some

274

mystical dimension in Don Juan's soul. Does this have a meaning? Is there a hidden message? In the third act, when Margarita returns to her convent, this little girl reappears with the light and hands it to Don Juan, who takes it from her. Symbolically, this means that his soul is saved. So, this work, which I am proud of reviving, is spiritually the diametrical opposite of Mozart's *Don Giovanni*.'

APPENDIX I

Plácido Domingo's Roles on Stage – Minor Parts

Borsa   (Rigoletto, 9-23-1959, Mexico City)

Chaplain   (Les Dialogues des Carmelites,
                       10-21-1959, Mexico City)

Camille de Rossillon   (The Merry Widow, 1960, Mexico
                       City)

Altoum   (Turandot, 9-11-1960, Monterrey)

Pang   (Turandot, 10-1-1960, Monterrey)

Normanno   (Lucia di Lammermoor, 10-5-1960,
                       Monterrey)

Gastone   (La Traviata, 10-8-1960, Monterrey)

Remendado   (Carmen, 10-15-1960 Monterrey,
                       Mexico City)

Cassio   (Otello, 10-17-1960, Monterrey)

Baron
Desiré   (Fedora, 7-2-1961, Mexico City)
Rouvel

Shuisky   (Boris Godunov, 8-8-1961, Mexico
Simpleton   City)

Abbé   (Andrea Chénier, 8-15-1961, Mexico
                        City)

Incroyable   (Andrea Chénier, 8-15-1961, Mexico
                        City)

Spoletta   (Tosca, 8-21-1961, Mexico City)

Goro   (Madama Butterfly, 9-15-1961,
                        Mexico City)

Arturo   (Lucia di Lammermoor, 10-28-1961,
                        Guadalajara)

Roles Performed Only In Concert

Lord Percy in Donizetti's *Anna Bolena*, 11-15-1966, New York

Viscardo in Mercadante's *Il Giuramento*, 9-9-1979, Vienna

Arrigo in Verdi's *La Battaglia di Legnano*, 6-30 and 7-3-2000, London

Appendix II

Discography

Beethoven
FIDELIO
TELDEC 3984-25249-2
Domingo, Meier, Struckmann, Pape; D: Barenboim

Bellini
NORMA
RCA GD 96502
Caballé, Cossotto, Domingo, Raimondi; D: Cillario

Berlioz
BEATRICE ET BENEDICT
DG 449 577-2
Minton, Domingo, Cotrubas, Fischer-Dieskau; D: Barenboim

LA DAMNATION DE FAUST DG 270 908-7
Minton, Cotrubas, Fischer-Dieskau, Domingo; D: Barenboim

LES TROYENS
PIONEER PC 94-048
Norman, Domingo, Troyanos, Monk; D: Levine (Met 1983)

Bizet
CARMEN
DECCA 414 489-2 (Complete); 458 204-2 (Highlights)
Troyanos, Te Kanawa, Domingo, Van Dam; D: Solti
DG 419 636-2 (Complete); 445 462-2 (Highlights)
Berganza, Cotrubas, Domingo, Milnes; D: Abbado

ERATO 2292-45207-2 (Complete); 2292-45209-2 (Highlights)
Migenes, Esham, Domingo, Raimondi; D: Maazel
RCA CVT 10530
Migenes, Esham, Domingo, Raimondi; D: Maazel

Boito
MEFISTOFELE
EMI CMS 566501
Treigle, Caballé, Domingo, Ligi, Allen; D: Rudel
SONY S2K 44983
Ramey, Marton, Domingo, Takacs; D: Patanè

Charpentier
LOUISE
SONY S3K 46429
Cotrubas, Domingo, Berbié, Bacquier, Sénéchal; D: Prêtre

Cilea
ADRIANA LECOUVREUR
SONY M2K 79310
Scotto, Obraztsova, Domingo, Milnes; D: Levine

Donizetti
L'ELISIR D'AMORE
SONY M2K 79210
Cotrubas, Domingo, Evans, Wixell, Watson; D: Pritchard

LUCIA DI LAMMERMOOR
DG 435 309-2
Studer, Domingo, Pons, de la Mora, Ramey; D: Marin

Garcia Abril
DIVINAS PALABRAS
LOH 545
Domingo, Egido, Pierotti, Baquerizo; D: Ros Marbà

Giordano
ANDREA CHÉNIER

RCA 74321394992
Domingo, Scotto, Milnes, Ewing; D: Levine
NVC Arts TXT 9034464
Domingo, Tomowa-Sintow, Zancanaro; D: Rudel

Gomes
IL GUARANY
SONY S2K 66273
Tian, Villaroel, Domingo, Haddock, Alvarez; D: Neschling

Gounod
FAUST
EMI CDS 747493 8 (Complete); CDM 763090 2 (Highlights)
Freni, Domingo, Ghiaurov; D: Prêtre

ROMEO ET JULIETTE
DG 270 908-7
Domingo, Swenson, Miles, Ollmann, Graham; D: Slatkin

Leigh
MAN OF LA MANCHA
SONY SK 46436
Domingo, Migenes, Patinkin, Ramey, Hadley; D: Gemignani

Leoncavallo
I PAGLIACCI
PHILIPS CD 411 484-2
Domingo, Stratas, Pons, Rinaldi, Andreolli; D: Prêtre
RCA 74321501682
Caballé, Domingo, Milnes, McDaniel; D: Santi
PHILIPS VHS 070 104-3
Domingo, Stratas, Pons; D: Prêtre (Zeffirelli-Production)

Mascagni
CAVALLERIA RUSTICANA
DG 429 568-2
Baltsa, Domingo, Baniewicz, Pons, Mentzer; D: Sinopoli
PHILIPS CD 416 137-2

Obraztsova, Domingo, Bruson; D: Prêtre
RCA 74321395002
Scotto, Domingo, Elvira, Jones; D: Levine
PHILIPS VHS 070 103-3
Domingo, Obraztsova, Bruson; D: Prêtre (Zeffirelli-Production)

IRIS
SONY M2K 45526
Domingo, Tokody, Pons, Giaiotti; D: Patanè

Massenet
HÉRODIADE
SONY S2K 66847 (Complete); SK 61965 (Highlights)
Domingo, Fleming, Zajick, Pons; D: Gergiev

LA NAVARRAISE
RCA 7432150167
Horne, Milnes, Domingo, Zaccaria, Bacquier; D: H. Lewis

LE CID
SONY M2K 79300
Domingo, Bumbry, Plishka, Bergquist; D: Queler

WERTHER
ORFEO C 464 9821
Fassbaender, Domingo, Seibel, Nöcker; D: Lopez Cobos
DG 413 304-2
Domingo, Grundheber, Moll, Obraztsova; D: Chailly

Meyerbeer
L'AFRICAINE
CV 2801
Domingo, Verrett, Diaz (San Francisco 1988)

Montemezzi
L'AMORE DI TRE RE
RCA 74321501662
Moffo, Domingo, Elvira, Siepi, Davies; D: Santi

Mozart
IDOMENEO
DG 447 737-2
Domingo, Bartoli, Vaness, Hampson, Terfel; D: Levine

Offenbach
LES CONTES D'HOFFMANN
DECCA CD 417 363-2
Sutherland, Domingo, Bacquier, Tourangeau; D: Bonynge
DG 427 682-2 (Complete); DG 429 788-2 (Highlights)
Domingo, Gruberova, Eder, Bacquier, Diaz; D: Ozawa
NVC Arts 0630-19392-3
Domingo, Baltsa, Cotrubas, Serra; D: Prêtre (Covent Garden 1981)

Ponchielli
LA GIOCONDA
CV 2812
Domingo, Marton, Semtschuk; D: Manugera (Vienna 1986)

Puccini
GIANNI SCHICCHI
SONY M3K 79312
Cotrubas, Scotto, Horne, Domingo, Gobbi, Wixell; D: Maazel

IL TABARRO
RCA GD60865
Caballé, Domingo, Milnes, Price; D: Santi
SONY M3K 79312
Cotrubas, Scotto, Horne, Domingo, Gobbi, Wixell; D: Maazel
DG 072 448-3
Domingo, Stratas, Pons; D: Levine

LA BOHÈME
RCA 74321394962
Domingo, Caballé, Milnes, Raimondi; D: Solti

LA FANCIULLA DEL WEST
DG 419 640-2
Neblett, Domingo, Milnes, Egerton, Lloyd; D: Mehta
SONY S2K 47189
Zampieri, Domingo, Pons; D: Maazel
DG 072 433-3
Domingo, Daniels, Milnes; D: Slatkin (Met 1992)
CGVL
Domingo, Neblett, Carroli; D: Santi (Covent Garden)

LA RONDINE
SONY M2K 37852
Te Kanawa, Domingo, Nicolesco, Rendall; D: Maazel

LE VILLI
SONY MK 76890
Scotto, Domingo, Nucci, Gobbi; D: Maazel

MADAMA BUTTERFLY
SONY M2K 35181
Scotto, Domingo, Wixell, Knight, Andreolli; D: Maazel
DECCA VHS 071-404-3
Domingo, Freni, Kerns; D: Karajan (Film)

MANON LESCAUT
DG 413 893-2 (Complete); DG 445 466-2 (Highlights)
Freni, Domingo, Bruson, Rydl, Gambill; D: Sinopoli
EMI CMS 764852 2
Caballé, Domingo, Tear, Van Allan, D: Bartoletti
ARTS D604105
Domingo, Te Kanawa, Allen; D: Sinopoli (Covent Garden 1983)

TOSCA
DG 431 775-2 (Complete); DG 437 547-2 (Highlights)
Freni, Domingo, Ramey, Terfel, Laciura, Veccia; D: Sinopoli
EMI CMS 566504-2 (Complete); EMI CDR 569827 2 (Highlights)
Scotto, Domingo, Bruson; D: Levine

RCA 7432139503 2
Price, Domingo, Milnes, Plishka, Grant; D: Mehta
TELDEC 0630-12372-2 (Complete); Teldec 0630-17367-2 (Highlights)
Domingo, Malfitano, Raimondi, Grant; D: Mehta
TELDEC 4509-90212-3
Domingo, Malfitano, Raimondi, Grant; D: Mehta (filmed in the original locations in Rome)
DG 072 426-3
Domingo, Behrens, MacNeil; D: Sinopoli (Met 1985)

TURANDOT
DG 423 855-2 (Complete), DG 410 465-2 (Highlights)
Ricciarelli, Domingo, Hendricks, Raimondi; D: von Karajan
DG 072 410-3
Domingo, Marton, Mitchell; D: Levine (Met 1988)

Rossini
IL BARBIERE DI SIVIGLIA
DG 435 763-2 (Complete); DG 437 841-2 (Highlights)
Battle, Domingo, Raimondi, Lopardo, Gallo; D: Abbado

Saint-Saëns
SAMSON ET DALILA
DG 413 297-2
Obraztsova, Domingo, Thau, Bruson, Lloyd; D: Barenboim
EMI CDS 754470 2
Domingo, Meier, Ramey, Fondary; D: Chung
CV 2820
Domingo, Verrett, Brendel; D: Rudel (San Francisco)

Strauss, J.
DIE FLEDERMAUS
EMI CDS 747480-8 (Complete); EMI CDR 569839 2 (Highlights)
Popp, Baltsa, Lind, Domingo; D: Domingo
NVC Arts 4509-992116-3
Te Kanawa, Prey; D: Domingo (Covent Garden)

Strauss, R.
DER ROSENKAVALIER
SONY M3K 42564
Ludwig, Jones, Popp, Berry, Gutstein, Domingo; D: Bernstein

DIE FRAU OHNE SCHATTEN
DECCA CD 436 243-2
Varady, Behrens, Runkel, Domingo, van Dam; D: Solti

Verdi
AIDA
DG 410 092-2 (Complete); 415 286-2 (Highlights)
Ricciarelli, Domingo, Obraztsova, Nucci; D: Abbado
EMI CDS 556246-2 (Complete); CDM 565572-2 (Highlights)
Caballé, Domingo, Cossotto, Ghiaurov, Cappuccilli; D: Muti
RCA 74321394982
Price, Bumbry, Domingo, Milnes, Raimondi; D: Leinsdorf
SONY S3K 45973 (Complete); SMK 53506 (Highlights)
Millo, Domingo, Zajick, Morris, Ramey; D: Levine
DG 072 416-3
Domingo, Millo, Zajick, Milnes; D: Levine (Met 1989)

DON CARLOS
DG 415 316-2 (Complete); 415 981-2 (Highlights)
Domingo, Ricciarelli, Valentini Terrani, Raimondi; D: Abbado
EMI CDS 747701 8 (Complete); CDM 763089 2 (Highlights)
Domingo, Caballé, Raimondi, Verrett, Milnes; D: Giulini

ERNANI
EMI CDS 747083 8
Domingo, Freni, Bruson, Ghiaurov; D: Muti
WARNER 450999213-3
Domingo, Freni, Bruson, Ghiaurov; D: Muti (Scala 1982)

GIOVANNA D'ARCO
EMI CMS 763226 2
Caballé, Domingo, Milnes; D: Levine

286

I LOMBARDI
PHILIPS CD 422 420-2
Deutekom, Domingo, Raimondi, Lo Monaco; D: Gardelli

IL TROVATORE
DG 423 858-2 (Complete); 415 285-2 (Highlights)
Domingo, Plowright, Fassbaender, Zancanaro; D: Giulini
RCA 74321395042
Price, Domingo, Milnes, Cossotto; D: Mehta
SONY S2K 48070
Domingo, Millo, Chernov, Zajick, Morris; D: Levine
RCA 7432161951-2
Cappuccilli, Kabaiwanska, Cossotto, Domingo, van Dam; D:
Karajan (Vienna 1978)

I VESPRI SICILIANI
RCA RD80370
Arroyo, Domingo, Milnes, Raimondi; D: Levine

LA FORZA DEL DESTINO
EMI CDS 747485 8 (Complete); CDC 754326 2 (Highlights)
Freni, Zajick, Domingo, Surian, Zancanaro; D: Muti
RCA 74321395022
Price, Domingo, Milnes, Cossotto, Giaiotti; D: Levine

LA TRAVIATA
DG 415 132-2 (Complete); 445 469-2 (Highlights)
Cotrubas, Domingo, Milnes, Malagú, Jungwirth; D: Kleiber
DG 073 120-3
Domingo, Stratas, MacNeill; D: Levine (Film)

LUISA MILLER
DG 423 144-2
Howell, Domingo, Obraztsova, Bruson, Ricciarelli; D: Maazel
SONY S2K 48073 (Complete); SMK 53508 (Highlights)
Millo, Domingo, Chernov, Quivar, Plishka; D: Levine

MACBETH
DG 449 732-2
Verrett, Cappuccilli, Domingo, Ghiaurov, Malagú; D: Abbado

NABUCCO
DG 410 512-2 (Complete); 413 321-2 (Highlights)
Cappuccilli, Domingo, Nesterenko, Dimitrova; D: Sinopoli

OTELLO
DG 439 805-2 (Complete); 445 867-2 (Highlights)
Domingo, Studer, Leiferkus, Vargas, Schade; D: Chung
EMI CDS 747450 8 (Complete); CDR 572105 2 (Highlights)
Domingo, Ricciarelli, Diaz; D: Maazel
RCA 74321395012
Domingo, Scotto, Milnes, Plishka, Little; D: Levine
VMP 5300
Domingo, Ricciarelli, Diaz; D: Maazel (Film)
CGVL 007
Domingo, Te Kanawa, Leiferkus; D: Solti (Covent Garden 1992)

RIGOLETTO
DG 415 288-2 (Complete); 423 114-2 (Highlights)
Cappuccilli, Cotrubas, Domingo, Obraztsova; D: Giulini

SIMON BOCCANEGRA
RCA RD70729
Cappuccilli, Domingo, Ricciarelli, Raimondi; D: Gavazzeni
DG 072 445-3
Domingo, Te Kanawa, Chernov; D: Levine (Met 1995)

STIFFELIO
DG 073 116-3
Domingo, Sweet, Chernov; D: Levine (Met 1993)

UN BALLO IN MASCHERA
DG 453 148-2 (Complete); 445 468-2 (Highlights)
Domingo, Ricciarelli, Bruson, Obraztsova, Gruberova; D: Abbado

DG 427 635-2
Domingo, Barstow, Nucci, Quivar; D: von Karajan
CGVL 024
Domingo, Ricciarelli, Grist, Cappuccilli; D: Abbado (1975)

Wagner
DER FLIEGENDE HOLLÄNDER
DG 437 778-2
Weikl, Studer, Domingo, Sotin, Priew, Seiffert; D: Sinopoli

DIE MEISTERSINGER VON NÜRNBERG
DG 415 278-2
Fischer-Dieskau, Ligendza, Ludwig, Domingo; D: Jochum

DIE WALKÜRE
TELDEC 3984-23294-2 (Act I)
Domingo, Polaski, Tomlinson; D: Barenboim

LOHENGRIN
DECCA CD 421 053-2 (Complete); CD 425 530-2 (Highlights)
Domingo, Norman, Sotin, Randová; D: Solti
RMA RTS VL 064
Domingo, Studer, Welker; D: Abbado (Vienna 1990)

PARSIFAL
DG 437 501-2 (Complete); 445 868-2 (Highlights)
Domingo, Norman, Moll, Morris, Wlaschiha; D: Levine

TANNHÄUSER
DG 427 625-2 (Complete); 429 789-2 (Highlights)
Domingo, Studer, Baltsa, Salminen, A. Schmidt; D: Sinopoli

Weber, von
OBERON
DG 419 038-2
Domingo, Nilsson, Hamari, Prey, Grobe; D: Kubelik

Zandonai
FRANCESCA DA RIMINI
PA 87-180
Domingo, Scotto, MacNeil; D: Levine (Met 1984)

Anthologies
BATTLE & DOMINGO LIVE
DG 419 038-2
Live from Tokyo 1988 with Kathleen Battle

BRAVISSIMO DOMINGO
RCA 07863570202
Operatic Arias and Duets with Price, Milnes, Kraft, Davies

BRAVO DOMINGO
DG 459 352-2
Operatic Arias (2 CDs)

CONCERT FOR PLANET EARTH
SONY SK 52570
Live from Rio de Janeiro 1992 with Winton Marsalis u.a.

COVENT GARDEN GALA
EMI CDC 7498112
Live from London 1988; Studer, Randová, Allen u.a.

THE YOUNG DOMINGO
RCA 74321533412
Operatic Arias Vol. 1–5, Box

THE UNKNOWN PUCCINI
SONY SK 44981
Piano and Organ; Domingo, Diaz, Rudel

DOMINGO – THE WOMEN IN MY LIFE
DG 415 120-2
Operatic Arias

DOMINGO AT THE PHILHARMONIC
SONY MK 44942
Live from New York 1988

DOMINGO FAVOURITES
DG 415 120-2
Operatic Arias

DOMINGO LIVE IN SEOUL
KOCH 365682P14
Live from Seoul 1995

DOMINGO SINGS & CONDUCTS TCHAIKOVSKY
EMI CDC 555018-2

DOMINGO!
SONY MK 74022
Operatic Arias and Duets with Scotto, Bumbry, Wixell

GOLD & SILVER GALA
EMI CDC 556337-2
Live from Covent Garden 1996 with Alagna, Gheorghiu, Vaduva,
Ramey, Morris, Eaglen, Gorchakova

GRANADA
DG 445 777-2
Domingo's Greatest Hits

GREAT LOVE SCENES
SONY MK 39030
Operatic Duets with Cotrubas, Te Kanawa, Scotto

LEONTYNE PRICE & PLÁCIDO DOMINGO
RCA 09026616342
Verdi & Puccini Duets

METROPOLITAN OPERA GALA
DG 2530 260
Live from the Met 1972 with Arroyo, Caballé, Corelli, Price, Tucker u.a.

MOZART ARIAS
EMI CDC 754329-2

NESSUN DORMA (CELESTE AIDA)
TELDEC 0630 13401-2
Operatic Arias

OPERA CLASSICS
EMI CDC 555017-2
Operatic Arias

OPERA DUETS
RCA 09026625952
Operatic Duets Milnes, Ricciarelli

OPERA GALA
EMI CDC 555554-2
Opertic Arias and Duets with Swenson, Hampson

OPERA HEROES
EMI CDC 555554-2
Operatic Arias; recorded 1970–85 with Freni, Scotto, Irwin, Milnes

PLÁCIDO DOMINGO – BAYERISCHE STAATSOPER
ORFEO C471971B
Live from Munich 1976–81 with Rysanek, Stratas, Brendel u.a.

PLÁCIDO DOMINGO CON AMORE
RCA GD84265
Operatic Arias & Songs

PLÁCIDO DOMINGO SINGS CARUSO
RCA 09026613562
Operatic Arias

PRELUDE TO A KISS
DECCA 460 793-2
Live from Chicago 1998 with Renée Fleming

PUCCINI
SONY SB2K 63278
Operatic Arias & Love Songs

RODRIGO: CONCIERTO DE ARANJUEZ
EMI 72435561752
Plácido Domingo sings and conducts with Manuel Barrueco, Guitar

SEMPRE BELCANTO
TELDEC 3984-23292-2
Operatic Arias

THE BEST OF DOMINGO
DG 415 366-2
Operatic Arias and Scenes

THE DOMINGO COLLECTION
SONY S2K 63027
Operatic Arias & Popular Songs

THE GREAT VOICE OF PLÁCIDO DOMINGO
DECCA 458 222-2
Operatic Arias

TOGETHER!
PLÁCIDO DOMINGO & ITZHAK PERLMAN
EMI CDC 754266-2
Duets for Tenor and Violin with Itzhak Perlman

VERDI HEROES
RCA 09026684462
Verdi Arias

VIENNA, CITY OF MY DREAMS
EMI CDC 747398-2
Operettas

APPENDIX III

Chronology

Opera/Part — City & Performance Dates
Adriana Lecouvreur/Maurizio
Mexico 1962; New York 1968, 1969, 1983; Caracas 1972;
Newark 1973; Paris 1975; Miami 1978; Munich 1985, 1989;
Barcelona 1989

L'Africaine/Vasco daGama
San Francisco 1972, 1988; Barcelona 1977; London 1978

Aida/Radames
Hamburg 1967, 1970, 1971, 1973, 1974; Fort Worth 1967;
Mexico 1970; New York 1971, 1976, 1988, 1989; San Juan, PR
1971; Miami 1972; Milan 1972; Munich 1972, 1979; Vienna
1973, 1974; Barcelona 1973, 1974; London 1974, 1977; Verona
1974, 1976; Madrid 1977; Newark 1980; Monte Carlo 1981;
Budapest 1987; Luxor 1987; Houston 1987

Amelia Goes to the Ball/Lover
Mexico 1961; Monterrey 1962

Andrea Chénier/Chénier
New Orleans 1966; Cincinnati 1967; Santiago, Chile 1967; New
York 1970, 1971, 1977; Madrid 1971; Mexico 1971; Barcelona
1973; Turin 1974; Saragossa 1975; San Francisco 1975; Bilbao
1977; Oviedo 1977; San Juan, PR 1978; Chicago 1979; Vienna
1981, 1982; 1986; Miami 1983; London 1985; Versailles 1989

Andrea Chénier/Abbé, Incredibile
Mexico 1961

Un Ballo in Maschera/Riccardo (Gustavus)
Berlin 1967; Chicago 1967; Miami 1968; Fort Worth 1970; New
Orleans 1970; New York 1970, 1971, 1972, 1980, 1981; Vienna
1971, 1987; Mantua 1972; Milan 1972, 1973; Barcelona 1972;
1973; Hamburg 1974, 1975, 1977, 1981; London 1975; Caracas
1975; Cologne 1981; Salzburg 1989, 1990; Seville 1992;
Yokohama 1993; Tokyo 1993; Los Angeles 1993

Il Barbiere di Siviglia/Count Almaviva
Guadalajara 1966

La Bohème/Parpignol
Monterrey 1960

La Bohème/Rodolfo
Mexico 1962; Tel Aviv 1962, 1963; Boston 1966; New York
1967, 1977, 1982, 1983; 1989, 1990, 1991; Hamburg 1967,
1968, 1969, 1970, 1971, 1975, 1980, 1985; Hamburg 1989;
San Francisco 1969; Fort Worth 1971; 1971; Milan 1971;
Munich 1972, 1977, 1980, 1984; Memphis 1972; Detroit 1972;
Vienna 1973, 1983, 1987, 1988; London 1974, 1987; Stuttgart
1974; Barcelona 1975, 1982; Valencia 1975; Saragossa 1976;
Elda 1976; Paris 1977, 1980; Denver 1983; Madrid 1986; Los
Angeles 1987

Boris Godunov/Shuisky, Simpleton
Mexico 1961

Madama Butterfly/Goro
Mexico 1961; Puebla 1961; Monterrey 1961

Madama Butterfly/Pinkerton
Torreon 1962; Tampa 1962; Tel Aviv 1963, 1964; Beersheba
1963; Binghampton 1965; New York 1965, 1966, 1967, 1968,
1969, 1991; Puebla 1965; Marseille 1965; Fort Worth 1966;
Los Angeles 1967, 1991; Hamburg 1969, 1972

Carmen/Remendado
Monterrey 1960; Mexico 1961; Guadalajara 1961

Carmen/Don José
Tel Aviv 1963, 1964, 1965, 1969; Haifa 1964; Kiryat Bialik 1964;
Washington 1965; New York 1965, 1966, 1967, 1968, 1971,
1974, 1975, 1976, 1986, 1996, 1997; Fort Worth 1965;
Cincinatti 1966, 1968; Santingo 1967; Saratoga Spring 1968;
Vienna 1969, 1973; Mexico 1967, 1978, 1980, 1982, 1984,
1992; San Francisco 1970, 1981; New Orleans 1971; Barcelona
1974, 1978; Las Palmas 1979; Monterrey 1979; Guadalajara
1979; Paris 1980; Hamburg 1980; Berlin 1981; San Juan, PR
1982; Chicago 1984; Milan 1984; Rio de Janeiro 1990; Los
Angeles 1992, 1998; London 1994; Zurich 1996; Munich 1996

Cavalleria Rusticana/Turiddu
Tel Aviv 1965; Haifa 1965; Jerusalem 1965; Kfar Atta 1965;
Cincinatti 1966; New York 1966, 1968, 1970, 1978; New Or-
leans 1968; Hamburg 1970, 1972, 1973, 1975, 1988; Atlanta
1970; Newark 1973; Hartford 1973; Vienna 1973, 1977;
Barcelona 1976; London 1976; Tokyo 1976; San Francisco 1976;
Verona 1977; Munich 1978, 1979; Milan 1981

Così Fan Tutte/Ferrando
Mexico 1962; Puebla 1962

Dialogues des Carmélites/Chaplain
Mexico 1959

Divinas Palabras/Lucero
Madrid 1997

Don Carlos/Carlos
Vienna 1967, 1968, 1970, 1972, 1992; Houston 1969; Verona
1969; Milan 1970, 1978; New York 1971, 1983; Hamburg 1974,
1975; Salzburg 1975, 1977; Los Angeles 1990

Don Giovanni/Don Ottavio
Tel Aviv 1963, 1964; Haifa 1963; Jerusalem 1963; New York
1966

Don Rodrigo/Don Rodrigo
New York 1966, 1967; Los Angeles 1967

El Gato Montes/Rafael Ruiz
Seville 1992; Orange County 1994; Los Angeles 1994

El Poeta/José de Espronceda
Madrid 1980

Ernani/Ernani
Milan 1969, 1982; New York 1971; Amsterdam 1972

Eugen Onegin/Lensky
Tel Aviv 1964, 1965; Haifa 1964

La Fanciulla del West/Dick Johnson (Ramerrez)
Turin 1974; Miami 1977; London 1977, 1978, 1982; Vienna
1979, 1988; Buenos Aires 1979; San Francisco 1979; Madrid
1983; Barcelona 1984; Berlin 1989; Chicago 1990; Milan 1991;
Costa Mesa 1991; Los Angeles 1991; New York 1991, 1992;
Bonn 1995

Faust/Faust
Tel Aviv 1963, 1964, 1965; Beersheba 1963; San Diego 1966;
Houston 1967; Orlando 1968; Vienna 1968; New York 1971,
1972; Boston 1972; Cleveland 1972; Atlanta 1972; New Orleans 1972; Minneapolis 1972; Detroit 1972

Fedora/Désiré
BaronMexico City 1961

Fedora/Loris Ipanov
Barcelona 1977, 1988; Madrid 1989; Milan 1993, 1996; Zurich
1994, 1998; Chicago 1994; Modena 1995; Vienna 1995, 1997,

1999; London 1995; New York 1996, 1997; Los Angeles 1997; Buenos Aires 1998; Washington 1998; Mexico City 1999; Rome 1999

La Forza del Destino/Alvaro
Hamburg 1969, 1970, 1971, 1972, 1974, 1975; Vienna 1971; New York 1971, 1977, 1996; Buenos Aires 1972; Valencia 1974; Frankfurt 1974; Paris 1975

Francesca da Rimini/Paolo
New York 1973, 1984; Washington 1984; Atlanta 1984; Memphis 1984; Minneapolis 1984; Detroit 1984; Toronto 1984; Cleveland 1984

Giuramento/Viscardo
Vienna 1979

Goya/Goya
Washington 1986

Hérodiade/Jean
San Francisco 1994; Vienna 1995

Hippolyte et Aricie/Hippolyte
Boston 1966

Idomeneo/Idomeneo
New York 1994, 1995; Frankfurt 1996; Vienna 1997; Chicago 1997

Il Guarany/Pery
Bonn 1994; Washington 1996

La Gioconda/Enzo
Madrid 1970; Berlin 1981; New York 1982, 1983; Vienna 1986

Le Cid/Rodrigue
New York 1976; Hamburg 1979; Paris 1981; Vienna 1987;

Madrid 1988; Chicago 1993; Seville 1999; Washington 1999

Les Troyens/Aeneas
New York 1983

Lohengrin/Lohengrin
Hamburg 1968; New York 1984, 1985; Vienna 1985, 1990; New York 1985

Lucia di Lammermoor/Arturo
Guadalajara 1961; Dallas 1961; New Orleans 1962

Lucia di Lammermoor/Edgardo
Fort Worth 1962; Guadalajara 1966; New Orleans 1966; Detroit 1970; New York 1970; Hamburg 1971; Piacenza 1972; Vienna 1979; Madrid 1981; Chicago 1986

Luisa Miller/Rodolfo
New York 1971, 1979; London 1979; Hamburg 1982

Luna
Valencia 1998

Manon/Des Grieux
New York 1969; Vancouver 1969

Manon Lescaut/Des Grieux
Hartford 1968; Fort Worth 1986; Verona 1970; Naples 1971; Barcelona 1971; Madrid 1978; Milan 1978; Hamburg 1979; New York 1980; Munich 1981; London 1983

Margarita La Tornera/Don Juan de Alarcón
Madrid 1999, 2000

The Merry Widow/Count Danilo
New York 2000

Norma/Pollione
New York 1981, 1982

Otello/Cassio
Monterrey 1960; Mexico City 1962; Hartford 1962

Otello/Otello
Hamburg 1975, 1976, 1977, 1985, 1988, 1992; Madrid 1976, 1985, 1991; Paris 1976, 1978, 1990, 1992; Milan 1976, 1980, 1982, 1987; Barcelona 1977, 1985; Munich 1978; Vienna 1982, 1987, 1989, 1991, 1992, 1997; St Petersburg 1992; San Francisco 1978, 1983; New York 1979, 1985, 1987, 1988, 1990, 1991, 1994, 1995, 1999; Verona 1994; Monte Carlo 1980; London 1980, 1983, 1987, 1990, 1992; Houston 1989; Lisbon 1989; Bonn 1993; Salzburg 1996; Mexico City 1981; Buenos Aires 1981; Bregenz 1981; Tokyo 1981; Chicago 1985; Los Angeles 1986, 1989, 1995; Berlin 1986; San Juan, PR 1990; Bilbao 1990; Stuttgart 1988; Santander 1991; Perelada 1991; Reggio Emilia 1992

Pagliacci/Canio
New York 1966, 1967, 1968, 1978, 1993, 1999; Pasadena 1967; Vienna 1968, 1970, 1973, 1977, 1985, 1987, 1993, 1994; Hamburg 1970, 1972, 1973, 1974, 1975, 1988; Philadelphia 1972; Barcelona 1976; London 1976; Frankfurt 1976; Tokyo 1976, 1997; San Francisco 1976; Verona 1977, 1993; Munich 1978, 1979; San Juan, PR 1979; Madrid 1979; Milan 1981; Berne 1982; Guadalajara 1982; Monte Carlo 1996; Los Angeles 1996; Nagoya 1997; Yokohama 1997; Washington 1997; Zürich 1998; Ravenna 1998

Parsifal/Parsifal
New York 1991, 1995; Vienna 1991; Milan 1991; Bayreuth 1992, 1993, 1995; Ravello 1997; London 1998; Rome 1998; Salzburg 1998

Les Pêcheurs de Perles/Nadir
Tel Aviv 1964; Haifa 1964; Kfar Atta 1964; Jerusalem 1964

Pique Dame/Hermann
New York 1999; Vienna 1999

Le Prophète/Jean
Vienna 1998

Rigoletto/Borsa
Mexico City 1959, 1961; Guadalajara 1961

Rigoletto/Duca
Hamburg 1969, 1970; San Antonia 1972; Vienna 1973; New York 1977

Roberto Devereux/Roberto
New York 1970; Los Angeles 1970

Roméo et Juliette/Roméo
New York 1974

Samson et Dalila/Samson
Chautauqua 1965; Milwaukee 1965; Binghampton 1966; Fort Worth 1967; London 1973, 1985, 1992; Orange County 1978; San Francisco 1980; Monterrey 1980; Madrid 1982, 1999; Nice 1985; Barcelona 1989; Chicago 1989; New York 1990, 1998; Vienna 1990, 1991; San Juan, PR 1991; Ravinia 1992; Hamburg 1996; Zürich 1997; Buenos Aires 1997; Mexico City 1998; Washington 1998; Los Angeles 1999

Samson et Dalila, II/Samson
Baden-Baden 1999

Samson II, Parsifal II/Samson, Parsifal
Berlin 1995

Simon Boccanegra/Gabriele Adorno
New York 1995, 1999; London 1997

Stiffelio/Stiffelio
New York 1993, 1994, 1998; Madrid 1995; London 1995; Los
Angeles 1995; Vienna 1997

Il Tabarro/Luigi
New York 1967, 1968, 1989, 1994; New Orleans 1968; Phila-
delphia 1972; Newark 1973; Hartford 1973; Madrid 1979;
Vienna 1993

Les Contes d'Hoffmann/Hoffmann
Mexico City 1965, 1967; Philadelphia 1965; New York 1966,
1973, 1982, 1988, 1992, 1993; Baltimore 1967; Shreveport 1968;
San Antonio 1968; Cincinatti 1968; Chicago 1976; Newark 1977;
Salzburg 1980, 1981, 1982; Cologne 1980; London 1980, 1981,
1982; San Francisco 1987; Tokyo 1988; Nagoya 1988; Osaka
1988; Los Angeles 1988; Vienna 1993, 1994

Tosca/Spoletta
Mexico City 1960

Tosca/Cavaradossi
Mexico City 1962, 1965, 1984; Tel Aviv 1964, 1965; Nahariyya
1964; Toledo, Ohio 1966; Dayton 1966; New Orleans 1966;
New York 1966, 1967, 1968, 1969, 1970, 1971, 1977, 1978,
1979, 1981, 1985, 1986, 1987, 1993; Hamburg 1967, 1968,
1969, 1970, 1971, 1972, 1974, 1975; San Diego 1967; Vancouver
1968; Cleveland 1970; Minneapolis 1970; San Francisco 1970,
1972; Vienna 1971, 1972, 1973, 1974, 1976, 1977, 1980, 1984,
1989, 1991; London 1971, 1972, 1981, 1991; Turin 1972; Rome
1992; Seville 1991; San Juan, PR 1972, 1985; Budapest 1973;
Paris 1974, 1994, 1995; Milan 1974, 1975; Saragossa 1974;
Moscow 1974; Verona 1974; Torre del Lago 1974; Barcelona
1975, 1983; Madrid 1975, 1984; Frankfurt 1975; Newark 1975;
Oslo 1989; Stuttgart 1976, 1990; Belgrade 1987; Munich 1976,
1977; Berlin 1977, 1985, 1987; Valencia 1977; Los Angeles 1985,
1992; Bilbao 1977; Toronto 1984; Oviedo 1977; Dallas 1984;
Las Palmas 1978; Washington 1984, 1988; Monterrey 1978;
Houston 1984; Cologne 1979; Newcastle 1983; Macerata 1979;

Chicago 1982; Manila 1979; Buenos Aires 1982; Naples 1981; Guadalajara 1981

La Traviata/Gastone
Monterrey 1960; Mexico City 1961

La Traviata/Alfredo
Monterrey 1961; Guadalajara 1962; Tel Aviv 1963, 1964, 1965; Haifa 1963; Jerusalem 1963; New York 1966, 1967, 1970, 1973, 1981; Cincinatti 1967; Los Angeles 1967, 1971; Cleveland 1972; Hamburg 1976, 1989, 1990

Il Trovatore/Manrico
New Orleans 1968; Hamburg 1968, 1970, 1971, 1978; Vienna 1968, 1969, 1971, 1978; New York 1969, 1973; Fort Worth 1973; Philadelphia 1970; San Francisco 1971; Paris 1973, 1975; Madrid 1973; Munich 1973; Zürich 1979; Frankfurt 1979; London 1989

Turandot/Altoum
Mexico City 1960

Turandot/Pang
Monterrey 1960

Turandot/Calaf
Verona 1969, 1975; New York 1970, 1987; Florence 1971; Madrid 1972; Newark 1974; Barcelona 1975, 1976; Cologne 1981; Milan 1983; Los Angeles 1984; London 1984

Ultimo Sueno/Enrique
Mexico City 1961

I Vespri Siciliani/Arrigo
Paris 1974; Hamburg 1974; New York 1974; Barcelona 1974, 1975

Walküre/Siegmund
Vienna 1992, 1993, 1996; New York 1993, 1996, 1997; Berlin
1993, 1996; Milan 1994; Salzburg 1995; Madrid 1996; London
1996; Munich 1998

Walküre I/Siegmund
London 1999

Walküre I, Parsifal II/Siegmund/Parsifal
Frankfurt 1995; St Petersburg 1998

Walküre I, Samson I/Siegmund, Parsifal
Paris 1998

Weber-Requiem/Tenor
London 1985

Werther/Werther
Munich 1977, 1978, 1979; New York 1978

INDEX OF NAMES

[In general fictional characters are entered first name, last name or first name only and actual persons are given last name, first name. Operas and other works of art are italicized.]